D1646886

GOOD SCHOOLS, EFFECTIVE SCHOOLS

GOOD SCHOOLS, EFFECTIVE SCHOOLS
Judgements and Their Histories

Harold Silver

CASSELL

Cassell
Villiers House   387 Park Avenue South
41/47 Strand   New York
London WC2N 5JE   NY 10016-8810

British Library Cataloguing-in-Publication Data
A catalogue record for this book is available from the British Library

ISBN 0–304–32971–1 (hardback)
     0–304–32973–8 (paperback)

Typeset by York House Typographic Ltd.
Printed and bound in Great Britain by
Redwood Books, Trowbridge, Wiltshire

Contents

Series Editors' Foreword

Concern with, and interest in, the factors that make some schools effective is so much part of contemporary educational agendas in different countries that there is often a neglect of the historical context that shapes such interest. Harold Silver's book reminds us in an authoritative manner of that context, and outlines in a fascinating historical travelogue the judgements, mechanisms and procedures that have been used to judge schools over time, particularly in Britain and the United States, from the early nineteenth century.

Crucially the book makes clear the origins of the now international effective schools research and practice community as an outgrowth of the concern for the education of the disadvantaged in the 1960s, a concern for *equity* which has recently seemed to have been replaced by concerns merely for *excellence*. The relationship between effective schools research and educational policy, the contemporary debates concerning *who* makes judgements and on what basis, the historical progression of effective schools research and the 'cutting edge' of the effectiveness and improvement traditions in both the United States and Britain are only some of the various themes interwoven in this multi-disciplinary and creative account.

The field has been waiting for someone to 'context' it historically, philosophically and educationally so that we can begin to concern ourselves with issues concerning the definition of effectiveness, our target groups and the political contexts of our research base. In this elegant, perceptive and authoritative account, Harold Silver has given us much to think about.

David Hopkins
David Reynolds

July 1994

Preface

The notion of 'good' schools, or their opposites, has a long history. The notion of 'effective' schools does not. The core of this book is an account of recent histories to explore these and other notions of what schools are or should be. The geographical frameworks for the discussion are complex. A long British and international setting leads into two centuries of British – mainly English – contexts and components of changing patterns and judgements of schools and schooling. The recent past has to take account of internationally important American developments over roughly two decades, as well as alternatives to 'effective' school developments in the United States, Britain and elsewhere.

In pursuit of these strands I have had particular help in Britain from David Reynolds, then of the University of Wales, College of Cardiff, and Peter Mortimore, who at the time was at the University of Lancaster. In the United States I had particular help from Carol Chelemer of the Planning and Evaluation Service of the US Department of Education, Joan Shoemaker of the State Department of Education, Connecticut and Chris O' Neil, Executive Assistant to the Commissioner, Rhode Island. People too numerous to mention in other American states and in Britain provided documentation or responded to telephone enquiries. What was then Oxford Polytechnic and is now Oxford Brookes University made an important contribution towards the American research costs. I am grateful to students and colleagues at Oxford Brookes University and the University of Plymouth for discussion of some of the issues involved.

Some material used here was included in 'Poverty and effective schools' (1991), *Journal of Education Policy*, **6** (3), in a joint paper with Charles Benson entitled 'Vocationalism in the United Kingdom and the United States' published by the Post-16 Education Centre, Institute of Education, University of London, and in a contribution to a *liber amicorum* for Henry Remak entitled 'Educational research and the policy environment: the case of "effective schools"', University of Indiana, 1991.

A special impetus was given to this study by the Rockefeller Foundation, whose invitation to spend six weeks at their Bellagio Center in Italy made it possible to reflect on the issues with Pamela Silver and other visiting scholars, and to combine work in progress with the Foundation's creative hospitality.

NOTE

In recent years there has been, most consistently in the United States, a move away from the use of the term 'school *pupils*' to the term 'school *students*'. I would have preferred to use *students* throughout this book, but in the countries and periods under discussion usage differed, and I have found it necessary to use both terms, reluctantly and interchangeably, according to the context.

Chapter 1

Threads and Meanings

Schools – and educational systems – have aimed to be effective. This may not have been their vocabulary, but they have tried to define or assert what they are about, and in some way to judge how well they succeed. In doing so they have historically had much in common. Schools have been a major agency for transmitting – mainly to children – the knowledge, traditions and values of the society. While relating to their society they have had degrees of isolation or separation from it. They have aimed to provide the society with the requisite skills for its continued economic existence, or the religious and social understanding needed for its stability. Schooling has broadly speaking been interpreted as providing a basic ('elementary' or 'primary') education, a more advanced ('secondary') education, and a higher ('post-secondary', 'college', 'seminary', 'university') education intended to provide intellectual, political and social leadership. Schools have both reflected their society and contributed to its dynamic.

Schools have also, however, been historically, geographically and nationally different. They have performed their functions with specific characteristics. They have served different social clienteles – defined by social class, sex, religion, race, talent or age. They have defined their aims in terms of human potential or economic growth, social status or financial success, service to God or to the social elite, liberal learning or athletic prowess, measurable knowledge or applied morality. Their corps of teachers have been recruited on different principles, and their curricula have had different shapes and contents. They have been open to different degrees of control, coordination, support or influence by states, organizations and publics. Schools have to different extents formed parts of 'systems'. They have been given or have won different levels of prestige, and have to different extents prepared for leadership or followership.[1] They have across time and distance been similar and different.

Judging how successfully schools accomplish their aims may lead to one kind of conclusion at a national level, and a different kind in the case of individual institutions. A school system may more or less well serve the nation's economic needs by providing suitably qualified manpower. It may more or less well serve the interests of a dominant political ideology. It may more or less well sustain opportunities for independent ideas and action. Within a system, however, there may be considerable variations of educational purpose, and of style and success in achieving it. Those who control schools as well as those whose children attend them or those who employ their products may hold critical views of the system or of individual schools or features of schools. There has historically been constant pressure to improve the secular or religious basis of schooling – through changes in

1

organization or administration, teacher training or recruitment, improved text-books or examinations, greater involvement by church or community, the alloca-tion of priorities by the state or overseeing authority. The criteria by which to judge how well an educational system serves the nation are not necessarily the same criteria by which the performance of a school or its management or its teachers may be judged.

Schools may be poor or inefficient or ineffective, but they do not normally aim to be so. They may have limited goals, or for various reasons they may fall short of the explicit or implicit goals they set for themselves or have set for them. A 'good' school has always been one which by some publicly available standard has consistently achieved known or assumed goals. That standard may have to do with the attitude or behaviour of its students, the rules by which the school conducts its affairs, the performance of its students in tests or examinations, on the playing field or the battlefield. It may be associated with neatness and deference, creativity and imagination, respect for tradition or commitment to change. A good school has been judged by the employability of its products, or by measures which have enabled schools to attract students or earn payment by revealed results. In stable and unchanging societies the nature of a good school may remain relatively uncontested and unchanged across long periods. In rapidly changing societies there may be deeply controversial and conflicting views of what constitutes the purpose of schooling, and what are therefore the characteristics of a good school. Social change brings a search for redefinition, for improvement, for 'better' schools.

A contemporary interest in explicitly 'effective' schools is an outcome of conditions in the late 1960s and 1970s, and has emerged mainly in advanced industrial countries. It has been partnered or paralleled by an accelerating interest – largely by governments, public authorities and researchers – in the meaning and means of school 'development'. This search for the criteria of effectiveness and development has differed from previous understandings of what constituted 'good' schools in the emergence of a research base for discussion, policy and planning. Not all advanced countries in the 1970s and 1980s, however, followed the specific path of 'effective school' research and policies, and those that did produced research literatures and policy directions often with somewhat different emphases. In the economic and political conditions of the 1970s and 1980s the industrially advanced countries generally – particularly those hardest hit by international competition and economic decline – looked for means of making their schools and higher education more cost effective or in some way improving their performance, with regard both to national economic equilibrium or recovery and to social stability and cohesion. The interests of researchers and governments proved to be close, but not identical. The researchers wanted explanations of what made schools different, and therefore more or less effective. Governments often wanted quick-fix solutions to pressing problems. Economic and social crisis produced rival remedies, including alternative strategies for achieving school reform, renovation, reconstruction, or 'effectiveness'.

Although the problems of low-income or developing countries were not dissimilar in some respects, attention to education inevitably took a different form. In this case the question was not primarily one of explaining how particular schools came to function badly or well, but one of devoting sufficient priority and resources either to the slow process of change or to the maintenance of existing conditions in difficult economic circumstances. The questions in many of these countries had more to do with sustaining basic education, contributing to tightly defined manpower needs often at relatively low levels of skill, and the tension between the provision of 'academic' education for all and 'vocational' education for some or most. In this situation there were few opportunities for the types of evaluation and research occurring in more developed countries, and limited possibilities of taking account of it or implementing curriculum change or teacher professional development, administrative improvement or the revision of educational goals.

One of the main sources of the contemporary interest in effective schools lies in the American 'War on Poverty' launched by President Lyndon Johnson in 1964. This wide-ranging set of programmes, with a strong emphasis on education as a means of combating poverty, looked to specific policies for pre-schooling and the early grades of the elementary school in particular in order to 'compensate' for environmental and family deficiencies which appeared to cause children to fail in school and therefore to have limited subsequent life chances. The educational components of the war on poverty, and of the research and experiments on which they were built, placed central emphasis on early childhood education and the early years of schooling as a crucial means of breaking the cycle of poverty. Head Start, Title I of the Elementary and Secondary Education Act, and other measures particularly in 1964–5, launched a war that was to be conducted by schools, and involved far-reaching changes in approaches to early schooling – as well as criticism of the existing school system and its failure to provide adequately for poor and racial and ethnic minority children. The new educational programmes were to be central to plans for President Johnson's 'Great Society'.

Under the new legislation Congress required the Commissioner for Education to arrange an enquiry into the relative conditions of schools which served the diverse communities of the United States. Amidst the massive new attention being given in the mid-1960s to compensatory education or the education of the disadvantaged, therefore, a substantial research project under James S. Coleman explored, and in 1966 produced a report on, equality of educational opportunity.[2] Its central message was that schools had far less impact on children's levels of educational attainment than did their family circumstances. Into the landscape of American educational debate erupted the apparent conviction that schooling did not matter. The school could not overcome the educational weaknesses that resulted from the poverty and resultant limitations of the family.[3]

In Britain, the sociology of the 1950s and 1960s pointed to the profoundly constraining influences of social class. A dominant sociology of education was concerned with the class bias of a divided public education system that had taken shape in the nineteenth century, and the strengths, weaknesses and promise of greater educational and social fairness through the comprehensive reorganization of the secondary schools. The long battle over reorganization reinforced the sense that schools *did* matter, only too well, in shaping the social and economic destinies of children. The Plowden Committee report, *Children and Their Primary Schools*, in 1967 emphasized the all-important influence of parental attitudes on children's performance, but did not undermine as dramatically as the Coleman findings had

3

done in the United States the previous year a prevailing certainty that schools 'mattered'.[4]

What appeared in both countries, and elsewhere, from this point was a slowly growing concern with the nature and causes of school differences, and with questions of whether or how such differences accounted for differences in learning, attainment and outcomes. By the early 1970s a scattered, often research-based attempt was being made to consider what characteristics of teachers, classrooms, administration, organization, principals or schools might be responsible for the 'success' or 'failure' of the students. Were social class, family and environment all-powerful obstacles to educational achievement by the majority of children from disadvantaged backgrounds? Were compensatory or enrichment strategies doomed to make short-lived and marginal impacts on the educational experience of such children? Were the efforts shaped in the mid-1960s misguided? Did school reorganization in Britain and elsewhere in Europe, for example, do more than transfer inequities *between* schools to the *interior* of schools? Were schools an inescapable mechanism for perpetuating the class system, perhaps even a deliberate mechanism by which to secure 'success' for the few and 'failure' for the many?[5]

Critiques of schools from many directions, reflecting these and related questions, put the purposes and possibilities of schools under prolonged and often controversial scrutiny. For many different reasons – even before the anxieties arising from intensifying world economic competition and recession thrust education to the very centre of the stage – the aims and competences of schools had been called severely into question. In Britain from 1969 and through the 1970s a series of 'Black Papers' attacked 'progressive' education and the comprehensive schools as responsible for the lowering of standards.[6] In the United States Admiral Rickover and others accused the schools of adopting a 'progressive' orthodoxy, to the detriment of the country's basic educational needs.[7] Attempts to analyse the elements of 'effective' schools were therefore one response both to a loss of confidence in what schools *could* do, and to growing disquiet about what they *were* doing.

The movement to define, identify and promote the purposes and practices of effective schools took shape internationally from the second half of the 1970s. It had roots in research and changing economic and political landscapes. Governments, for other reasons and with different objectives, were looking for ways to make schools more effective in contributing to the policies for economic security and social stability that became basic to the conservative political agendas of the late 1970s and 1980s. Researchers and educationists were looking for ways to make schools more effective in serving both their fundamental educational purposes and their clienteles, and the accountability purposes being defined with increasing urgency for schools and other educational institutions. In the United States particularly, the 'effective schools' definitions directly addressed, however differently from the compensatory education movement of the 1960s, the problems of the same constituencies: school students from poor, minority and disadvantaged backgrounds. The effective school was in fact often defined as one which enabled such students to register the same level of educational achievement as those from more affluent and advantaged backgrounds. The effective school was being promoted as one which served all students well.

What these threads illustrate is the complexity of establishing what in fact constitutes an effective school. The effective school movement from the 1970s has a distinctive vocabulary and range of aims. The itemized components of the 'effective' were a new focus of research, debate and attempts to influence policy. They competed with but to a degree also meshed in with other and often related interests in 'school improvement', 'school reform', 'restructuring', the nature of teaching styles, the purposes and practices of tests and assessment, changes in school-teacher education or school curricula, and moves towards a national curriculum or new forms of school financing. Although there were major, new and distinctive aspects of the effective schools approach, the movement illustrated an old dilemma contained in the centuries-old concern with what constitutes a 'good' school.

Defining a good school over the centuries, and in different countries and localities, has been a question not only of the way a school has operated, but of the way its aims have been established, by whom, and with what intentions. Re-enacting the conduct and aims of schools in the past raises the considerable problem faced by historians in establishing the motivation of the participants. Motives are rarely as pure as historians often suggest. Controversy in recent decades has sometimes focused on the aims of those who established schools or school systems – whether as philanthropic gestures or as a means of control, to extend or to limit access to knowledge, to promote democratic development or to prepare a docile labour force. Contemporary experience would suggest, however, that even the most committed politicians have mixed motives. Raising the school-leaving age, introducing a vocational programme, extending pre-school provision, planning a core curriculum – these and other changes may have a dominant but rarely an exclusive purpose. Governments and benefactors may be single-minded, but may serve more purposes than they recognize. Controversy may persist over the reasons why British mass schooling was developed in the late eighteenth and early nineteenth centuries, or why American city school systems were centralized in the late nineteenth century, or why schooling in colonial territories took the forms it did, but single-cause explanations rarely provide an answer. What has been a good school in such circumstances is therefore related to the multiple expectations and judgements of multiple constituencies.

The problem then is to establish over time who has been largely or solely responsible for defining standards for schools, for monitoring them, for making decisions about the components of standards, including the work of teachers, the approach to teaching and learning, the curriculum, organization, the relationship of the school to its parent or controlling body – the church, local political authority, patrons, or others. There have historically been few objective criteria by which standards have been set or evaluated, and those that have appeared have either failed to survive, have not been generalized, or have undergone frequent and substantial change. Payment by results in late-nineteenth-century England was a discrete chapter in educational history. Neither the appointment of Her Majesty's Inspectors of schools nationally in Britain from the 1830s, nor the later development of a system of advisers or inspectors by local education authorities, was adopted in precisely these forms in other countries. Systems of public examinations, group

5

testing and student assessment of various kinds have undergone regular and considerable changes. 'Good' schools have been recognized historically mainly by their conformity to explicit standards of student control and behaviour, expressed in terms of 'discipline' or 'order', and by outcomes in terms of public examination results or – in the United States – numbers and qualities of 'graduates'. Systems of inspection or accreditation have evolved in order to provide publicly available and acceptable forms of accountability. Parents and communities have judged schools by the appearance and 'performance' of teachers and students, or the school's record in the numbers of students entering prestigious universities. Increasingly in the twentieth century schools have been judged by the standards of students as judged by employers at the point of recruitment. The ability of the schools to inculcate attitudes appropriate to the state, the church, the employer, the community, has in one form or another been central to judgements about schools in all countries over the centuries. Good schools have been ones which trained girls to be good wives and mothers, or which trained boys to serve the commercial ethic or the Empire. 'Good' has been an infinitely adaptable epithet, used of schools of many kinds, by interested parties of many kinds.

Since few of these judgements have involved the use of objective or sometimes even public criteria, a good school has normally been one which satisfies the subjective sentiments of its controllers, participants or clients. To proclaim a school to be good implies approval of its aims, procedures and achievements. To be effective, in the terms of those developing the concept and its implications from the 1970s, a school has to meet known, explicit criteria. To announce a school to be effective in this context is to say something more precise and circumscribed than to say it is good. A school is effective if, after adopting the programme and procedures suggested, it is then successful in those and its own terms. It would be possible for a parent or a community to accept that a school is effective without being good. There may be other criteria of success that the school does not meet, which could relate, for example, to particular aspects of the happiness or well-being of its students, or their opportunity for creative expression or sport. What the literature of effectiveness has shown is that there is a core of important criteria concerning such aspects of schooling as the role of the principal, the curriculum and the total environment of the school – though the relationship of such criteria to one another and to student attainment is not always easy to demonstrate.

Although there are substantial variations in the characteristics of effective schools as identified by different researchers, the core was sharp enough to have made it possible in the 1980s for an international effective schools movement to develop. Within it, its publications, its conferences, its scholarly networks, enough common ground emerged for analyses of effective schools in Louisiana or the Netherlands to sit comfortably with work on schools in London or New Zealand. International projects became possible, and conferences focusing on school effectiveness and school development could take place in Wales or Israel or Canada, with scholars, administrators and school people from a wide variety of countries taking part. The international literature of school effectiveness grew rapidly in the 1980s, with constant reference by analysts in one country to research in other countries. The work of Michael Rutter and colleagues in *Fifteen Thousand Hours* (1979) or Peter Mortimore and colleagues in *School Matters* (1988) was as well known in some other countries, including the United States, as in their native Britain.[8] The American work of Ron Edmonds was seminal and constantly footnoted in Britain and Europe.[9] Reviews or critiques of the effective schools research, such as those of Purkey and Smith (1983) or Larry Cuban (1983 and 1984), became essential reading for workers in the effective schools field elsewhere.[10] Identifying the organizational, curricular and pedagogic principles of effective schools, as compared with those which were either less effective or ineffective, did not necessarily mean that there were simple recipes available for creating them. The rapid development of effective schools policies in various American states, and in 1988 by Congress itself,[11] involved a search for suitable implementation strategies, the means of working with schools to secure change, the roles of the state, the school district, superintendents, principals and teachers, in moving schools in the new directions – at the same time as other research and other policy imperatives indicated other choices.

In both Britain and the United States, as in continental Europe, Australia and elsewhere, the effective schools movement was accompanied by different pressures for school improvement. A number of studies of American schooling resulted in the establishment of consortia, state programmes, and other versions of reform which paralleled effective schools developments, and channelled resources in other ways.[12] Reform movements of various kinds appeared in all of these countries in the 1980s. The one that swept the United States in the mid- and late 1980s produced statewide decisions to lengthen the school day or term, tighten up graduation or college-entry requirements, or reconstruct curricula to give greater and more consistent emphasis to language, mathematics, science and other basic knowledge and skills. A Congressional Act of 1988 mandated – amongst many other things – that a proportion of federal funding available for school development should be devoted to the promotion of effective schools according to precise criteria – in fact the same as those defined by Ron Edmonds in 1979.[13] Effective schools had entered policy vocabulary and action alongside other intended strategies of school reform.

In Britain the contribution to a body of effective schools literature by David Reynolds, Michael Rutter, Peter Mortimore and others was not as directly incorporated into educational policy-making as was that of their counterparts in the United States. The increasingly centralized educational policies of the British Conservative government after 1979 pointed in directions which also intended significant change or reform, but the situation and the emphases were often very different. Government policy vocabulary was that of 'value for money', a 'national curriculum', parental 'choice', schools' ability to 'opt out' of local authority control, and other means of changing the established patterns of school finance, management, relationship to the world of work, and public accountability. By the late 1980s the message of the effective schools movement was being heard in the context of conferences and workshops, some local authority planning and – particularly in Scotland – the work of the Inspectorate. The relationship to school-based review and improvement plans was important, but not consistent, and the effective schools effort was having to try to penetrate structures and procedures whose priorities had been massively determined by government aims and policies of a different kind and with different central power from those of the United States.

What was certainly true of the effective schools developments of the 1980s in the countries where they took place was their refocusing of attention to the internal processes of schools. The literature addressed concepts of school culture or ethos, bridged across to a strong international interest in analysing teacher effectiveness, and drew upon and influenced the work on school administration and management that had been strongly developed in previous decades. It is to some extent true that the British and American educational policies against poverty that emerged in the mid- and late 1960s distracted attention from the internal features and weaknesses of schools, or made undue assumptions about the ways schools operated or could operate given new policies and resources. The Coleman Report, for example, was able to make judgements about schools on the basis of their level of resources, but did not make – and would not have been able to make – judgements based on the ways in which schools differed in their use of those resources, or the ways in which internal school organization and relationships contributed to school differences. The focus on pre-school provision, important though this was in these and many other countries, was not adequately matched by an understanding of the capacity of schools to continue and to build on pre-school achievements. The pressure in Britain to establish comprehensive schools in order to mitigate the effects of social class was overwhelmingly concerned with access to secondary schools and the basic structure of the schools, and very little with the specifics of curricula or teaching methods. The educational literature of the 1960s and early 1970s had other preoccupations.

The effective schools movement of the late 1970s and 1980s was not the only contributor to the redirection of attention to the internal working of schools, and therefore of differences amongst schools and their ability to influence their students' levels of attainment. It did, however, help to establish that too little was known about, and too little research interest was taken in, how schools worked, how and why they differed, why some succeeded by certain criteria in difficult circumstances more than others, what it was in the school culture that determined its, and its students', success rate, and by what measures to make that judgement. It could be argued, however, that in focusing attention on such questions the effective schools movement weakened commitments of other kinds – notably to the promotion of social equity. Focusing on the correlation of detailed factors could make it difficult to see the school and its sub-units as dynamic processes, and substitute weakly combined emphases on specific features of schools for the richer, more complete understandings of some other approaches to school improvement.

The discussion of effective or good schools, for these and other reasons, needs to take historical account of the research and political backgrounds from which they sprang. It needs to take account of contexts and alternatives, the strengths and weaknesses of the effective schools movement and its relationship to other strategies of system reform, school development, teacher empowerment or changes in approaches to curricula, assessment, teaching and students. This is all part of an unending need to review what schools are, what they succeed and fail in doing, and what that means, what judgements can be made about them, and by whom. What judgements can be made, and by whom, about a school that declares itself to be child centred and 'progressive', and a school that has a strong, structured, 'academic' commitment? One that pursues a 'vocational' programme as a means of student motivation and one committed to a firm religious orthodoxy? How does the recent concern with effectiveness relate to past efforts by schools to set and achieve stated goals, teaching to a particular curriculum and towards a specific pattern of assessment and examinations, producing gentlemen or ladies, aiming at equity or caught in a pattern of inequity, responding to the need for skilled or unskilled manpower, or for an informed and participating, or passive, citizenry? How good or how effective have schools ever been, are they now, and how do we know?

To search for answers to such questions means looking in many directions. The discussion in this book has to take as one of its centrepieces the emergence and implications of an American effective schools movement, but looks for a longer perspective in some aspects of mainly British experience in the nineteenth and twentieth centuries. The importance of the American development is considerable since the United States was not the only country where dominant voices were proclaiming it to be almost in a state of educational siege.[14] The interest of the British perspective lies in the struggle not just of schools but of national policy-making to grapple with questions of standards and the machineries for ascertaining and enhancing them. The essential context for the American theme from the 1970s is one of a fragmented system within which a concept such as the effective school must take root, build a constituency, compete, and become part of an immensely complex process of policy evolution. The context for the British theme is that of concepts confronted more directly by a nineteenth- and twentieth-century development of strong national policy-making. In 1988 the American Congress legislated for some limited support for effective schools as defined in the research. In the same year the British Parliament approved an Education Reform Act which, amongst other things, endorsed a National Curriculum accompanied by national testing. The two experiences open up different approaches to the essential questions with which we are concerned: how good or how effective have schools ever been, are they now, and how do we know? And what do we mean?

NOTES

1 This distinction is drawn in Eric Eaglesham (1967). *The Foundations of Twentieth-Century Education in England*. London: Routledge & Kegan Paul (chs 4 and 5).

2 James S. Coleman *et al.* (1966). *Equality of Educational Opportunity*. Washington, DC: Department of Health, Education, and Welfare.

3 The issues are discussed in Harold Silver and Pamela Silver (1991). *An Educational War on Poverty: American and British Policy-Making 1960–1980*. Cambridge: Cambridge University Press.

4 Central Advisory Council for Education (England) (1967). *Children and Their Primary Schools* (Plowden Report). Vol 1. London: HMSO.

5 This view was summarized most influentially by Samuel Bowles and Herbert Gintis (1976). *Schooling in Capitalist America: Educational Reform and the Contradictions of Economic Life*. New York: Basic Books.

6 The first of these was C. B. Cox and A. E. Dyson (1969). *Fight for Education: A Black Paper*. London: Critical Quarterly Society.

7 For example H. G. Rickover (1963). *American Education: A National Failure*. New York: E. P. Dutton.

8 Michael Rutter *et al.* (1979). *Fifteen Thousand Hours: Secondary Schools and Their Effects on Children*. London: Open Books; Peter Mortimore *et al.* (1988). *School Matters: The Junior Years*. London: Open Books.

9 For example Ronald Edmonds (1979). 'Effective schools for the urban poor', *Educational Leadership*, **37** (1).

10 Stewart C. Purkey and Marshall S. Smith (1983). 'Effective schools: a review', *Elementary School Journal*, **83** (1); Larry Cuban (1983). 'Effective schools: a friendly but cautionary note', *Phi Delta Kappan*, **64** (10); Larry Cuban (1984). 'Transforming the frog into a prince: effective schools research, policy, and practice at the district level', *Harvard Educational Review*, **54** (2).

11 Public Law 100–296 (the Hawkins–Stafford Elementary and Secondary School Improvement Amendments).

12 For example the Coalition of Essential Schools, based at Brown University and developing from ideas contained in Theodore R. Sizer (1984). *Horace's Compromise: The Dilemma of the American High School*. Boston: Houghton Mifflin (particularly 1985 edn with Afterword).

13 Public Law 100–296 (cf. sections 1541–2).

14 The best known of such voices is The National Commission on Excellence in Education (1983). *A Nation at Risk*. Washington, DC: US Department of Education.

Chapter 2

Towards Complexity

Schools, and the philosophers and providers of schooling, have always been concerned with outcomes. For Plato the outcome was 'better men', 'guardians' or overseers of the state, prepared by 'right education'. It was a state in which people were fashioned for their roles, and this way the city state 'develops and is ordered well, each class is to be left to the state of happiness that its nature comports'.[1] For Plato the school directly serves the state, is an instrument of state cohesion, relates differently to different social strata, and is to be judged by its performance of the ascribed functions. For the welfare of the state it *needs* to be efficient, within prescribed curricular limits. The Platonic version of education has parallels in schooling across the continents and centuries, though it was not everywhere the same concept of the state, or necessarily the state at all, that the school was to serve. Confucian China needed a stable bureaucracy, Judaism, Islam and Christianity a priesthood. Schools of different kinds were developed to serve versions of Plato's differentiated state, to fulfil different functions in the church, or to provide the levels of literacy required for public administration, private management or commerce.

In a precise sense, therefore, schools were created and functioned to achieve demonstrably vocational purposes. They trained choristers for cathedrals, prepared limited numbers for the lower ranks of officialdom. The functions of schools which served wider constituencies were perceived in different but no less vocational terms. 'Grammar', 'petty' or various kinds of charity school, for example, might have varied populations, but their foundation documents, the qualifications and terms of reference of their teachers, and the nature of their curricula, defined precise outcomes – in relation to church doctrine, social position or occupational duties. The school in Europe – broadly speaking until the end of the eighteenth century – was a servant of some explicit interpretation of social stability and continuity. It sent its products with basic or more advanced literacy towards traditional employments and acceptance of established order, or towards the university or seminary or apprenticeship to the law, the guild, the craft. A good school was therefore one which adhered to precise definition and regulation, was appropriately taught on the basis of an established curriculum, and prepared its students for such precise outcomes – and survived.

'Education', of course, was always wider than 'schooling', and what was learned in other ways could contribute to social conservatism, but also to a search for change. The gentry might have their private tutors and libraries, girls might have their governesses, the populace might have their sermons. Social and political continuity might be disturbed, however, by oppositional or heretical or radical movements drawing on other forms of knowledge and understanding – self-taught, spread by grievance and political action, filtered down from the writings and actions of popular figures, the reassertion or reinterpretation of oral traditions, what was heard from the pulpit or the market-place. The promotion of literacy might be greater in Protestant than in Catholic Europe, amongst white American settlers than amongst black slaves, but its encouragement and denial might both be directed towards explicit functional ends – respect for the social order, respect differently perceived as buttressed by popular ignorance or by popular access to the literature of religion.

Historically, however, the school was everywhere inseparably associated with wider relationships within the community, and with expectations of its service to the monastery or the cathedral, the synagogue or the city, the squire or the patron. Other versions of education and its purposes, schools and their curricula, aims and practices, did of course emerge within movements seeking forms of religious, social and political change. Humanism or Protestantism, for example, offered wider educational perspectives. Seventeenth-century educationists argued the merits of education in the vernacular, the importance of scientific knowledge, the matching of education to the growth of the child, education for wider personal and humanitarian purposes than those of traditional schools. Comenius, Milton and others altered the tone and content of educational debate. New approaches to the curriculum and pedagogy were being formulated, new texts being written, new traditions of educational thought being established. Changes in the practices of schooling were, however, limited in Britain and Europe generally until the late eighteenth and early nineteenth centuries. The expectations and functions of schools were too settled to admit of radical change until other factors basically affected the political and social configurations of countries and the continent. The endorsement or criticism of schools, their efficiency, their effectiveness, their rightness or goodness, continued to relate to their ability to accomplish the precise outcomes built into the formulas by which they were founded and supported.

For Britain, as for the rest of Europe, the crucial sources of change lie in the eighteenth-century Enlightenment and the radical and revolutionary economic, social and political changes of the late eighteenth and early nineteenth centuries. Out of the European Enlightenment came vigorous, systematic attacks on outmoded institutions, including education, and the antiquated curricula and processes which seemed inefficient in working for old ends or responding to new ones. The Enlightenment philosophers of France or Scotland, or Locke in England, identified education as a cornerstone of progress, and the existing bases of education as legacies of obscurantist social structures and theories they sought to replace. From the 1770s and through the American and French revolutions new social programmes gave added momentum to the search for new dimensions and contents of schooling. Education – not always interpreted similarly – in the writings of a Tom Paine, a William Godwin or a Jeremy Bentham became synonymous with political and social change. In the debates of the French revolutionary parliaments schools were central to planning, as they were to the founding fathers of the American revolution and the particular energies of Thomas Jefferson. For some revolutionary and radical thinkers schools were perceived as serving a renewed and democratized state, for others as serving communities or the populace – sometimes in opposition to the notion of 'the state'. For a Mary Wollstonecraft a conception of popular education was part of a programme for the liberation of women.

The changes associated with political reform and revolution were accompanied, and for the most part inextricably related to, changes in the economic and social – and in some cases military – complexion of Europe. In the late eighteenth and early nineteenth centuries major changes related to conflicts both between and within states, changes which helped to transform the map of schooling across Europe. At the beginning of the nineteenth century Napoleon remodelled French education, and Prussia, after being defeated by Napoleon, inaugurated Europe's first state-provided system of elementary education. Following a revolt in Russia in 1825, Nicholas I sought to eliminate 'foreign influences' by introducing a new system of laws covering all levels of education. The statutes of 1835 aimed to construct an education system 'that would be instilled with a new national "spirit" and that promised to preserve the "existing order" '.[2] Education had become a key element in European moves to establish or strengthen statehood, to modernize within the framework of essentially conservative structures and ideologies.

There were important differences amongst the new generations of educational proponents and activists in Europe and the United States. Jefferson's proposed structure of popular education in Virginia, or Horace Mann's work to establish a statewide system in Massachusetts, was different from the conception of a Humboldt or a Fichte in Germany in a different context of the actual or proposed role of the state. All differed in many respects from the essence of what was being presented by Rousseau and some of those who used Rousseau as the basis for 'progressive' versions of schooling. All of these ideas and plans fall nevertheless within an emerging pattern of nationhood and statehood, different versions of the adaptation of schooling to a changing order, or to an old order under threat. The most obvious challenges to established social and political structures met with educational responses often violently opposed to one another – to teach or not to teach writing to the poor; to make or not to make schooling compulsory; to separate or not to separate public education and religion; to bring or not to bring the state into the training of teachers. Debate, whether in Britain or Prussia, the United States or Russia, moved in general, however, from considerations of *whether* popular education was desirable to *what forms* of education should be provided, by whom, and with what degree and forms of state intervention.

Schools were being created for new purposes, old ones were being castigated for their failure to modernize, and across the early decades of the nineteenth century there were pressures for reform and system building. Whether established schools were 'efficient' was not too difficult to determine. If an endowed grammar school had a lax teacher and few pupils, or if a school of any kind failed to keep order and was prey to riot and abuse, the case – at least for the reformers – was clear. As circumstances changed, whether schools were 'good' or 'effective' was becoming a more complex set of issues.

Britain provided a particularly revealing case of a conflict of educational ideologies, failing for most of the century to construct a 'national' system of education. Throughout the period the British state was one of the arenas where the contending forces clashed, but it was especially clear in Britain that judgement of school processes and outcomes was a critical component of the competing attempts to understand, control or influence social and political change. Public attacks on the lamentable weaknesses of the long-established 'great' – or what came to be known as the independent 'public' – schools in the early decades of the century were one expression of feelings aroused by the inadequacies of schools at many levels, including the social and academic profiles of England's only two universities until the 1830s – Oxford and Cambridge. Eton and other schools were under attack in the early century for their rote-learned Latin curriculum, their educationally unsound and unacceptable conditions and procedures. The critics judged such schools to be poor because they failed to educate either for traditional purposes or in response to the conditions of the new century.

Britain in the early nineteenth century had inherited a rapidly and radically changing economy and environment. The world's first industrial nation was facing the problems of uncontrolled urban growth and population movement, the disruption of the traditional rural patterns of authority through church and squire, the conflict of ideologies as radical movements confronted the authority of the state machine and campaigned for freedom of the press, the suffrage and improved conditions of life. Britain had become a testing ground for new social theories and political programmes in the world's most rapidly changing economy.

Conservative responses distrusted the state, sought to rely on the good sense and good will of the new industrialists, submitted slowly and reluctantly to parliamentary regulation of industrial and urban conditions, and looked to the church, philanthropy and established institutions to make adaptations. The evangelical wing of the Church of England looked to strategies of moral regeneration, including through education; the utilitarian movement looked to rational programmes of political and civic change, including through education. Radical movements looked to a variety of possible sequences of reform, either through political action leading to popular control of the processes and implications of change, or – as in the case of Robert Owen and the Owenites – through forms of cooperative production and community organization which would make obsolete political structures irrelevant. All of these included changes in society and the individual through education.[3] Amidst the warfare of social and political theories, programmes and movements, education was invariably a salient issue, as a form of social protection, child rescue and moral strength, or as a lever of reform, or some mixture of these and other motives. The purposes and practices of schools were never far from political and social debate, and what had changed profoundly from the late eighteenth century was the translation of social theories into educational action.

At the level of popular action, initiatives and movements to establish schools between the 1780s and 1830s took many and different forms, aiming at a range of clienteles. Existing provision of charity schools for the children of pauper families was an inadequate model for any pattern of mass education for the children of the densely populated industrial and commercial towns. The prevailing model across this period – one of its outstanding innovations – was the monitorial school developed from the end of the eighteenth century by Joseph Lancaster and Andrew Bell, the former through what became the British Society and the latter the National Society. Lancaster's work benefited from primarily nonconformist and political radical support, Bell's from those wishing to support an organization dedicated to educating children 'in the principles of the Established Church'. Both aimed, using a single teacher and a system of 'monitors', to teach large numbers of children inexpensively a simple curriculum for basic literacy and morality.

Visitors to the schools judged them by their economy of scale, the effective use of rewards and punishments, the internal operation of the process by the young monitors – taught by the teacher, and themselves drilling their peers in what they had been taught. The schools were also judged by their public image – how the children comported themselves, for example on 'open' days, or when paraded to church. The schools were a new phenomenon, targeted at a mass population, supported by voluntary donation and subscription, using a method into which teachers could be quickly and easily inducted, and offering education of a kind and in a form visibly adapted to the new conditions. The schools aimed at literacy and the preparation of children for some of the precise features of the new adult world – punctuality, the performance of routine tasks, the acceptance of authority. The schools were aware of the immediate society their children were to enter, and for both girls and boys this normally meant servanthood, the factory or other local employments. The new mass education placed girls on a footing of equality with boys, so far as the provision of schooling was concerned. The curriculum was sometimes and increasingly extended, providing needlework for girls, for example, but in some cases a wider vision developed. One such school in London is known from the start to have seriously addressed questions of the children's health and welfare, and acted as a focus for local efforts to improve the environment and combat cholera,[4] and it is probable that others went beyond the most restricted definition of the monitorial school's purposes.

These and other forms of popular education often, of course, achieved more or differently than what was specifically intended. Some of the working men who played active leadership roles in the Chartist or other popular and radical movements of the 1820s and 1830s recorded their debt to such schools in laying a basis for their continued education, often literary and political in scope. The 'self-educated working man', an important phenomenon of the nineteenth century, frequently found the starting point for his reading – and writing – of poetry, his use of such historical models for political action as John Ball and William Tell, in the education provided by the monitorial or some other school, an education that was limited but nevertheless acknowledged as 'effective'.

Versions of popular schooling which paralleled the monitorial schools included the Sunday schools, which spread rapidly from the movement's beginning in the 1780s. They aimed to provide a basic education of some kind – the amount of secular instruction varied – for those children who did not or could not attend any other form of school, or whose schooling needed to be supplemented with something more directly biblical and catechismal. Factory schools, varying considerably in quality, were opened by some employers, who were required by law from the early 1830s to provide part-time education for their employed children. Ragged schools attempted to provide for the most destitute. 'Dame' schools were a largely unrecorded, sporadic, alternative to the more formal versions of schooling, probably varying enormously in the talents of the 'dames' and in the nature and quality of what was provided in the informal schoolroom.[5] Since schools of all kinds generally charged a fee, the dame schools formed part of a continuum of schools presumably judged by parents, wherever there were choices, to provide some sort of value for money. The value might be different in different schools at the children's different ages: either they were being kept out of harm's way, or they were being trained in right habits or useful skills. Frequently, however, the school was in competition with the field or the factory or other means of boosting the family income.

Given the uneven distribution of literacy, and the relatively low level of culture represented by most formal schooling, various kinds of adult education were often also crucially important. Some had long histories, and self-educated working men were able, for example, to draw on Methodist traditions of class discussion and reading. Adult schools were a feature of the early nineteenth century, and from the early 1820s mechanics' institutions offered what amounted to 'continuation' rather than basic education. The institutes, like the Sunday schools, had a variety of patronage, including employers and working people themselves. Working-class and radical movements from the 1780s were forces for self-education and mutual education, and often structured themselves round activities aimed at literary and political education or 'useful knowledge'. Increasingly in the early and mid-nineteenth century they also created their own schools. It was in this context that some of the Enlightenment and 'progressive' education traditions came together, in the educational energies particularly of Robert Owen.

In Europe others also fostered such a development, notably around Rousseau's ideas of education for individuality, and the caring approach to children's education associated particularly with Pestalozzi. Rousseauite ideas circulated in England and gave rise to experimental schools.[6] What Owen did was create an 'infant school' at New Lanark that won considerable Europe-wide publicity and interest. He made *A New View of Society*[7] an educational manifesto of child-centred, community-related education, and gave rise to a movement which, through the work of Samuel Wilderspin in particular, carried the infant school to many parts of the world. Owen initially supported the Lancasterian monitorial school, but abandoned it for a wider and deeper vision of schooling which was intended to shape children's fullest talents and train them as rational people. By the 1820s and 1830s, therefore, yet another approach to popular schooling had become a major contributor to debate and to some extent to the practice of education.

Within the Owenite movement, as more widely in radical and popular movements, attention was often directed to the issue of educating girls and women. The most publicized efforts of the nineteenth century to develop education for girls were those relating to the secondary and higher education of largely middle-class girls, but in terms of popular education there were other traditions. This applied not only to the equal provision of infant or monitorial education for girls and boys, but also to the educational activities for and by women that often developed in the political and social contexts of Owenism and Chartism.

Judgements of the quality of schooling were therefore being made in the early part of the nineteenth century from a range of competing viewpoints, using widely different criteria of the nature and outcomes of different kinds of educational institution. The criteria might relate to jobs or character, curricula or child development, a contribution to protecting the status quo or promoting a new state of society, service to the Christian or the secular, or 'value for money' expressed in many and widely different ways. Providers and customers looked for efficiency, which could be a different conception when applied to Eton, to factory 'half-time' education or to an Owenite infant school. The British and National school organizations attempted to influence and monitor their affiliated schools, including through the school texts they recommended (for example those of the Society for Promoting Christian Knowledge), the brief training they gave their teachers, and those they recommended to the managers of schools. School managers or committees, which might in practice mean the local vicar or a group of subscribers, would to different extents supervise or intervene in the life of their schools. The British and National Societies began rudimentary inspection arrangements, but it was not until the end of the 1830s that there were the serious beginnings of a national attempt to monitor 'standards' in mass schooling.

The story of attempts to provide popular education in early industrial England and Wales is one of complex voluntary initiatives. Scotland provided a distinctively different pattern of schooling, based on a long Calvinist tradition of public education and a commitment to widespread elementary education. Britain differed from France, Prussia and some other European countries in not moving towards a legislated, multi-level state system. It is for this reason that Britain adopted other machineries of support, influence and quality control, some of which were exported, others not, to colonial territories and other countries. While in Europe it was common for governments to develop control over the pattern of provision and the mechanisms for ascertaining at least basic efficiency, in the United States these became city-wide or state-wide functions. The effectiveness of schools in delivering adequate levels of literacy and a workforce for the increasingly complex demands of later nineteenth-century industry and public life slowly became major issues in Britain, and government was haltingly driven to take part in legislating for different aspects of education, and to evolve mechanisms for monitoring the state of provision at different levels.

This is an increasingly complex picture of educational provision and purposes in a developing and changing society. The two essential points that emerge are the diversity of schools and their intentions, and the distribution of the power to define their intentions and operations. The next chapter will consider some of the strategies adopted in the British case to monitor the quality of schooling, but as countries around the world developed more sophisticated and diversified school systems, other strategies or other versions of the British strategies were also adopted.

The three main elements in the British nineteenth-century pattern of 'quality assurance' at the school level were the investigative role of parliamentary and other commissions, the Inspectorate, and a system of public examinations. The machinery of commissions became important in some of the British colonies, notably Canada. Public examinations became a prevalent educational tool in many countries. In the United States a widespread commitment to the power of testing was developed, and from the 1880s a system of voluntary accreditation for schools and higher education provided a form of self-imposed accountability for standards. Various kinds of bureaucratic control and inspection were built into European school systems. The relationship between forms of public accountability and increased state involvement in and funding of education was strengthened. Other agencies became involved in influencing and ascertaining standards – including church authorities for their schools, and universities in order to assure the quality of their entrants. For independent schools, an examination system together with success in clearing any other hurdles for would-be entrants to higher education became crucial measures of their success. The strategies of quality assurance and accountability also became important for new sectors of education as they emerged, in post-primary or post-secondary education, part-time and adult education and the education of girls. Developments in provision of education for new constituencies, using different modes of attendance or curricula, became inseparable from examinations or other means of demonstrating that in joining the repertoire of education new institutions were capable of competing on the basis of appropriate, known standards.

Education, understood in a sense wider that what took place in schools or other formal institutions, had become an important battleground on which struggles to change or preserve the shape of nineteenth-century society took place. Major aspects of these struggles did, however, concern the establishment and modification of schools, and the activities taking place within them. What was good or otherwise about a school was a judgement based on the perceived needs of its principal constituents, divided in a number of ways – by social class and local characteristics, and relating to gender and employment, and criteria established by the church, the universities, educationists and other specialists, social movements, political parties or agencies of the state.

Considerable changes in the basis on which judgements are made have taken place in the final decades of the twentieth century, and it is to the critical international example of effective schools that we shall turn. Before we do so, however, it is important to establish a perspective on the factors governing judgements of schools in the nineteenth and earlier twentieth centuries by looking more closely at the experience of one country. Countries differed in their structures of schooling, the rhythm with which school systems were established or filled out, and the details of their pattern of school organization, teacher recruitment and pedagogy, curriculum and the values underlying relationships and behaviour. In the British case there was much that was not formally replicated in other countries, but the factors affecting the formation of judgements at different levels of education, in state and private sectors, and amidst the changing pressures and requirements of urban, industrial, political and social change, have parallels of many kinds in other countries. The intention in the next two chapters is not to write a history of educational provision and change, but to outline what, in one country, governed judgements about the quality of schooling.

NOTES

1 Plato, *The Republic*, translated Paul Shorey (1963). London: Heinemann, Vol. 1, pp. 310–21, 329–31; first published 1930.

2 Cynthia H. Whittaker (1984). *The Origins of Modern Russian Education: An Intellectual Biography of Count Sergei Uvarov, 1785–1855*. De Kalb, Ill.: Northern Illinois University Press, pp. 128–31.

3 For Owenism and other social and political movements see Harold Silver (1965). *The Concept of Popular Education: A Study of Ideas and Social Movements in the Early*

Nineteenth Century. London: MacGibbon & Kee; Brian Simon (1960). *Studies in the History of Education 1780–1870*. London: Lawrence & Wishart (reprinted as *The Two Nations and the Educational Structure 1780–1870*).

4 Pamela and Harold Silver (1974). *The Education of the Poor: The History of a National School 1824–1974*. London: Routledge & Kegan Paul, ch. 5.

5 Cf. Paul Gardner (1985). *The Lost Elementary Schools of Victorian England* (London: Croom Helm) for a study of the dame schools.

6 Cf. W. A. C. Stewart and W. P. McCann (1967). *The Educational Innovators 1750–1880*. London: Macmillan, ch. 1.

7 Robert Owen, *A New View of Society and Other Writings*. London: Dent (written 1813–14; this Everyman edn first published 1927).

Chapter 3

The Nineteenth Century, I: Elementary Standards

The schools which England and Wales, and to a lesser extent Scotland, inherited and developed in the early nineteenth century were divided by social class and to a large degree by gender. The types of school and kinds of provider, curriculum and outcome all related to their class and gender identities. They did not, however, do so totally, in that from the late eighteenth century and throughout the nineteenth century there were experiments with schooling and with curricula, and there were variations within categories of schooling regarding the ways in which they were provided and the aims identified for them. The patrons of Sunday schools and mechanics' institutes, for example, could be essentially and narrowly middle class, or could extend more widely, and include degrees of influence or control by the 'clients' themselves.[1] In the first half of the nineteenth century, even though the basic pattern of mass schooling was fairly fixed, there were within the system schools – probably only small numbers, however – which pushed at the edges of the curriculum towards, for example, nature study and elementary science. Although dominant forms of popular schooling appeared, provided by religious bodies and with increasing public financial support, the nature and content of schooling remained a contested area, with attempts, for example, to include basic economics or social studies or other subjects in the curriculum, and efforts to provide alternative forms of education for children or adults, and to extend provision for girls and women.

Parliament debated education under various kinds of impetus from the first decade of the nineteenth century, but not until 1833 did it begin to make decisions that would directly affect the schools and interpretations of their aims and quality. The decision in that year to allocate a small amount of government funding to support the voluntary schools, through the British and National Societies, led six years later to the appointment of the first of Her Majesty's Inspectors of Schools, whose responsibility was to be to make judgements about the standards of those schools in receipt of such funds. HMIs were to be the main agency for determining whether schools could be said to be setting appropriate standards in their secular curriculum, and whether the standards of teachers and teaching, management and resources, justified public support. The small number of these relatively independent HMIs worked intensively within their allocated geographical areas to visit schools, pass judgement, report and be the eyes and ears of government. Their very existence was intended to encourage schools to achieve appropriate standards, and managers to be aware of their role in ensuring standards that would ensure favourable reports and continued financial support. The HMIs reported in considerable detail to the Committee of Privy Council responsible for educational matters, and the inspectors' reports represent the first substantial attempt in Britain to investigate – albeit erratically at first – the features of schools which could lead them to be judged favourably or otherwise. In many respects for the first three decades of their existence the HMIs were determining what constituted the culture of popular education, and how to make judgements about its constituent parts.

The key purpose of the development of school inspection was to check on the use of government grants and the quality of the education provided. Sir Joshua Fitch, former Chief Inspector of Training Colleges, reflected at the end of the century that 'at first the duty of Her late Majesty's inspector was simply to ascertain if the conditions laid down by the Treasury had been duly fulfilled. He visited each school, inquired into the qualifications and status of each teacher, verified the statistical returns, and reported in very general terms on the order, intelligence, and efficiency of the school.'[2] The early inspectors appointed (with the approval of the Church in the case of the National schools) were therefore to exercise the right of inspection of those schools in receipt of public funds. Although the inspectors were expected to provide 'accurate information as to the discipline, management, and methods of instruction pursued in such schools', they were to have 'a more comprehensive sphere of duty', which included encouraging local efforts to improve and extend elementary education, and to do so by indicating to the providers what improvements in equipment, management, discipline and teaching methods were taking place elsewhere. Their role was defined as ensuring government and local cooperation in disseminating good practice, without interfering with the internal working of schools or pressing suggestions upon the providers 'which they may be disinclined to receive'. The aim was not control but assistance.[3] An 'instructional letter' sent to one of the first two HMIs appointed, the Rev. John Allen, asked him to obtain information 'as to the state of Elementary Education in the mining districts of the counties of Durham and Northumberland'. What he was to do was 'ascertain the number and character of the schools for the children of the poorer classes', including dame, day, Sunday, evening and all other schools whether connected with the societies or churches or not. HMIs were to find out the number of children on the books of each school and the average attendance, as well as

> the nature and extent of the instruction given; the books used; the
> qualifications and salary of the teacher; the methods of instruction
> adopted; the annual income of the school; and such other particulars
> as may tend to afford the most complete information upon the
> subject.[4]

These, clearly, were initial enquiries, and what the inspectors could report on the quality of schooling was at first extremely limited. John Allen's inquiry in this district took six weeks, and he visited 150 schools (plus 20 'school-rooms and masters'), covering a whole range of single-sex and mixed schools, church and Lancasterian, dame and Sunday, private venture and other schools (including one in Durham gaol). He described many of the visits as 'merely rapid glances, from which little could be gathered except general impressions as to the orderly behaviour, cleanliness and attention of the scholars'. Most of the teachers in the day schools of these colliery districts were 'ill educated', the deficiency of books was 'most lamentable', and 'of education, in that sense of the word which includes the training and the endeavour to perfect the faculties of the entire man, there is none'. The physical facilities, including ventilation, were poor, though the parochial schools were better ventilated and their children generally cleaner.[5]

On some of these initial visits the inspectors sat in on the lessons. When the Rev. Baptist W. Noel inspected day schools in Birmingham and some Lancashire towns in 1840, the number of boys present at the lessons he heard ranged from 67 to 218, and the number of girls ranged from 31 to 150, the average being 120. In one case as he sat by the monitor he could not hear the girl who was reading aloud from the New Testament: 'several children were laughing to each other . . . the only symptom of reverence in the whole class was, that every time the name of our Lord was pronounced the whole class made a short rapid courtesy', and the 'irregular popping down' this occasioned, combined with the levity, 'was extremely unpleasant'. On another occasion a girl out of her place received a blow of the fist without warning on the back of her head. Answers to questions from the inspector or the teacher produced such answers as the following:

> In what country do we live? – Europe.
>
> What are the chief kingdoms of Europe? (Silence)
>
> What is Liverpool? – An island.
>
> What are the chief towns of England? – London, Manchester, Lancashire.

Questions about the Gospel often produced either silence or nonsense answers.[6]

How much more systematic the work of the inspectors soon became, and the degree of depth and judgement they attained, can be seen from the example of the work of Joseph Fletcher, who took over responsibility for inspecting the schools of the British and Foreign School Society in 1844. After some preliminary reports he reported on the state of all such schools in 1846. He began his procedure at each school (sometimes consisting of a boys' school and a girls' school under the same roof) by obtaining from 'the most active members of its committee' as much information as possible about the school's 'financial and moral' history, and about the current state of its property and finances. He then

> obtained a rough measurement plan and survey of the schools, and obtained an outline of their working constitution, and of the school agency. . . . An inspection of the schools . . . occupied the remainder of the day, protracted much beyond the ordinary school hours with the elder classes.

He sent the 'salient points' in a weekly report on the schools visited to the Committee of Council.

Fletcher's inspection was 'not a hasty one' directed only to the older pupils. He indicated his procedure and intentions in some detail, going through each class

> so as to form a fair estimate of what was *doing* in each school . . . Dwelling more upon the state of the upper classes, I there revised the results of the operations below; and upon any simple text in their reading-books, found no difficulty in proving to what degree of analytical precision in the use of language before them their faculties

had been cultivated, or to what extent a consistent intelligence upon
the subject matter of it had been awakened among them; to what
higher rules of arithmetic each could proceed after commencing with
the lower; what was the character of their writing and their capacities
of expression; and what was the extent to which their elementary
knowledge of the globe which they inhabit, and of the physical and
moral elements around them, had, in fair sequence, been carried.

Fletcher reported not only on individual schools, but also on what he deduced to be
the essential educational purpose of a Christian education as conceived by 'the
ablest supporters of the schools which I have been commissioned to inspect'. The
purpose appeared to be to make its recipients 'good' and 'wise'. Education was
therefore concerned not only with 'physical strength' and 'intellectual vigour', but
also with 'passions' and 'affections':

Education, in this, its highest sense (embracing physical, intellectual,
industrial, moral and religious education), they are well aware is not
the work of the school only, but likewise of the church, the Sunday-
school, the home, the playground, the street, the workshop, the field,
the mine, the tavern, and the court-house. They are equally aware that
no sane individual, in any conceivable state of society, can escape
education in every branch, either to truth or error, to good or evil.

The choice was not one between 'education' and 'no education', but between 'good'
and 'bad' education. A school for the children of the poor should therefore be 'a little
artificial world of virtuous exertion'.[7]

What the inspectors found in these early decades was governed by the
intentions of the providers and their ability to implement them, differentiated by the
nature of the district and its employments, differences between town and
countryside and amongst towns, provision for boys and girls, the ability to recruit
and retain competent teachers, and the structure, management, teaching processes
and curricula of the schools themselves. The inspectors found themselves looking
not only for basic information and 'good practice', but also for change, and the
conditions of change. They were seeking to influence schools and their providers
(with the reservations imposed upon them), and to report accurately to the
Committee of Council in order to influence the extent and allocation of resources,
and policy more widely. Their visits did not remain as peremptory as those of John
Allen in 1840, but they always faced the problem of extensive visits and the fact that
they had inadequate time to do all that was required of them consistently and
thoroughly. They recorded what they could about standards, and the elements that
affected standards, but at the same time they passed judgement, and not only
reported what others considered to be a 'good' education but also influenced those
perceptions themselves.

They reported on the quality of schooling, and on those of its contributory factors
that it was possible for them to determine and comment on briefly. In their summary
comments on the schools they visited they were making absolute judgements,
but by implication comparative judgements with other schools. The inspectors'
comments in the same year on the Southern District, which included such

essentially rural counties as Berkshire, Buckinghamshire, Kent, Sussex and Wiltshire, and on the Northern District, which included both the rural areas and the growing industrial towns of Lancashire and Yorkshire, give an indication of the range of school quality being perceived. Mr Allen, in the former case, found, for example, schools at all points on the spectrum. In Buckinghamshire he found one school ('chiefly supported by squire and clergyman') that was

> An excellent school in all respects, and best in the most important matters. Children well exercised in composition. Maps drawn with remarkable skill. Two of the boys have made some progress in algebra. A separate classification for arithmetic, which answers well.

At another, in the same county,

> Instruction and discipline highly satisfactory. Children taught with intelligence and thoroughly the Scriptures and the doctrines of the Church. Composition very good. Arithmetic first rate. Some knowledge of geography and grammar. Teachers such as one should rejoice to see at their work.

One Hampshire school was described as having 'excellent attendance. School in all respects in a highly satisfactory state. Master appears to love his work.' Another, in Sussex, was 'an excellent specimen of what may be effected in a district reclaimed from the waste, by the constant pains of the clergyman, with very humble means'. The instruction here was 'very satisfactory' and 'carried beyond the ordinary rudiments'. The children were 'clean and very orderly'. There were many schools described in such positive terms, and using similar criteria. Mr Watkins, reporting on the Northern District, recorded more peremptory judgements. Schools were 'very pleasing', 'very successful', 'excellent'. One Yorkshire village school was 'very successful for the time it has been open; master very zealous, but has need of assistance in teaching so many children'. Another was a 'pleasing village school; mistress devoted to her work, and succeeding in it'; a third was 'proceeding very well . . . teachers intelligent'. A school in Sedbergh was 'thriving', and in many places there were 'improvements', 'devoted teachers', and 'much promise of good'.

In many cases, Allen in particular reported on schools of intermediate or mixed quality. One Kent school had boys who 'read distinctly' and the writing was 'respectable', but he thought the younger children should be in an infant school, and that the standards of discipline and cleanliness 'might be improved'. In another, the instruction of the boys was 'better than their discipline'. In schools everywhere there was a mixture of good and bad to report:

> – Children quiet and orderly. Instruction somewhat scanty. . . .

> – Boys read well; more might be done by questioning to bring out their intelligence.

> – Instruction needs improvement. Arithmetic fairly done. . . .

> – Children are intelligent. Compose and work sums well; spelling well done; writing fair. Room for improvement in the reading and discipline.

> – A few of the elder ones well taught. Room for improvement in the instruction of the rest.

'Room for improvement' and 'more might be done' were constantly used phrases. Watkins constantly found 'promising' schools where there were too many children under one master or mistress. A school might have 'many good points, both in the children and teachers', but 'reading bad, and singing coarse and loud', or it might be 'good on the whole' or 'fair in progress'. Watkins made constant comparisons with his previous visit and found schools making progress, or not much progress, or little progress, or none. He made allowance for 'discouraging circumstances', the short time since the school was opened or the teacher appointed. A large number of schools were 'fair' or 'tolerable'.

In terms of discipline, progress, instruction, quality of teaching, 'intelligence', performance in individual subjects, moral tone, or whatever other criterion was used, substantial numbers of schools were neither excellent nor fair. Allen reported schools where the instruction was 'imperfect' or 'somewhat scanty', the master 'overtasked', or discipline 'more the result of fear than affection'. On the whole he was generous to schools, indicating the need for or possibility of progress rather than condemning – which he was able to do when he felt it necessary, as where a school had a small endowment which was 'apparently of little service to the place' and the children were poorly taught, and the 'discipline imperfect'. Instruction might not be 'intelligently given', by masters who could be 'negligent or severe'. In both boys' and girls' schools, however, Allen's negative judgement tended to be 'room for improvement'.

Whether Watkins saw poorer schools or was prepared to be more critical it is not easy to say. There were more outright condemnations in his case:

> – An ignorant school of disorderly children.
>
> – Little knowledge, and no discipline in this school . . .
>
> – Altogether wanting in discipline.
>
> – Bad in all respects; master not qualified for a teacher; few and ignorant children.
>
> – Very bad school in all respects; children ignorant and undisciplined; master incapable.

More of the rural schools in the Southern District were probably in settled village or small town communities, and the National Society, in more predominantly Anglican communities, was by far the larger of the two societies providing support. In the more changing and unsettled conditions in the Northern District, Watkins was undoubtedly encountering schools faced with more difficult circumstances, including poorer financial support and fewer trained or competent teachers.[8]

Central to the inspectors' judgements on the quality of schools were discipline, the curriculum (including, where appropriate, knowledge of Scripture), and the qualities of the master or mistress. The curriculum was for most elementary schools in the middle of the nineteenth century the basic one of reading, writing and arithmetic, with some other teaching 'above rudiments' in some cases, and needlework for girls (which was reported by some inspectors as being excessive, especially where the girls fulfilled orders for the church or other patrons). Reporting on the National schools of the Midland District in 1846 the Rev. Henry Moseley calculated that of the 10,042 children present in the schools he had inspected 1,373 (781 boys and 592 girls) could 'read with ease and correctness in the Epistles, being 1 in $7\frac{3}{10}$ of the whole number, or, if the infant-schools be left out of the calculation, 1 in 6'. He attributed a decline from the previous year to a more rigorous standard he had set for the reading test. Teaching to read was 'the principal occupation' of the National schools, and since it was a 'drudgery' that began as soon as the child's 'intelligence' opened and continued until the child left school he marvelled that 'so imperfect and so inadequate a result is obtained'. One in five of the children he saw was learning to write on paper, about one in four was learning the first four rules of arithmetic, one in 12 had advanced to the compound rules, and one in 47 to the rule of three (of these 220 pupils only five were girls). Approximately one in 11 children was learning English history and English grammar: 'very many are, however, said to learn them, who possess, nevertheless, no knowledge of them'. This was the full range of the curriculum on which Moseley commented.[9]

In all schools, whether monitorial or not, the inspectors judged the teachers against what one of them described as the need for children to be not merely 'schooled but educated; not alone be drilled to perform their manoeuvres with military precision, but be trained to intellectual and religious habits'.[10] The inspectors repeatedly commented on the inadequacy of rote learning, and praised teachers who attempted, and often achieved, more than 'schooling'. Amid a catalogue of depressing comments on schools in the Midland District the inspector in 1845 found teachers to commend. In one school a Committee of Council grant had improved the buildings and apparatus, and the knowledge of the children was 'in many respects highly creditable to their teachers'. Schools were being successfully taught without monitors, but with the new generation of pupil teachers. One village school provided 'distinct evidences of careful and persevering attention on the part of the master'. In another the mistress was 'well educated and intelligent; the management of the school liberal and enlightened'. One master of a school in a coal-mining area was 'an intelligent man, a good musician, a good teacher'. A mistress in another school had 'taught the first class vocal music, by note, with much success'. Some teachers were described as 'devoted to their work', many as having much improved since the last visit.[11]

Joseph Fletcher, after his 1845 inspection of British and foreign schools, analysed what constituted an 'inferior' school, even though in the schools on which he was commenting there was no lack of 'energy or industry among the teachers'. The inferiority lay not in the numbers of children attending such schools, but in 'classification, order, discipline, methods, and even the cleanliness of the children, after making due allowance for the character of the population surrounding each'. The teachers were 'much too "intellectual", in the most perverse sense', and Fletcher summarizes the effects of their teaching:

> Children shut up within four walls from the spontaneous use of their senses on the objects around them, here obtain no cultivation of their faculties of observation in connexion with the language which they are taught, beyond being occasionally required to give hard names for

the qualities common to *every* object with which they come in contact, as 'natural, artificial, opaque, elastic, inflammable, porous,' &c. But they are required to work very doggedly in reading-drafts on the old plans, and to learn off by heart texts and recitations, which they do not understand, to be repeated, *in display*, before the whole school; a method of which the ill effect is not lessened by Scripture words and sacred subjects furnishing the matter of its exercise.

What a 'sympathizing teacher' does, in Fletcher's view, is help the children to understand the functions of real objects (a plant, a flower, a picture of an animal) and their parts, to show how all is arranged 'by a beneficent Creator', or relate passages of Scripture to the children's own lives in the school or playground.[12] The monitorial system, commented another inspector, provides a teacher, as 'an educated man and an enlightened instructor, no place in the school, but only with reference to his skill as a disciplinarian, and a man of order and authority. It intends no contact of his mind with the minds of the children of his school'. His only contact was vicariously, through the monitors.[13]

Generally speaking the inspectors of the 1840s painted a bleak picture of those schools still using monitorial methods. In 1840 one described the monitors as boys of 10 or 11 years old 'who have only been two or three years in the school, and have little separate instruction, are almost as ignorant as the classes whom they instruct; scarcely know how to read well themselves and are utterly incapable of exercising the intellect of the children on the lessons which they read.'[14] Another, in the same year, described monitors aged 12–13 teaching the younger children 'long rows of unconnected and often difficult words, to which neither they nor their master seek to attach a meaning'.[15] In 1846 Joseph Fletcher analysed in some detail the different ways in which monitorial teaching might work, with different outcomes. In the best cases teachers had as much of the school as possible under their own 'direct instruction', selecting some of these children as monitors, and 'compensating' them by 'extra instruction at over-hours'. The weaker teachers did neither of these things. Any village school could do as well for a minority of children as bad British schools, but the schools needed to be judged by what they were doing for 'the greater number . . . and therefore for the mass of the surrounding population'. Fletcher had come to the conclusion that there was nothing in a monitorial school arrangement that was necessarily 'fatal to the moral tone of a school', though excessive numbers, the consequent neglect, and over-reliance on the arrangement produced much that was 'injurious'. He had obviously seen some successful practice:

> The best masters . . . know how to treat their monitors as their young friends, privileged as such above the mass of the school, and yet completely amenable to discipline, where the friendship of their teacher brings them in contact with a mind itself humble, pure, affectionate, and earnest.

While recording how the system could degenerate, and had degenerated, he gave due emphasis to the way well-instructed monitors 'of sufficient age and character' in a well-organized school could sustain a reasonable level of instruction. The key to the system was the teacher's ability to manage the school, relate directly to the monitors, and help them to become adequate proxies for the qualities he brought to bear: 'in every good school the monitors are taught to teach by mutually questioning each other under the master's correction, but seldom to convey *every* lesson with which they are intrusted'.[16]

Good schools were often associated in the inspectors' reports with the various forms of training, often of a fairly basic kind, being developed for teachers. The National and British Societies and a variety of other organizations had been attempting to provide some form of preparation for teachers in the expanding system of mass education, but until the development of the new pupil teacher system from 1846 the supply of 'trained' teachers remained small. The inspectors constantly referred to the improvement that would be effected in specific schools if the teachers could have some training, or if the school could obtain trained teachers. In some instances there was little difference amongst 'dame schools', which were commonly criticized by the inspectors, village schools, and the less efficient large monitorial schools. One of John Allen's reports in 1840 commented on 16 National schools visited, attended by children of both sexes, and taught by masters with, in some cases, female assistance in teaching older girls to knit and sew. Of the 16 masters, only five 'could be said to have received any proper training . . . six of them taught on no system, without any arrangement of the children into classes, and these results, as far even as mere instruction went, seemed to me inferior to that which is obtained in a good dame-school'.[17] Joseph Fletcher commented in 1846 on the Sunday schools of manufacturing districts, 'doing the work of the day-school on the Sabbath' in an attempt to provide a modicum of education for those otherwise deprived of any.[18] Against such complex backgrounds the inspectors were often hard put to know how to make judgements about schools – often meriting praise for doing anything at all, sometimes being praised for outstanding efforts or successes, either on some absolute standard, in some kind of vague comparison, on simply elaborated criteria, or merely 'making due allowance for the character of the population'. From the beginning of inspection in the 1840s it was clearly of importance to inspectors to record changes, hopefully improvements, from year to year, in terms of new or renovated buildings, new apparatus, new or improved teachers, better school organization and discipline, greater interest by managers and parents. They struggled to estimate whether in fact such improvements were taking place, either as a result of the grants the school received, or for any other reason.

School by school and across the system, therefore, the inspectors were passing judgements of many kinds, and recording recommendations in their reports. The latter might relate, for example, to ways of using registers to abstract statistics which would help a school's promoters 'judge of the progress it is making', or to the teaching of 'the penal laws' to promote an understanding of their benefits and the avoidance of 'fruitless and criminal opposition'. In the latter case the inspector was undoubtedly interpreting his role as one of providing strong advice: 'I have taken pains to press upon teachers the propriety of making boys, previous to their withdrawal from school, acquainted, at any rate, with the great facts of our constitution.'[19] The latter inspector, the Rev. F. C. Cook, is interesting in this connection for the explicitness with which he describes his procedures and criteria, when reporting on the Eastern District in 1845. This was his second report, and on each visit in his second tour of inspection he wrote a short account of the school's progress and read it to the school's committee or managers, 'at the same time offering such advice and suggestions as they might express a willingness to entertain'. His 'favourable indications of increasing efficiency' in the schools included:

1 The sound practical character of the religious teaching.

2 The improved style of reading.

3 The greater attention bestowed upon the rudiments of English composition.

4 The advance in the practical application of arithmetic, and the introduction or extension of various subjects, such as geography, grammar, and history.

5 The improvement of the discipline, and the diminution of corporal punishment.

Cook makes a detailed analysis of all of this in relation to the church schools he was visiting in the district, and of particular interest is a discussion of the use of the terms 'sound', 'practical' and 'satisfactory' in his reports. By 'sound', in relation to religious teaching, he meant that 'due pains are taken to teach the leading facts and doctrines of Christianity in accordance with the authorized formularies of the Church'. His judgement was that, after making 'every allowance for the defects inseparable from the monitorial system', this was being achieved more than commonly believed, especially where the teachers were 'actively superintended by the clergy'. He took the word 'practical' to imply that the teacher was 'not contented with general statements of doctrine. . . . A good teacher, whose heart is in the matter, takes care that every word shall convey a meaning . . . nothing has caused me so much surprise and gratification as the answers which a large proportion of children, both in infant and National schools, have given to questions of a simple practical character.' By the term 'satisfactory' Cook meant that the instruction was not only sound and practical, but also 'fairly diffused through the several classes'. In this last case he was excluding those schools where religious knowledge was confined to the more advanced pupils, and those where the general tone of the school belied a superficial acquaintance with such knowledge. In relation to reading, composition and other subjects Cook also tried to establish criteria of judgement, and account for improvements he detected in each of them.[20] Cook, like all the inspectors, was ultimately concerned with establishing the characteristics of a good school in the conditions of the development of mass schooling, and doing so amid a confusion of available criteria, prejudices and prescriptions. The inspectors were struggling to define what might constitute acceptable standards of schooling in terms of the achievement of basic literacy and other skills, discipline, and moral and religious targets of attainment, as well as negatively in terms of the weaknesses and unacceptable characteristics of the prevailing patterns of schooling for the rural and urban poor.

The inspectors of schools, like those of factories, were part of what became a strong investigative tradition in Britain, particularly from the 1830s. This included the establishment of local and national statistical societies, a 'social science' movement, and the work of a range of individuals to explore and explain the poverty, ill-health, crime, illiteracy and all other aspects of growingly urban, industrial and conflict-ridden Britain. Royal Commissions on Oxford and Cambridge in 1850 were the first of a late-nineteenth-century sequence of commissions to report and recommend on aspects of education. In 1858 a Royal Commission was created under the Duke of Newcastle 'to inquire into the present state of popular education in England, and to consider and report what measures, if any, are required for the extension of sound and cheap elementary education to all classes of the people'. It reported in 1861, and its proposals prompted revised codes in that and the following year, inaugurating what became known as payment on or by results. This and other commissions promoted consideration of what constituted quality or requisite or appropriate schooling of various kinds, and the deficiencies and possibilities of aspects of the curriculum, including science. The Newcastle Commission and payment by results relate specifically to the attempts made by the inspectors from the 1840s to determine and improve the quality of mass schooling.

The Newcastle Commission addressed the question of what, in describing the standards of schools, was excellent, good, fair or bad. It did so on the basis of a mass of evidence it collected, primarily from the ten assistant commissioners it appointed to examine the condition of education in the specimen districts to which they were assigned. The Commission considered the inspectors' reports to have been important, but insufficient for its purpose: they were 'Inspectors of Schools, not of education'. They had no experience of uninspected or private schools, and they had no overview of the numbers of children not educated.[21] The Commission sent the Rev. Mark Pattison and Matthew Arnold to inquire into the state of education in Germany and France, and considered evidence from some other countries. In coming to conclusions about the kind and extent of popular education needed, the Commission addressed such issues as the role of inspection and examination in determining and improving standards and how best to improve instruction for different ages of children in the schools. It published and commented extensively on the evidence of the assistant commissioners, many of whom, of course, reinforced views that had been expressed by the inspectors.

The evidence suggested to the commissioners that, for example, the education of very young children depended on the teachers' 'special taste for the occupation . . . tact, patience, and ingenuity. . . . In the best infant schools much is done, and even much is taught', and there were examples of the reading, dictation, geographical and other skills of very young children. The children from infant schools 'made better scholars than those from dames' schools', according to one assistant commissioner, and 'they exhibit a marked superiority, both in intelligence and in manner'. Another, not untypically, considered that a child should be able to 'read, write, and cipher fairly, applying the four rules, and understanding their principles, on leaving a good infant school at the age of seven'. The commissioners welcomed the infant school because it did not interfere with the demands of employers of labour (as was the case with many children over the age of seven), and because the schools were 'comparatively cheap, as they are usually taught by mistresses'.[22] Judgements about these schools related to their processes and outcomes, and in the generality of schools inspected this was also true. The commissioners were in fact concerned with the motives of the teachers and their pupil teachers (a system developed from 1846), and the combination of the factors relating to teachers and their examination successes, alongside other factors, that contributed to the 'humanizing and civilizing influences of the school'. They pieced together these basic ingredients:

> The reputation of the school and the augmentation grant, and
> certificate of the teacher, depend upon the general character and
> management of the school. If a fair average number of children are
> ascertained by examination to be well taught, if the school is well
> arranged, if its general appearance, and, as the inspectors say, its
> 'tone' is satisfactory, if the pupil-teachers are well trained, and if the
> master or mistress teaches in a skilful and intelligent manner, and
> maintains discipline kindly and firmly, nothing more is required.[23]

There were two crucial elements – the children's mastery of the basics of education, and the dependence of judgements on the character of the school 'as ascertained by examination' – at a time when the development of examinations was becoming a major issue in the educational system generally.

Having scattered judgements of this kind throughout their report, the commissioners in their general conclusions included what was to be an influential section on the 'standard of efficiency in the inspected schools'. They considered the evidence they had received and the meanings of the standards as classified by inspectors in the categories of excellent, good, fair and bad. On the basis of their scrutiny of this evidence they concluded that the inspections that normally took place were inspections 'of schools rather than scholars'. Their important second conclusion was that judgements about schools depended more on the inspection of the first class (the senior class) than of other classes. They concluded that the existing system of inspection and examination had the 'tendency to make the first class the measure of the value of the whole school', and they criticized the opinion that teachers' successes should in fact be judged by the proficiency of children in the first class.[24] The commissioners were therefore convinced that any new system (and this was one of the intentions of the payment by results introduced after the Newcastle Commission Report) must deploy the inspection and examination system in elementary schools in such a way as to improve the proficiency of those other classes. The report aimed at overcoming what it considered to be a failure of the elementary schools – the majority of children did not 'receive the kind of education they require'. The Commission concluded that the schools provided instruction that was 'commonly both too ambitious and too superficial in its character . . . it has been too exclusively adapted to the elder scholars to the neglect of the younger ones . . . it often omits to secure a thorough *grounding* in the simplest but most essential parts of instruction'. The teaching and the form of examination were both to blame.[25]

From the evidence to the Commission and its report there is continued confirmation both of the variability of standards in the schools in the second half of the nineteenth century, and the difficulty of applying what often appeared to be commonly acceptable standards of judgement. One of the most perceptive of the assistant commissioners, W. B. Hodgson, reported a statement he had heard made by one of Her Majesty's Commissioners, to the effect that he knew schools 'in which he could estimate a pupil's length of stay by the stupidity impressed upon his countenance; the longer the stay the more stupid did the child appear'. Hodgson himself believed that there were schools where 'more is done to stupify than to arouse, in which even what little knowledge is taught is purchased at the cost of the love of knowledge; schools greatly inferior in intellectual, and not much superior in moral, influence to the rough but vigorous teaching of the streets and highways'. The question of quality, he affirmed, 'scarcely admits of determination by means of figures'.[26] In this, however, Hodgson was moving in a direction contrary to the prevailing opinion presented to and espoused by the Commission, and by other bodies concerned with other levels of education, and seeing the examination and figures as the necessary means of determining quality. The evidence most readily accepted by the Commission about that quality pointed to the view that means must be adopted to spread efficient teaching and measurement throughout the schools. Many of the inspectors' reports in the 1840s and 1850s had testified to the view now being accepted by the Commission that teachers were focusing on the older children.[27] The codes embodying the 'payment by results' that followed the report contained other fragments of ideology, but using the inspectorial and financing system to tighten up the standards of elementary schools as a whole was an important one.

The essence of the system of payment by results introduced in 1862 was a payment to inspected elementary schools for each child, one-third of which was for attendance; the remainder was a payment that was reduced by one-third in each of the three areas of reading, writing and arithmetic if the child failed to satisfy the inspector. The children had to be presented for examination in set 'standards'. The regulations also provided for further reductions in grant if the buildings were inadequate, sufficient pupil teachers were not employed, or other infractions. The declared intention was for the inspection to continue to take account of the school as a whole, and its religious and moral tone were to be taken into account by the inspectors. Payment by results was to be, as Fitch later summarized it, 'a business-like and sensible plan for apportioning the public grant among school managers, and . . . a satisfactory assurance to the taxpayer that he was receiving a good educational equivalent for his outlay'.[28] There was at the time much controversy surrounding the new code, and over the next three decades it was gradually amended to bring a wider curriculum into the regulations and to relax some of their provisions. It was abandoned in the 1890s.

There was strong opposition to the system from some of the inspectors, particularly Matthew Arnold, on the grounds that it would weaken attention to the general culture of the school, in favour of mechanically preparing the children for individual examination. Others welcomed the emphasis it would place on bringing larger numbers of the younger children up to standard. The Committee of Council report for 1864–5 suggested that of the 26 inspectors' reports two-thirds commented favourably on the working of the new code, and improvements in the standard of instruction.[29] In general teachers were probably opposed to the system, and later judgements, while recognizing that it had aimed to remedy weaknesses in the schools, condemned it strongly. A retired Inspector of Schools for the London County Council, G. A. Christian, wrote in 1922 of 'the reactionary influence exercised by the Revised Code of 1862'. For nearly 30 years education 'lay deep within the shadow of an influence that was pernicious at the best and poisonous at the worst'.[30] Fitch described in 1902 how the system had been gradually widened to enable other subjects to earn grant, but as the years went by the disadvantages of the system were seen more and more clearly. It had led teachers to concentrate on the number of passes rather than on 'general mental improvement'. It had 'substituted a hard and arithmetical test of the efficiency of the school for a true estimate of its worth as a place of intellectual training and moral discipline'.[31] Since the teacher's income depended on the grant, there was a temptation to abuse the system in a variety of ways, for example by fraudulent attendance figures. In spite of precautions to prevent this, it was alleged in Wales that, when the inspector came, 'capable children likely to earn a grant were passed on from school to school to be examined under the names of less capable children on the books of the recipient school. . . . Detection would be almost impossible.'[32] The inspectors were generally conscientious, but given the volume of work or other factors, they might treat their visits as routine and perfunctory. The inspector 'would be always in a hurry'.[33] In 1887, one master interviewed by the Cross Commission on the working of the elementary education Acts was asked about the method of distributing the grant, and thought it had 'a very harassing effect upon the teachers'. The teaching of children was 'very much pleasanter' before the introduction of the present code, which was not as 'beneficial to the moral training of the children' as the old system used to be. Pressed further about the role of the inspector's visits the witness responded as follows:

> Do you ever have visits without notice from the inspectors? – I have not had one for I should say three years, to the best of my recollection.
> Had you visits without notice formerly, before the last three years? – I used to have visits occasionally.
> But not every year? – No.
> Were those visits without notice of any service to the school or to yourself? – None whatever.
> What did the inspector do when he came? – He simply came in and looked at the log book and said, 'I suppose I must sign the log book,' and he is supposed to count the register; somehow or other he never did count mine, but I have known of his doing so; and then he would simply say, 'Good afternoon,' and it was all over.

The witness was reminded that from 1878 inspectors had been instructed to make visits without notice, and to make them 'an encouragement to teachers'. The witness replied that he would have welcomed such visits and advice, but 'I have never known anything of the sort'.[34] Not too much should be made of a single instance. Given the anxieties of the managers and the teachers, the pressures upon the children, the difficulties faced by the inspectors, and the competing demands on schools to meet the criteria of payment by results and attend to 'general mental improvement', judgements made about the performance of individual schools have to be treated with some caution.

The crucial development represented by the establishment of the HMI system, the use of assistant commissioners, and the construction of a funding mechanism based on 'objective' measurement, was the principle of external investigation and judgement. The schools inspectorate reporting to the Committee of Council on Education was not the only form of inspection in the nineteenth century. It was preceded and paralleled by the inspection of the religious education in denominational schools by agents of the respective bodies. Following the 1870 Elementary Schools Act and the establishment of School Boards local inspection arrangements began to emerge. The London School Board, for example, decided to set up its own inspectorate immediately after the board was created, and in 1873 the Leeds School Board included in its regulations:

> In order to provide for the complete supervision of the schools, in addition to official visitation, there shall be appointed . . . as visitors any members of the Committee or the Board who are willing to undertake the duty, and such persons . . . as may be approved by the Board. The schools shall be visited from time to time.[35]

The concept of school 'visitors' was also not new. Charity and monitorial schools had been informally and irregularly 'visited' by subscribers, patrons, managers, the clergy and their wives, and others, either simply to show interest, or to ascertain that the teachers and the children were doing what was expected of them. In some cases the visit was to supplement the work of the teacher, by contributing to either the religious or the secular curriculum. One example appears very clearly in responses to a circular distributed by the Newcastle Commission to many people involved in education. One was Barbara Bodichon, née Leigh Smith, whose MP father had been what she described as a 'great supporter of British schools'. He had deputed her

> to see that the money he gave the schools at Hastings, Sussex, was well used. I was in the habit of visiting the schools, teaching sometimes; but gave most of my time to cultivating the teachers, and trying to help them. In London I have visited National, British, secular, Catholic, ragged, and other schools, and for a year before I started the school in Carlisle Street, I studied the question of education in books, and discussed it with many teachers and others interested in education.[36]

Patrons and managers were, as in this case, also 'visitors', whether formal or otherwise, and their judgements about the detailed procedures, the abilities of the teachers, the behaviour and performance of the children also counted in judgements about the school in general. These were local judgements, and the views of the church or the managers were important to the continued operation and success of the school, as measured by enrolments, attendance, and the active support of the appropriate constituency of benefactors or others – all reflected in the outcome of inspectors' visits in the case of grant-receiving schools. At all stages of the development of mass education there were managers – of charity, industrial, ragged, British, National, Sunday and other voluntary schools, and then under the boards created by the 1870 Act – who made enormous efforts to secure adequate resources, and to support the work of the schools. All of the contexts affecting local judgements, however, changed during the nineteenth century. There were monitorial schools where there was a struggle for involvement and support, and there were others with active supporters who treated the school as an important adjunct to the church or as a centre for community action.[37] The same was true of Sunday schools or mechanics' institutes. The Board schools of the late nineteenth century had elected managers, and church and other schools in receipt of grant were also supposed to have managers. One HMI recorded that in rural districts before the turn of the century the signatures required for the necessary returns would in some cases be obtained by 'Squire Broadlands' calling in 'his wife and gardener. They put their names where they were told, and asked no questions.' In the new century the 'so-called managers', he added, 'have the shadow of power without the substance',[38] the real power having passed to the new local authorities. However diverse the schools, however diverse their controllers and stated aims, and however diverse the involvement of the managers, the overall intention was to ensure the recruitment of teachers who could implement the aims, and satisfy them and the parents as fully as possible that standards defined somewhere were being met as well as could be expected, given the type of children and the resources.

It is, of course, impossible to generalize about parents' opinions of the schools. The range of social background of the parents even for the elementary schools was wide. Differences of attitude to voluntary and then compulsory schooling, religious and secular education, type of school and the nature of the teaching and the curriculum, attendance and length of stay at school, employment prospects and the educational qualities needed for them, the limits of teachers' authority and the willingness to pay fees – these and other variations prevent meaningful generalization. There is no doubt that in the conditions of urban, rural, industrial and social change in the nineteenth century the attitude of the poor to elementary schools was often dictated by economic need, and the length of schooling and daily attendance were conditioned by domestic, employment or climatic conditions.[39] Against the often described difficulties of providing schooling for the poor and securing regular attendance and educational progress, there are clear indications, however, of parents' support for and serious interest in the condition of the schools attended by their children, and the implications for the children themselves. While a systematic analysis is not possible here, some clues – however uncertain their reliability – are helpful.

In 1845 the Rev. Frederick Watkins, Inspector for the Northern District, reported on the use of monitors, whose inadequacy injured the school and removed from parents 'all hope of the improvement of their children taught on such a method'. The teacher at one of his schools in Lancashire reported the objection of parents to their own children being used as monitors, because the parents 'fancy that the boys would be kept back by acting as monitors', and could not agree to extra lessons after school 'as compensation for their labour'.[40] Mr Fletcher, reporting on British Society infant schools in the same year, thought that nothing was more hopeful in 'our uneasy social state' than 'the promptness with which the parents have availed themselves of the advantages of infant education thrown open to them'.[41] The following year Mr Fletcher said of communities where there were rival schools that 'a vast mass . . . do not care to send their children to any school', but those parents who did send their children to school 'are shrewd enough to know which is the best, so far as the secular instruction is concerned, about which alone they care'.[42] The evidence to the Newcastle Commission of its assistant commissioners suggested that 'almost all the parents appreciate the importance of elementary education', that the 'respectable parents are anxious to obtain it for their children', and that they were reluctant to pay fees or keep the children at school when there was an opportunity to earn wages. One of the assistant commissioners reported that when possible he asked working men whether education was useful to their children: 'they seemed to doubt whether I was serious; or, if they supposed that I was, they seemed to consider the question rather insulting'. He considered that schools which supplied 'the kind of education required by the poor' were likely to be filled, and that parents were just judges of the qualities of a teacher in particular – teachers affecting their interest in a school more than buildings or other factors. The Commission concluded that parents could not be blamed if they withdrew their children from school if, after years of schooling, they had not obtained 'a knowledge of reading, writing, and arithmetic . . . the elements of religion, and. . . . the principles of good conduct'. The assistant commissioners also reported on the evening classes held in the schools in some places, where young children and adults were keenly attending and reluctant to talk to a visitor since 'they had come to study, and they meant to study'.[43] One assistant commissioner, reporting on Rochdale and Bradford, commented that 'the inefficiency of the schools which are accessible frequently discourages parents from seeking education'. Some parents thought it was enough merely to send their children to school, others were not themselves educated enough to judge their children's progress, but generally 'the poor are keenly anxious that their children should be "got on", and like to see some visible signs of progress . . . a good school quickens, and a bad school deadens, the desire for instruction within the range of its influence'.[44]

It may not be possible to generalize about parents' opinions, but it is likely from this and similar evidence that parental judgement on the quality of schooling was based largely on these 'visible signs of progress', and obviously an important measure would be the ability of children to master the basic functions which might have some bearing on their employment opportunities. Managers, inspectors and commissioners might give priority to the moral influence of the schools, and though parents might do the same, the impact on employment and the family economy would rank high among their criteria. Before and after 1880, when elementary schooling from the age of five became compulsory (and the compulsory age of attendance gradually rose from then through the remainder of the nineteenth and into the second half of the twentieth centuries) there were undoubtedly parents looking for visible signs of right behaviour and religious outlook in their children, but Mr Fletcher was probably right that for most working-class parents it was secular instruction 'about which alone they care'.

We are not attempting here to rewrite a history of popular or elementary education in the nineteenth century. The emphasis has been on some aspects of that emergent system which highlight the way judgements were arrived at by particular constituencies, within frameworks established by the most powerful and influential. A systematic account of the system would require an analysis of the establishment from 1870 of a state-regulated pattern of School Boards and Board schools, alongside a continuing voluntary sector. Such a study would consider the ways in which 'standards' were set and perceived as elementary education became compulsory and free, as the School Board electoral process unfolded with the involvement of new constituencies, including women and working-class candidates. In particular, the study would be concerned with the development within the elementary system of moves towards 'post-elementary' education, resulting in the establishment of central schools and other attempts to provide an alternative to the separate system of 'grammar' or 'secondary' schools, which were linked to the elementary schools in England only by the most tenuous but gradually expanding scholarship ladder of opportunity. By the end of the century the definition of 'good' elementary schools was being influenced by new social contexts and pressures. The structure, content and aims of schooling were becoming salient elements of political organizations and campaigns. Sharpening international economic competition was bringing education to the centre of public policy-making in America and Europe, and in Britain increasingly to the attention of commissions concerned either directly with schooling or indirectly through concern with industrial and agricultural change, and its effects on the contours of social and political life. European competitors were successfully developing technical education on the basis of longer- and better-established systems of elementary education, and compulsory elementary education had become the norm by the late century in the American states.

Judgements of the quality of schooling were affected by these and other economic, social and political changes. The constituencies making the judgements were themselves changing – as trade unions, new political organizations such as the Fabian Society and the Independent Labour Party, women's organizations and reform movements of various kinds saw elementary education and its integration into a more complete system as a focus of attention. From the first decade of the twentieth century multi-purpose local authorities were to take over responsibility for the publicly provided schools. With the expansion of teacher training and the emergence of a 'child study' movement in the 1890s the 'judges' of schooling were to include a widening range of experts and professionals.

It has been argued that it was with the 1870 Education Act that the 'education of the poor' became 'the education of the people'. Since the Act made the provision of an adequate level of education for all children the centrepiece of a major development in the activities of the state, its 'most far-reaching effect was to give the child a special status and set in train a chain of measures which revolutionized his position in society'.[45] What is certainly true is that the agenda of public concern about education was changing, and whether or not they were 'revolutionary', the chain of measures affected the structure and expectations of education. The 'chain' suggests an inevitable sequence, but this was far from being the case. The provision and quality of schooling were items in political and social conflict. They were argued over, refined and redefined. As in other countries, the establishment of national systems of elementary education laid the basis for twentieth-century battles for extensions of provision and improvement of levels or standards. The clamour was to be not just for more schools or the raising of the leaving age, but for curriculum changes to reflect the changing demands of more democratically active communities, the changing manpower and skill needs of employment, the growth of service sectors, and changed understandings of what was meant by 'education'.

NOTES

1 Thomas Walter Laqueur (1976). *Religion and Respectability: Sunday Schools and Working Class Culture 1780–1850*. New Haven: Yale University Press; Malcolm Dick (1980). 'The myth of the working-class Sunday school', *History of Education*, **9** (1); Ian Inkster (1976). 'The social context of an educational movement: a revisionist approach to the English Mechanics' Institutes, 1820–1850', *Oxford Review of Education*, **2** (3).

2 Joshua Fitch (1901). 'The inspection of secondary schools'. In Laurie Magnus (ed.), *National Education: Essays towards a Constructive Policy*. London: John Murray, p. 78.

3 *Minutes of the Committee of Council on Education: with Appendices, 1840–41* (1841). 'Instructions to inspectors of schools'. London: HMSO, pp. 1–2.

4 Ibid., p. 124.

5 Ibid., pp. 125–30.

6 Ibid., pp. 182–8.

7 *Minutes of the Committee of Council on Education: with Appendices, 1846* (1847). London: HMSO, Vol 2, pp. 3, 48–9.

8 Comments from Allen and Watkins, *Minutes of the Committee of Council on Education: with Appendices, 1845* (1846). London: HMSO, Vol 1, pp. 17–57, and Vol. 2, pp. 133–41.

9 *Minutes . . . 1846*, Vol 1, pp. 162–4.

10 Report by Rev. Baptist W. Noel on Birmingham and other towns in Lancashire, in *Minutes . . . 1840–41*, p. 177.

11 *Minutes . . . 1845*, Vol. 1, pp. 287–95.

12 Ibid., Vol. 2, pp. 221, 228.

13 Ibid., Vol. 1, pp. 244–5.

14 Rev. Noel, in *Minutes . . . 1840–41*, pp. 175–6.

15 Seymour Tremenheere, ibid., p. 458.

16 *Minutes . . . 1846*, Vol. 2, pp. 69–73, 76–7.

17 *Minutes . . . 1840–41*, p. 314.

18 *Minutes . . . 1846*, Vol. 2, pp. 28–9.

19 Rev. Moseley, ibid., Vol. 1, pp. 154–5; Rev. F. C. Cook, report on the Eastern District, in *Minutes . . . 1845*, Vol. 1, p. 145.

20 *Minutes . . . 1845*, Vol. 1, pp. 138–57.

21 Education Commission (1861). *Report of the Commissioners Appointed to Inquire into the State of Popular Education in England*, Vol. 1, pp. 7–8.

22 Ibid., pp. 30–2.

23 Ibid., p. 156.

24 Ibid., p. 238.

25 Ibid., pp. 295–6.

26 Education Commission (1861). *Reports of the Assistant Commissioners*, Vol. 3, p. 509.

27 For example, *Minutes . . . 1845*, Vol. 1, pp. 21, 25, 33, 45, 49, for the 'first class' being 'well taught', and the rest 'imperfectly'.

28 Fitch, 'The inspection of secondary schools', p. 79.

29 B. J. Johnson (1956). 'The development of English education, 1856–1882, with special reference to the work of Robert Lowe, Viscount Sherbrooke'. MEd thesis, University of Durham, pp. 175–8.

30 G. A. Christian (1922). *English Education from Within*. London: Wallace Gandy, p. 116.

31 Fitch, 'The inspection of secondary schools', p. 79.

32 E. M. Sneyd-Kynnersley (1910). *HMI: Some Passages in the Life of One of HM Inspectors of Schools*. London: Macmillan, pp. 10–11.

33 Ibid., p. 11.

34 *Second Report of the Royal Commissioners Appointed to Inquire into the Working of the Elementary Education Acts, England and Wales* (1887). London: HMSO, pp. 74–5.

35 Christian, *English Education from Within*, p. 166; E. L. Edmonds (1962). *The School Inspector*. London: Routledge & Kegan Paul, pp. 89–90.

36 Education Commission (1861). *Answers to the Circular of Questions, 1860*. London: HMSO, p. 103. For her other school activities see Hester Burton (1949). *Barbara Bodichon 1827–1891*. London: John Murray, pp. 49–52, 130–2.

37 For the latter, see Pamela and Harold Silver (1974). *The Education of the Poor: the History of a National School 1824–1974*. London: Routledge & Kegan Paul, ch. 5: 'The schools and the community to 1860'.

38 Sneyd-Kynnersley, *HMI.*, p. 122.

39 For a survey of schools and conditions see J. S. Hurt (1979). *Elementary Schooling and the Working Class 1860–1918*. London: Routledge & Kegan Paul. For the earlier period see Silver, *The Education of the Poor*, chs 1–4.

40 *Minutes . . . 1845*, Vol. 1, p. 113.

41 Ibid., p. 216.

42 *Minutes . . . 1846*, Vol. 2, p. 31.

43 Quoted in Herbert S. Skeat (1861). *Popular Education in England: Being an Abstract of the Report of the Royal Commissioners on Education*. London: Bradbury & Evans, pp. 37–8, 70–1.

44 *Reports of the Assistant Commissioners*, Vol. 2, p. 206.

45 Nigel Middleton (1970). 'The Education Act of 1870 as the start of the modern concept of the child', *British Journal of Educational Studies*, **18** (2), 172–3.

Chapter 4

The Nineteenth Century, II: Some Recognized Authority

'Secondary' education, often known as 'higher education' in nineteenth-century Britain, is a story of the increasingly close definition of what constituted a 'grammar' or a 'public' school, the latter becoming part of the 'independent' school sector of the twentieth century, when a state sector of secondary education was created. The medieval and later grammar school foundations often included 'poor scholars' amongst their clientele, though there has been much historical controversy about the meaning of the term. What is certainly clear is that the nineteenth-century grammar school became more firmly middle class, to some extent as other forms of schooling became available for the children of the lower or working class. Their curriculum remained essentially classical for much of the century, as attempts early in the century to diversify the curriculum came up against a legal obstacle based on the need to continue to respect the wishes of the original founders. Only from 1840 were the endowed schools fully free to develop 'modern' subjects if they so wished.[1] In spite of continual controversy over the moribund nature of many grammar schools and their curricula it was only in the 1860s that their operation was scrutinized by a Schools Inquiry Commission and recommendations for substantial changes made. At the same time throughout the nineteenth century a sector of such schools with particular attributes and status came into increasing prominence as the elite 'public schools', and these also were the subject of scrutiny in the early 1860s by a Public Schools Commission. These schools, which were for the most part residential, had become nationally visible – mainly through the activities of particularly prominent headmasters – dominated entrance to the two elite universities of Oxford and Cambridge, and recruited nationally. They had mostly developed into high-status institutions from their past as grammar schools, and in the nineteenth century they were joined by new public schools either modelled on existing schools or setting out to match their status but operating on different lines. From the early decades of the century 'proprietary' schools, free of traditional legal restrictions, were developed mainly in commercial towns to rival the grammar schools and to provide an essentially modern curriculum. From the 1860s grammar and public schools for girls joined the 'secondary' landscape.

The changes in fee-paying school provision at these levels therefore changed considerably across the century, in response to the considerable social and economic changes which sustained them and which they in turn sustained. The range of considerations affecting judgements of what constituted an appropriate school for children of middle-class or aristocratic families was wide and complex, and mapping the concept of standards is a difficult exercise. Public schools were increasingly copied by the grammar schools, aspiring to the public school status, competing with them for clienteles and entrance to the universities (the map of which itself expanded across the century), and often reflecting (as did new public schools) the aim of the newly affluent to be seen to espouse the traditions and values of the established gentry. Schools aimed to establish criteria of right behaviour and values, instanced by Thomas Arnold's introduction of a 'prefect' system at Rugby, to induct older boys into the practice of responsibility and a direct relationship with the values being inculcated by the headmaster. Since schools were either unable to widen their curricula, did so reluctantly, or set out in new directions, parents and the public could to some extent interpret what constituted a good school either in terms of the successful delivery of the classical curriculum – as a passport to the traditional aristocratic cultural norms, to the university and to high-status employment – or in terms of a successful modern curriculum, as a gateway to commerce or the newly emerging professions.

The curriculum was not the only criterion of success, but it was a major one. After the commissions and reforms of the 1860s a good girls' school could be seen as one that sought to copy and be equal to a boys' public or grammar school, one that differed from them and was adapted to the needs of girls (for example, by teaching biology), or one that continued to provide the 'finishing school' education that pointed to marriage and the culture of, or culture that was modelled on, an upper class. In the latter decades of the century, as the schools responded to reform by Parliament or the pressures of parental demand, some of the public schools pioneered the establishment of science laboratories. A good school was therefore one that might serve essentially 'liberal' or essentially 'vocational' ends, as the terms themselves changed implication and meaning, and as complicated mixtures of the two appeared. Was a classical education which pointed to government or the church not 'vocational'? Was science a 'liberal' or a 'vocational' subject? Were modern subjects like foreign languages and geography both liberal and vocational, depending on the manner in which they were taught, the type of school, and the occupational destinations for which they prepared? The advent, at the end of the century, of a 'progressive' schools movement involving the establishment of independent schools based on approaches to child study, child-centred pedagogies, concepts of freedom or coeducation or more practical curricula, yet further widened the range of interpretations of what a good school for the children of middle- and upper-class Britain might be.

What had developed was a confused sector of education, within which segments and hierarchies were clearly evident, aiming at traditional outcomes, modified traditional outcomes, or the new outcomes associated with a rapidly changing society. Pressure for entry to the increasing number of universities and university colleges (very small by modern standards) placed many of the schools in competition with one another, as did the introduction and expansion of competitive entry to such employments as those of the civil service in Britain and its equivalent and other occupations in the colonies. In this market-place what all the schools had in common was that their very survival and expansion were the hallmarks of success. At the end of the century, for example, F. W. Sanderson rapidly built up Oundle, with new buildings and increased numbers: 'numbers were important for they showed the methods adopted were successful'. Growth indicated that a public demand was being met, but more boys also made possible more choice and experiment: 'a growth in numbers makes some experiment possible, the success of the experiment brings an increase in numbers, this again renders a further experiment possible, and so the process goes on'.[2] If growth was a basis for experiment, it was equally vital for the continuation of schools with settled traditions.

There were indeed throughout the nineteenth century changes of emphasis in the value systems underpinning the schools. Those at the top of the hierarchy produced 'the men who ruled England as a moral elect'.[3] Settled traditions were one aspect of serving this purpose; the study of the classics was held to buttress right opinions and right attitudes. That curriculum, or in some cases the methods of teaching it, came under increasing criticism, and the place in it not only of modern subjects but also of religion, for example, was a focus of concern. The schools confronted the need to meet the requirements of social service and the virtues appropriate to the stabilizing effect of a 'moral elect' in the changing society. One of the central developments in the life of the public schools was an increasing emphasis on athleticism and games. In the second half of the century games became an established feature of the curriculum of the public and increasingly the grammar schools, and critics identified a 'disturbing athleticism' at Oxford and Cambridge in the 1860s.[4] The Clarendon Commission praised the public schools for providing 'bodily training' not by the gymnastic exercises common on the Continent, but by 'athletic games', which served both that and other purposes. Games were not merely for exercise or amusement; the cricket and football fields 'help to form some of the most valuable social qualities and manly virtues, and they hold, like the class-room and the boarding-house, a distinct and important place in public-school education. Their importance is fully recognized.' The Commission approved of the schools which taught swimming and had a rifle corps. Although there were dangers in making games, particularly cricket, too prominent a part of school life, the Commission clearly welcomed the emergent emphasis on this contribution to 'social qualities and manly virtues'.[5]

The quality of the elite public schools and their imitators involved a variety of judgements about their formal curriculum and its classical core, their moral, Christian code, and increasingly their inculcation of an outlook involving 'playing the game', manliness and a complex balance between individual prowess and a collective ethic. These were values which pertained not only to the codes of behaviour that the families which sent their children to these schools expected, but also to the roles they expected their children subsequently to play. For their boys there were the traditional outlets of Oxford and Cambridge, the inheritance and management of estates, government or the church. In the last two decades of the century Wellington was described as an 'uncommonly good place . . . a splendid institution for the Nation and for the Empire'. Its main aim was 'to turn out a hardy and dashing breed of young officers'.[6] At these and other public schools the expansion of empire was obviously of considerable importance, presenting opportunities (or, as some would see it, obligations) not only in the army, but also in political and administrative roles. For the lower ranks of the public schools too there were opportunities in this process of what some historians have called 'cultural imperialism' in colonial government, the church and the colonial imitations of the English public and grammar schools – though not all historians agree that it was purely a unidirectional process of the imposition of imperial values.[7] The schools certainly changed to accommodate new needs. Imperialism had 'put a new premium on discipline, authority, and team spirit'. Its modified aims included a discipline which would 'create responsible, honorable boys, willing to give their lives unquestionably to the preservation and expansion of empire'.[8]

So the tone was set for the 'secondary' sector by a widening group of elite schools which perpetuated a set of aristocratic values, but adapted them to new national and imperial imperatives. The tone was set by forms of school organization (notably their 'house' structure) and curriculum, the responsibilities (and licence) given to prefects, and the later emphasis on manliness, sporting prowess and team spirit. Embedded in these structures and values were assumptions about particular forms of *noblesse oblige* and public service as well as rewards. The public school in general 'taught its boys to compete' and in this way 'schools "socialized" their middle-class recruits . . . a balance was struck between competition and social co-operation'. In doing so, however, they did not develop a critical awareness of the meanings of leadership and responsibility, and 'the public school outlook was itself complacent', unable to respond to major change, including the approach of war.[9] But the major public schools did retain a firm public image as guardians of gentlemanly and civic values.

The girls' public schools of the later nineteenth century developed their own ethos of 'girlhood' and gentility,[10] and curricula which attempted some sort of balance between the perceived needs of girls and the need to be seen to compete successfully with boys' schools in the increasingly important public examinations. Throughout the century, however, there was resistance of various kinds to the secondary and higher education of girls.[11] An important indicator of the way in which judgements were made of the education of middle-class girls was the evidence received and conclusions reached by the Taunton Commission, indicating in the 1860s the 'general indifference of parents to girls' education'. Since most parents saw marriage as the means of providing for their daughters, 'the gentler graces and winning qualities of character will be their best passports to marriage'. In the Commission's returns 'the girls' school is often spoken of as intended to be more a home than a school'. The witnesses uniformly underlined the weaknesses of girls' education:

> Want of thoroughness and foundation; want of system; slovenliness
> and showy superficiality; inattention to rudiments; undue time given
> to accomplishments . . . want of organization.

However deficient boys' schools may have been, the girls' schools were in most respects worse. In suitable conditions girls could be seen to have an aptitude for most subjects. The Commission concluded that there was 'weighty evidence . . . that the essential capacity for learning is the same, or nearly the same, in the two sexes'. In mixed schools it was reported that there was 'no noticeable difference of attainments'.

In the girls' schools it was the poor teaching that held them back. Mathematics, reported Mr Fitch, 'are not taught *mathematically*'. In selecting a school, middle-class parents looked for music as a 'leading subject of instruction', however little interest in it the girls might have. Needlework occupied too much time, and physical exercise was 'imperfectly attended to'. The schools were mainly small, and the women teachers 'not fully equal to their task'.[12] It was with the reforms of charities and endowments and the establishment of new girls' schools, notably by the Girls' Public Day School Trust, that the boarding and day education of middle-class girls was placed on a more secure footing from the 1870s. The Trust schools 'organised and popularised a sound education for girls, and greatly influenced public opinion in favour of giving to them the same advantages which had been given for years to boys only'. The teaching in the new schools was superior 'to that given in any private school or procurable at home', and the fees were described – with some exaggeration – as being low enough to provide 'an excellent education . . . within the reach of all but the very poor'.[13] Attitudes to the schooling of middle-class girls were being affected in the final decades of the century by significant changes in the family and the social position of women and by campaigns for improvements in women's higher education, and new employment opportunities – including in teaching. As with the secondary education of boys, judgements of the quality of schools were being conditioned by the combination of changes in the schools and in the wider society.

Crucial to understanding not only the condition of schools but also the nature of the evidence and the ways in which opinion was influenced was the development in Britain of the use of commissions of inquiry – a development that was to be important also for Britain's colonial territories and later Commonwealth countries. What some parliamentarians sought to obtain from the early decades of the century, and what some social activists attempted to provide, was accurate information about the state of educational provision. In Parliament and the published literature in the first half of the century there were occasional and less than reliable pictures of the numbers of schools and pupils, and – especially in relation to the Factory Acts – descriptions of working-class childhood, the family, children's employment, and attendance at school. By the 1850s the government or Parliament began to adopt a more systematic practice of appointing commissions to investigate the range of institutions or issues of current concern. Across the 1850s and 1860s such commissions considered and reported extensively on Oxford and Cambridge, popular education, the major public schools, and other 'secondary' schools. Assistant commissioners, as we have seen, reported to some of the commissions on detailed scrutiny of institutions, and the commission reports formed a significant tradition of public description and analysis that was to be a continuing feature of British practice through the late nineteenth and the twentieth centuries. The reports revealed gaps, weaknesses and trends, and yet further indicated components and perceptions of educational standards – in the system and in specific institutions – and they often had direct influence on policy and legislation. They influenced government action, for example, to reform specific aspects of the public schools and universities, and the Newcastle Commission Report of 1861 was the foundation on which the policy of payment by results was built.

The criteria used by the commissions in judging the educational standards partly reflected and partly shaped changing perceptions of the realities and needs of the emergent pattern of 'secondary' education. The Clarendon Commission on the major public schools laid enormous emphasis not only on what they could describe regarding the schools themselves, but also on the standards of scholarship of the schools as perceived from Oxford and Cambridge:

We have found no difficulty in ascertaining what is taught at these
schools; to discover what and how much is learnt in them is difficult.
... The range and methods of teaching have been amply explained to
us; the success of these methods can only be tried by imperfect tests.
... The class-lists and lists of prize-men at the two Universities
furnish something like a criterion of the attainments in scholarship
and mathematics of the abler and more industrious boys.

The assumption here, of course, is that only two universities counted in making
judgements about the outcomes of public school teaching (London and Durham
universities had been created in England in the 1830s, the first of the new university
colleges was being created at the same time as the commission, and Scotland had
four universities). 'Scholarship', similarly, meant classical scholarship. The
Commission deduced that those entering Oxford and Cambridge 'from the highest
forms of these schools are on the whole well-taught classical scholars'. That,
however, was a modest claim. Those who succeeded well at the universities
'notoriously form a small proportion of the boys who receive a public-school
education. The great mass of such boys expose themselves to no tests which they
can possibly avoid, and there are hardly any data for ascertaining how they acquit
themselves in the easy examinations which must be passed in order to obtain a
degree.'

The Commission looked at various university requirements, including 'matriculation' at the point of entry – a test not applied by all colleges, and of different
kinds at those which did. Since the public school curriculum was overwhelmingly
classical the evidence to the Commission often constitutes a very direct form of
judgement. Candidates for matriculation at Christ Church, Oxford, were expected
to construe passages of Virgil and Homer that they had seen before, to write a little
Latin prose, to answer some simple grammatical questions, and to show 'some
acquaintance with arithmetic'. The Dean of the College gave the Commission the
following picture:

Very few can construe with accuracy a piece from an author they
profess to have read. We never try them with an unseen passage. It
would be useless to do so. Tolerable Latin prose is very rare. Perhaps
one piece in four is free from bad blunders. ... The answers we get to
simple grammar questions are very inaccurate.

Standards of arithmetic had improved, but 'the answers to the questions in
arithmetic do not encourage us to examine them in Euclid or algebra'. The
Commission found that the proportion of candidates who failed varied, but at
colleges which were not full 'and have a direct pecuniary interest in being lax, the
test, a slight one at best, obviously vanishes altogether'. Other witnesses gave facts
and figures which did not, the commissioners concluded, 'indicate an average of
classical attainment which can by any stretch of indulgence be deemed satisfactory.
We are further told that there is a great want of accurate "grounding", perceptible
sometimes even in elegant scholars; that the knowledge of history and geography,
though better than it was, is still very meagre; and that there are great deficiencies
observable in English composition, reading and spelling.'

There was mixed evidence as to whether matters were in general improving or deteriorating, but the Commission's conclusions were clear. For large numbers of students the work of the first two years at the university was 'simply school work – work proper for the upper forms of a large school'. The best students came from the well-established old public schools and those like Marlborough and Cheltenham modelled on them – though the public schools in general, particularly Eton, also sent 'the idlest and most ignorant men'. In mathematics the public schools held 'a position of marked inferiority' to other schools which taught the subject. On the basis of their inquiries the Commission arrived at six carefully phrased conclusions:

> That boys who have capacity and industry enough to work for distinction, are, on the whole, well taught, in the article of classical scholarship, at the public schools;
> But that they occasionally show a want of accuracy in elementary knowledge, either from not having been well grounded, or from having been suffered to forget what they have learnt;
> That the average of classical knowledge among young men leaving school for college is low;
> That in arithmetic and mathematics, in general information, and in English, the average is lower still, but is improving;
> That of the time spent at school by the generality of boys, much is absolutely thrown away as regards intellectual progress, either from ineffective teaching, from the continued teaching of subjects in which they cannot advance, or from idleness, or from a combination of these causes;
> That in arithmetic and mathematics the public schools are specially defective, and that this observation is not to be confined to any particular class of boys.[14]

Whatever parents might have wished in terms of the social expectations of the public schools, it is clear that only with certain boys at particular schools could there be expectations of significant academic success. The Clarendon Commission looked, as we have seen, at physical exercise and games at the schools, as it did at the balance of classical and modern studies, but ultimately it was the classical basis of the curriculum, and the general ethos of the schools, that it saw as the most significant and durable features of the schools. It described these features in terms which must have been firmly present in the judgements made by parents and influential middle- and upper-class England of the schools as a whole, and of the performance of particular schools:

> Among the services which they have rendered is undoubtedly to be reckoned the maintenance of classical literature as the staple of English education, a service which far outweighs the error of having clung to these studies too exclusively. A second, and a greater still, is the creation of a system of government and discipline for boys, the excellence of which has been universally recognized, and which is admitted to have been most important in its effect on national character and social life. It is not easy to estimate the degree in which

the English people are indebted to these schools for the qualities on
which they pique themselves most – for their capacity to govern
others and control themselves, their aptitude for combining freedom
with order, their public spirit, their vigour and manliness of character,
their strong, but not slavish respect for public opinion, their love of
healthy sports and exercise.

The public schools had been 'the chief nurseries of our statesmen', and they and the
schools modelled upon them had perhaps 'had the largest share in moulding the
character of an English gentleman'.[15]

A body like the Clarendon Commission not only collected information and
presented evidence. It defined. It helped to regulate the criteria by which schools,
their components and their outcomes were to be judged. The Taunton Commission
on the 'endowed', or what came to be called the 'grammar', schools also looked at
the record of their students entering the universities, and was similarly concerned
with 'judgment by curriculum'. The circumstances and the clienteles were different,
but the conditions of the 1860s were reflected similarly. It looked at the extent to
which the schools (which excluded the nine investigated by Clarendon) reflected
their founders' intentions and at how their curricula had changed:

We find 340, or about 43 per cent. of the whole number of schools in
our list . . . which do not teach either Latin (except possibly to only
one or two boys), or Greek. And in very few of these cases is any
effective instruction given in mathematics, French, or natural science.
By far the majority, though not quite all, give no better education than
that of an ordinary national school, and a very great number do not
give one so good.

Twenty-seven per cent of the schools could be considered 'classical schools', a
number which was much larger than the number which 'can on any showing be
credited with a single University student in three years'. Many of the endowed
schools, in a return to the House of Commons, had listed a broad curriculum. Mr
Fitch compared the returns with schools he visited. One listed its subjects as 'Greek,
Latin, English, French, mathematics, geography and history', and another 'English,
classics, and mathematics'. Both of them he found on his visit 'to be elementary
schools of the humblest class, and nothing beyond reading, writing, and arithmetic
was taught in either of them'. In Yorkshire and Durham he had counted 38 schools
claiming an 'ample and varied curriculum, including Greek and Latin, and other
advanced subjects', but which in 1865 were found to have 'no scholars . . . learning
the subjects so described'.[16] Again, the Taunton Commission was not merely collecting
evidence and suggesting improvements – it was helping to define what counted as
legitimate criteria for judging schools. The same had been true of the Newcastle
Commission, and was to be true, for example, of the Secondary Education
Commission (the Bryce Commission), in the 1890s, when exploring the nature of
secondary education, its relationship to technical education, changing patterns of
social structure and employment, or greater educational and other opportunities for
girls.[17]

From the mid-nineteenth century a further and ultimately crucial element in judgements of school quality was the development of the examination system. Examinations and testing were a distinctive feature of the development of nineteenth-century educational systems. In the United States, for example, testing emerged as an alternative to other countries' more centrally directed procedures for securing quality control. The sources of the American testing movement included 'the effort of school administrators at the central district or supervisory level to monitor the performance of administrators and teachers in local schools', and 'the efforts of reformers external to the system to devise ways for schools to do their job of instruction more effectively and at a lower cost'.[18] 'Objective' guides to the performance of schools and their personnel were being devised in different educational structures, and testing ran parallel to the development in Britain of judgement by nationally appointed inspectors and the regulations that governed their work. At a different level in Britain the creation of public examinations between the 1850s and 1870s in particular served as a means of attempting to ascertain and to regulate the shape of curricula and the standards of teaching and attainment. The university-controlled examination served as a means of identifying mainly grammar school pupils for entrance to the universities and university colleges (more of which were being founded from the 1860s), or as a means of selecting candidates for the British or Indian civil service. They were an important step in bringing the concept of merit into the process of educational and social selection, and by establishing clear targets they applied the notion of standards to both schools and individuals. Examinations played an important part in the development of curricula for arts and sciences, and a number of bodies established in the nineteenth century – such as the Royal Society of Arts and the City and Guilds of London Institute – used examinations as a means of regulating the standards of classes taught in a variety of schools and other institutions – full-time and part-time. What was rapidly developing for the grammar school was the role of examination results as the central means of making relative judgements about schools.

The increasing importance of public examinations as a passport to higher education and professional careers affected the public schools as well as the grammar schools. Although the social selectiveness of Oxford and Cambridge remained basically secure, increased demand for university entrance – including for girls as the male exclusiveness of the universities began to be breached in the 1870s – meant growing competition for entry to the expanding university system. The competition also affected the curriculum, as the range of modern subjects in the universities widened and opportunities for higher education in the arts and humanities, science, and other claimants for university legitimacy attracted students and reshaped entry requirements. Judgements of schools increasingly took account of their potential for access to a diversifying pattern of further study and professional preparation and entry. Examination results became vital to those looking for progression of this kind. The proportion of grammar school pupils proceeding to university, the civil service or the professions remained small, but external examinations directly affected the structures and culture of schooling for secondary education generally.

The university examination system was being either introduced or extended at Oxford and Cambridge in the first half of the nineteenth century. The Oxford and

Cambridge 'locals' were the first in the field of external examinations for secondary schools, the Oxford Local Examinations Delegacy being created in 1857 and holding its first examinations the following year, the Cambridge Syndicate for Local Examinations following several months later.[19] The basic principle of the examination process was competition, as the *Cornhill Magazine* underlined in 1861:

> Competitive examinations . . . are put forward with great zeal as providing a new profession for modest and unacknowledged merit, as a stimulus to general education, as a remedy for political jobbery, and as a means of securing efficiency in the public service. . . . Scholastic competitive examinations are at present universal in all places of education in this country, and are even more popular and more rigorous in some parts of the continent; this is especially the case in France.[20]

Young John Eames, in Trollope's *The Last Chronicle of Barset*, found the other young men in his civil service office 'a little cold', and since 'competitive examinations had come into vogue, there was no knowing who might be introduced'. He was 'very averse to the whole theory of competition'. His Chief Commissioner, however, was a 'great believer in competition, wrote papers about it, which he read aloud to various bodies of the civil service, – not all to their delight, – which he got to be printed here and there, and which he sent by post all over the kingdom'. The competition, of course, had to do with a development which enabled middle-class candidates to enter the civil service – resulting, said Mr Eames, in the Devil taking the hindmost, and since 'the hindmost candidates were often the best gentlemen . . . the Devil got the pick of the flock'.[21] By 'all places of education' the *Cornhill* article had middle-class education specifically in mind, though a definition of examinations which included the results of inspection in the elementary schools would make the claim of universality broadly true.

The question of inspection and/or examination was widely debated in the late nineteenth century, with the former emphasizing an assessment of standards by scrutiny of the processes of schooling, the latter emphasizing outcomes – a distinction and controversy that were still to be part of educational debate a century later. The Bryce Report in 1895 chose a combination of the two, concluding that 'one test of efficiency' was 'the soundness of the scholar's attainments, more especially in the final school stage; and a certificate attesting this has a value for the individual scholar which makes such a test otherwise desirable'. Perhaps more important: 'Success in a final examination, it should be noted, is a test of school efficiency that parents individually understand.' The Commission was in this reflecting the widespread acceptance of external examinations by schools, and by the middle-class public in particular. The Commission had its reservation, however, based on the principle of inspection – which had proved less acceptable to secondary schools:

> Some other test, either by inspection or examination, is generally admitted to be also necessary to ensure that the work of the school is sound throughout, and that the results in final examinations are not gained by concentration of attention on the senior forms.[22]

49

In the elementary schools, the principle of inspection had by the 1860s become in fact two competing principles – inspection of the 'condition of the school' and examination of individual children. As one inspector pointed out in the late 1860s:

> it may be proper to state that the condition of a school is not
> necessarily indicated by the number of passes. A very inferior school
> may rank with the highest in this matter. The one may just satisfy the
> claims of the Revised Code, while the other exhibits all the life,
> activity, and excellence which alone can be called education, but
> which is not indicated by the number of passes.

The report of the Committee of Council responded to this by underlining the question that remained: 'What other method will equally well secure that the greatest possible number of the scholars shall be raised to the point of passing?'[23] Evidence to the Bryce Commission suggested consistent support for the inspection of secondary schools, though the Commission favoured inspection of a 'more general' rather than a 'complete systematic detailed' type. One sentence in the report sums up a view gaining ground, and combining the experience of different approaches to evaluating the condition and standards of schools: 'If a school undergoes a general inspection and has its pupils periodically examined by some recognised authority reporting the result, this test of its efficiency ought to suffice.' Inspection and examination were both part of the nineteenth-century search for the means of making judgements of schools on the basis of 'some recognised authority'.[24]

To some extent the vocabularies of inspection and examination had become interchangeable. St Olave's grammar school in Southwark, for example, had employed 'private examiners' since earlier in the century. St Olave's instituted its own system of outside examiners in 1823 to report on the success of its use of the monitorial system. From 1858 this system of private examiners continued side by side with the introduction of the Oxford local examination, which was seen as an objective standard 'distinct from the haphazard standards of private examiners'. These had been described to the school as almost worthless since the 'examiner' was normally reluctant to make serious criticisms of the school.[25] The trustees of Sir Thomas Rich's School in Gloucester appointed a committee in 1842 to investigate the school, which was not reaching what were considered to be suitable standards. The committee, and the trustees themselves, were still active in investigating the school through to the 1860s and employing outsiders, including other schoolmasters and clergymen, to conduct 'examinations' of the school and to report.[26] The *Cornhill* recommended to parents that if a school principal preferred 'private examiners' to public examinations, 'you should know their names and position, and that they are *not*, if possible, his private friends also'.[27] In one way or another judgements by trustees or other responsible bodies, parents and communities had come to depend on externally obtained evidence. The government-appointed inspector, the private examiner, the test, the written examination, had become critical to the perception of what made or failed to make a good school.

The nature of the evidence obtained in elementary schools and secondary schools differed, but formed part of the general search for objective judgements, what the *Cornhill* called 'the moral relations of measures', which in 1861 were 'generally invested with far greater prominence than was formerly the case'.[28] There were, however, penalties to be paid for the examination system. The Taunton Commission recognized that 'there is a great deal of school work which cannot be tested by any but skilled examiners; there is also a great deal which cannot be tested by an examination at all'. No examination could 'take account of the moral training, which a good school ought to have'. One witness told the Commission that examinations might be a necessary evil but became 'injurious to a school' when 'the school follows the examination, and not the examination the school'. Another said that examinations such as those for the Indian civil service were 'sitting like a blight on education', and a third thought that the effect of examinations was to 'strain the boys and make their knowledge not permanent'. In all cases the witnesses were commenting not on examinations conducted by the teachers themselves, but on external examinations, which compelled schools to do what some outside body dictated.[29] The *Cornhill*, in one article, advised parents that if the school principal submitted boys for public examinations they should find out 'not only how many succeed, but how many he sent up'. In another article the magazine (which claimed a million readers) condemned competitive examinations as 'useful in proportion to the immaturity, the languor, and the absence of the higher qualities of mind in the persons examined; and . . . there is a point, which is soon reached, at which they become positively injurious to students of a higher kind'. Examinations favoured a 'rather low level of mediocrity'.[30] There were criticisms of examinations from various directions, many part of a continuing controversy. This was true of the long debates about the education of girls, and the virtues of examinations as demonstrating their equal capacity to learn, or their negative effects on girls' physical and mental constitutions.

By the end of the century there were mixed views of examinations as a source of benefit to schools. On the debit side, there were still voices like those which spoke to the Taunton Commission about examinations leading the schools. In 1901 Laurie Magnus, a champion of secondary and technical education, described the proliferation of examinations, without a central authority, as chaos. Possibly only in the Chinese Empire had there been more deference paid to examination marks: 'Where there is teaching there is examination; indeed, it may seriously be said that there is more examination than teaching in the common experience of an English schoolboy.'[31] On the credit side, the Bryce Commission could congratulate the universities, ancient and modern, on their part in developing examination schemes, all of which had undoubtedly 'done much to raise the standard of teaching in the lower and higher grades of secondary schools. They have provided an impartial test of attainment.'[32]

By the beginning of the twentieth century the constituencies that would be looking to inspection and examinations for evidence of the attainment of adequate standards had come to include not only the various bodies of trustees and managers who controlled the independent schools, the parents and patrons, and the church and other bodies which established and managed networks of schools, but also the public bodies with devolved responsibility for schools. The School Boards were to give way in the early new century to local education authorities with responsibility not only for the elementary schools, but also for the development of publicly provided secondary schools. Judgements of state-supported schooling were increasingly to be made in the context of health and welfare arrangements made by local authorities and channelled through the schools. As 'scholarship' opportunities were established, judgements were to include elementary schools' records in sending their products up the ladder to grammar schools. How parents, managers, politicians and others judged the schools had become vastly more complex than in the conditions of the early nineteenth century. Magnus talked of 'the unrest in education . . . chiefly due to the changing conditions of modern life'.[33] As was the case internationally, given the rapidity of economic and social change, the 'unrest' was widely reflected in a growing difficulty in generalizing about the aims and attainments of schools. Debate and controversy became widespread and common-place amongst educationists, politicians and the public.

Schools and systems had declared and undeclared aims, and over such questions as coeducation, progressive school organization and teaching methods the need for and content of teacher training, discipline, or 'wastage', aims were now defined in widely different ways. Neither examinations nor commission reports and parliamentary debate and action produced well-founded, commonly acceptable approaches to what a good school should be. At a given moment in time a 'successful' public school might be one that was seen to fulfil its mission of recruiting 'qualified' teachers (itself not an easy concept) and an appropriate, continuing level of students ('level' more often judged socially than educationally), maintaining a suitable environment and atmosphere, justifying its choice of curriculum and extra-curriculum, and preparing its students well for whatever its mission suggested: university entrance or a station in life. It would announce successes either in examinations or in numbers going to university. Such a school would therefore flourish on the basis of reputation translated into parental support and student fees, and it would have at its head someone able to represent the strength and status of the school. Either declared or undeclared would be a range of school characteristics recognized as important to the constituency – the games ethic, character training and social skills that mattered for the milieu and occupation that lay ahead. The school would be 'effective' (without using that vocabulary) if it steered its charges through the processes it designed and operated, and delivered them with identifiable characteristics into the world for which their parents and social class intended them.

A 'successful' elementary school, say a Board school, might be one whose mission (rarely made explicit) was to prepare its students, over a relatively short period of school life, for entry into a different social world from that of the middle-class grammar and public schools. Its clientele was defined by geography and social class, it was not residential, it had neither the resources nor the relationship to parents that the public schools had, though the form of its relationships to its local community could be very important. Its curriculum was framed either by payment by results or by other national and Board pressures or requirements, and its teachers were qualified by virtue of their attendance at training college, not university. Such a school would be orderly, and its ethos would be one of regular attendance and disciplined work within a curriculum which provided the basic skills of literacy and numeracy together with some other elements of general culture useful for adult life and employment. Parents did not pay fees, and had few or no local choices of school. The status of the school in the community depended on its delivery of an educational programme which it did little to determine. It was 'effective' if it satisfied the regulations and expectations of the inspectors and the Board.

The provision of popular education moved increasingly from voluntary to state initiatives. Scotland provided a distinctively different development of school provision, based on the Calvinist tradition of public education and a greater commitment than in England to widespread and thorough elementary education. Britain differed from France, Prussia and some other European countries in not moving early towards a legislated, multi-level state system, and therefore in adopting different machineries of establishing and monitoring standards. Whilst in Europe it was common for governments to have control over the pattern of provision and the mechanisms for ascertaining at least basic efficiency, in the United States these fast became city-wide or state-wide functions. From the 1870s, however, questions of standards in Britain were affected by the entry of the state more directly into establishing the framework of schooling. The 1870 Elementary Education Act required the establishment of School Boards where there was a deficiency in the provision of places by voluntary bodies. Through the following decades attendance became compulsory, public elementary education became free, and the school-leaving age began to rise – all of these being features of those other countries which made efforts in the late nineteenth century more firmly to establish their educational systems – including the United States. In England at the end of the century, as quasi-secondary classes or schools were emerging within the elementary system, the machinery of state prevented the creation of such an 'alternative' structure of secondary education. In the first decade of the new century Parliament instead extended the grammar school system and laid down a modernized version of an established grammar and public school curriculum in doing so. What was a good school was still related to the differentiated purposes of schools serving the realities or aspirations of different social groups. The state was increasingly the arbiter of how these differentiated purposes would be embodied in school structures.

Extending the questions involved in 'effectiveness' historically to other countries of course complicates the issue very considerably. For example, was a version of English schooling transplanted to Australia or India or West Africa aiming at a simple transfer of efficient methods or forms of control, or did it serve other ends instead or simultaneously – a degree of social mobility, the preparation of a reliable local leadership, the strengthening of an indigenous elite, or a disregard or negation of local cultures and traditions? Judgements of a school in such conditions could be as varied and controversial as in Britain. What was 'effective' meant: 'effective for whom?', and 'as judged by whom?' Did it provide opportunities for girls or working-class children, was that its aim, was it generous or restrictive in attempting to achieve it? In the United States a clear example would be the emergence from the 1840s of an ideology, policy and pattern of 'public' education, publicly provided, publicly financed, but in the presence of church-related, mainly Catholic parochial schools. The declared mission of the American public school was to provide secular or non-denominational elementary education for all children, but the system was accused by the Catholic community of having the undeclared mission of 'Protestantizing' the children of Roman Catholic families. 'Non-denominational' was seen as meaning 'non-denominational Protestant', an attempt to impose, in the name of the state, a secular or minimally religious education that was anathema to and would undermine the Catholic church.[34] Judgements of the 'effectiveness' of such a school would therefore be quite different when coming from Catholic leaders or parents, or the proponents of publicly provided education, regardless of other, more 'academic' considerations. What was good, successful or effective about a school in the nineteenth century depended on its mission and procedures, how it presented them and how they were monitored, but equally on the diverse directions from which judgement might come.

A discussion of the history of reading has raised similar questions. The purposes of reading have been described as assuming

> many different forms among different social groups during different eras. Men and women have read in order to save their souls, to improve their manners, to repair their machinery, to seduce their sweethearts, to learn about current events, and simply to have fun.[35]

A description of that kind could well fit the diverse reasons for providing or acquiring education in the nineteenth century.

NOTES

1 R. S. Tompson (1970). 'The Leeds grammar school case of 1805', *Journal of Educational Administration and History*, **3.**

2 (1923) *Sanderson of Oundle*. London: Chatto & Windus, pp. 31–3.

3 Rupert Wilkinson (1964). *The Prefects: British Leadership and the Public School Tradition*. London: Oxford University Press, p. 16.

4 David Newsome (1961). *Godliness and Good Learning: Four Studies on a Victorian Ideal*. London: John Murray, p. 205.

5 *Report of Her Majesty's Commissioners Appointed to Inquire into the Revenues and Management of Certain Colleges and Schools, and the Studies Pursued and Instruction Given Therein* (Clarendon Report) (1864). London: HMSO, pp. 40–1.

6 G. F. Berkeley, quoted in Newsome, *Godliness and Good Learning*, p. 201.

7 See J. A. Mangan (ed.) (1988). *'Benefits Bestowed'?: Education and British Imperialism*. Manchester: Manchester University Press, including a discussion of the issues by Clive Whitehead, 'British colonial policy: a synonym for cultural imperialism?' and an editorial discussion on 'Imperialism, history and education'.

8 Edward C. Mack (1941). *Public Schools and British Opinion since 1860: The Relationship between Contemporary Ideas and the Evolution of an English Institution*. New York: Columbia University Press, pp. 107–8.

9 Wilkinson, *The Prefects*, pp. 21, 90.

10 See particularly Joyce Senders Petersen (1987). *The Reform of Girls' Secondary and Higher Education in Victorian England*. New York: Garland, ch. 9.

11 See Joan N. Burstyn (1984). *Victorian Education and the Ideal of Womanhood*. New Brunswick, NJ: Rutgers University Press.

12 Schools Inquiry Commission (1868). *Report of the Commission* (Taunton Report), Vol. 1, pp. 546–53, 560–1.

13 Lilian M. Faithfull (1924). *In the House of My Pilgrimage*. London: Chatto & Windus, p. 75.

14 Clarendon Report, Vol. 1, pp. 23–6.

15 Ibid., p. 56.

16 Taunton Report, Vol. 1, pp. 131–2.

17 Secondary Education Commission (1895). *Report* (Bryce Report). For example, Part II, pp. 75–8, Part III, pp. 130–44.

18 Daniel P. Resnick (1984). 'Educational policy and the applied historian', *Journal of Social History*, **14** (4), 540.

19 James A. Petch (1953). *Fifty Years of Examining: the Joint Matriculation Board 1903– 1953*. London: Harrap, ch. 1 (and *passim* for the early and later development of examinations). See also John Roach (1971). *Public Examinations in England 1850– 1900*. London: Cambridge University Press (especially Part I, 'The competitive principle established').

20 *Cornhill Magazine* (1861). 'Competitive examinations', **4** (December), 692–3.

21 Anthony Trollope (1909). *The Last Chronicle of Barset*. London: Everyman, pp. 124–5; first published 1867. For Trollope's view of 'the perils of competitive examination' and 'that much loathed scheme' cf. his *An Autobiography*. London: Williams & Norgate, 1883; 1946 edn, pp. 50–2, 110–11.

22 Bryce Report, Part II, p. 161.

23 *Report of the Committee of Council on Education . . . 1868–69*. London: HMSO, p. xxv (the inspector was the Rev. Mr Mitchell, reporting on Church of England schools in London and the Home Counties).

24 Bryce Report, Part III, pp. 163–4.

25 R. C. Carrington (1971). *Two Schools: A History of St Olave's and St Saviour's Grammar School Foundation*. London: The Foundation, pp. 150–1, 164, 181.

26 D. J. Watkins (1966). *The History of Sir Thomas Rich's School Gloucester*. Gloucester: The School, pp. 44–57.

27 *Cornhill Magazine* (1861). 'Middle class and primary education in England: past and present', **4** (July), 52.

28 Ibid., 'Competitive examinations', p. 692.

29 Taunton Report, Vol. 1, pp. 322–3.

30 Ibid., p. 712; *Cornhill Magazine*, 'Middle class and primary education in England', 50, 52.

31 Laurie Magnus (ed.) (1901). *National Education: Essays towards a Constructive Policy* ('Editorial'). London: John Murray, p. 11.

32 Bryce Report, Part III, p. 239.

33 Magnus, *National Education*, p. 16.

34 See Lloyd P. Jorgensen (1987). *The State and the Non-Public Schools 1825–1925*. Columbia: University of Missouri Press.

35 Robert Darnton (1989). 'Toward a history of reading', *Wilson Quarterly*, Autumn, 92.

Chapter 5

Expertise and Ignorance

In one sense the twentieth century represents more of the same, continuing to combine complex educational realities with diverse judgements of schools from diverse constituencies. In another sense, however, the picture changes, as the extent and powers of the constituencies change, as structural changes take place in systems and school organization and control, as the role of the state and public agencies increases or changes, and as education becomes a growing subject of research and professional concern – at the same time as opportunities increase for the expression of popular and media opinion. In many countries greater parental and community involvement with schools was often accompanied, as described in Queensland, by 'an ingenuous belief in the efficacy of education', and 'widespread ignorance of schools as they are today, particularly among those groups and individuals who have no regular contact with schools through their children'. As a result, 'vocal minority groups' became able to use 'the sensationalism of the media'.[1] The vociferous were very often at the opposite end of a spectrum from the researcher, and could be in government as well as in the market-place or the editorial office. The pluralism of western societies, the conditions of the democratization of educational and other social processes, the competition of values, enabled parallel but widely different approaches to education to evolve, and only rarely to coalesce. Care could be paralleled by arrogance, ways forward by retreats, policy by counter-policy, applause by denunciation. What made a school 'good' remained a set of issues relating to schools serving different social groups, to the choices made by those parents able to make them, and to the collective judgements of those who administered or guided or taught in schools. Across school systems, however, the growing and diversified profession of educational researcher and evaluator – especially in the first half of the century – spread considerable influence. Judgements of the quality of schools were no longer contingent purely on the relatively unsystematic accounts of inspectors, or the outcomes of external examinations which gave insights into the performance of only a scholastic minority, but also on criteria stemming from the enhanced status of expert opinion. University education departments in Britain or research bureaus in the United States, international contributions to a science of education, sustained analysis of 'progressive' organization and methods, studies of backwardness and child development, social disadvantage and child guidance – these and the complete range of educational processes at all levels and of all kinds had become a crucial new feature of the context of thinking about schools. It was a feature that could, of course, be derided or ignored.

It is not necessary here to attempt to trace the twentieth-century trajectories of all the nineteenth-century components of judgement-making that we have considered. By the end of the nineteenth century, clearly, forms of inspection and examination had become established, and in Britain the system of national and local inspectorates was to be sustained in the new century. The mix of public and private schooling was to change, but to remain essentially unchallenged, and however much the aims of different categories of schools might be modified, essential social and academic cores remained. It will be useful to focus on those aspects which were most affected by new policies, structures and theories, and fed most into the contexts which helped to shape opinions of schools. It is particularly important to emphasize the roles of expert opinion and the state, and to outline the directions established in the first half of the century that were to help explain the changes of approach to good or effective schools in the later century. Two preliminary points need to be stressed. The first is that the expert and research community was itself not homogeneous, and across time pre-eminence was ascribed, for example, to the educational psychologist, the sociologist, the evaluator or the curriculum developer. The second is the increasingly international nature of educational development and debate in the twentieth century. Intelligence tests were a product of Europe and the United States, 'progressive' ideas moved influentially from the United States to Britain in the writings of John Dewey, and from Britain to the United States through the reputation of A. S. Neill and Summerhill, and ideas and experience in curriculum development or the influence of family and social class on school learning moved from country to country. In 1950 the growth of American educational research was described as 'one of the conspicuous educational developments of the last half-century'.[2] This was true internationally, though not on the same scale. Not at the same times or with the same shape and emphases, researchers and educational systems targeted issues of language or intelligence, race or gender, science education or creativity. Key research findings and educational literature had an international audience, whether dealing with nursery or 'special' education, grading or credentials. Given the range of the issues affecting judgements about schools, and the international stage on which criteria were debated and set, it is possible only to suggest some of the most pertinent developments of roughly the first half of the twentieth century, as a kind of prehistory of important strands that were to appear in the later decades of the century.

The economic and social contexts of education, of course, changed dramatically in the first half of the century, and against the background of expansion and slump, the growth of service industries and higher education, new technical and skill requirements, educational systems and schools moved in new directions. Lord Eustace Percy, former president of the Board of Education, summarized the uncertainties amidst the economic tremors of 1930. The 'ordinary Englishman of average ability', who Percy seemed to take to be an upper-class or middle-class public schoolboy,

> no longer finds it easy, on the strength of a public school and
> university education, to govern the peoples of India, to sway
> Parliament by his eloquence, to satisfy the nation with simple reforms
> in legislation and administration, or to build up a prosperous business

in foreign trade. A public school education, even backed by more than average abilities, is to-day no guarantee against unemployment, let alone a passport to success.

In all walks of life careers required 'much deeper knowledge, greater skill, more exact training and stronger character'.[3] Percy knew that the public schools were deeply in competition with the grammar schools for university places, and believed that the boys who 'finished' their education at schools of all kinds 'have indeed finished it . . . they are as good at sixteen or eighteen or twenty-one, as the case may be, as they ever are afterwards':

> Employers who are asked by 'educationalists' to say what they want from the schools will hardly think it necessary to say that they want educated men. They assume that, as the ordinary Englishman traditionally assumes it. The danger, the really desperate danger, at the present day is that this is just the one thing that schools and colleges and universities may fail to supply.[4]

Magnus's 'unrest in education' never ceased to be an unrest, in Britain or elsewhere in the western world, precisely because of the rapidity of economic and technological change, and the zigzags of economics and politics. Neither in 1930 nor at many other points in the later century was it clear how these or other schools were to avoid the 'desperate danger' of failure in terms that had been mounting in importance from the late nineteenth century. The failure was that of not supplying 'educated men' (women were rarely included in this kind of commentary) who could both make their own way and sustain the country in international competition. Not that the public schools in Britain ceased to represent the educational basis of a powerful elite. Their students continued to dominate the Cabinet, and indeed their 'success' as schools continued to be judged to a considerable extent by their ability to permeate the country's dominant political, commercial and professional circles. In the 1930s the poet W. H. Auden, who had himself attended one of the schools, thought that the most important condition 'for a successful school is a beautiful situation'. Their *raison d'être* was 'the mass production of gentlemen'. When other contributors to the same collection of essays reported on the mass production of ladies they did so acknowledging that the girls' public schools 'run on a male system imperfectly adapted to female needs. We were terribly, terribly keen on games'; this promoted various kinds of 'almost inevitable idiocy', including a shyness which made the girls play games when ill. The school was implying: 'Run about, girls, *like* boys, and then you won't think *of* them.'[5]

Resistance to the development of popular education had not disappeared. For one of the contributors to Magnus's book in 1901 (a former Member of Parliament) there were 'still some people who dispute the value of education, and who affect to believe that it unfits certain classes of the community for what these censors are pleased to consider their proper station in life'. He quoted the chairman of a large manufacturing company as saying he did not consider 'that this country suffered any disadvantage by reason of deficient education . . . the craze for education would disappear with its votaries . . . the workshop was the best and cheapest education. There was only room under modern conditions for a very few experts.'[6] Thirty-three years later Bertrand Russell considered that 'the prejudice against popular education died hard. . . . Nor is the prejudice extinct even now.'[7] What opposition to extensions of popular education amounted to across these decades, however, was essentially opposition to the amount of education, the extension of compulsory schooling, the diversification of curricula into 'fancy' subjects, the raising of social or career aspirations. There were mixed views amongst parents, employers or politicians as to the 'proper' functions of an elementary school, the 'right' amount of public resources or scholarships to take the appropriate small segment of elementary school children into the grammar schools. The main debates of the twentieth century were not about whether to educate, but in what kinds of school, with what kind of curriculum, with what aims, for how long, and in what ways, taking account of sex, race, age or ability differences. Access to secondary education, and therefore to the qualifications for entry to higher education or occupations increasingly requiring them, became particularly important in the 1920s and 1930s in Britain as demands and proposals for changes to the system of state-provided education moved to the top of the educational agenda. Expansion and structural changes affected the work and perceived functions of elementary or primary or secondary schools in many countries.

What countries shared was a growing length of school life, and a strengthening of the sense of 'adolescence' (a term in use only from the outset of the twentieth century) as a 'problem' period of life. With the shrinking of apprenticeship, the raising of the school-leaving age and legislation further to curtail children's employment and therefore contribution to family budgets, together with the uncertainties of employment, the continued decline of churchgoing, urban expansion, and the impact of war on families, behaviour or conduct became more prominent social issues. The life of the streets or juvenile delinquency or youthful misconduct were not invented by the twentieth century, but they became issues which related to perceptions of the roles of social institutions. Pressures inevitably increased for schools to respond to demands for their acceptance of wider social responsibilities, and public attitudes to schools took more account of their ability to 'solve' adolescent and other problems.

At one level this meant judgements about how school students behaved out of school as well as in the classroom. Later in the century schools were to be asked to serve as a, even the, defence against sexual promiscuity or drug abuse or delinquency, and their public image – certainly as presented in the media – was often more concerned with portraits (sometimes caricatures) of the degree to which these problems were present inside schools themselves. At another level this meant stronger perceptions of the school as an academic-cum-social institution, as a conduit for measures relating to health and disadvantage, counselling and access to other public services. In the nineteenth century in the United States, despite resistance to government involvement, education became what has been described as an anomaly, 'one public service widely accepted in the North as a proper function of public agencies. Advocates of spending for public schooling portrayed the common school as the great preemptive social service, the public good that made other forms of social spending less necessary if not superfluous.'[8] It was often argued in European countries in the nineteenth century too that schools were cheaper than prisons, but the 'social service' function of schools in any sustained sense was a development of the next century. Judgements of schools in this respect had therefore often to be tempered by the extent to which public authorities were responsible for enabling the schools to fulfil this role, the extent to which services were adequately supplied or supported by the authorities concerned. Judgements about private or church-related schools might therefore in many places and at many times contain an element of comparison with public education and access to resources or services that had come to be seen as desirable or essential ingredients of schooling.

Judgements of the quality of individual schools were, of course, profoundly affected by the position of schools in relation to changes in the system of which they were part. They might be seen as better or worse than similar schools, as good or poor preparation for the next stage of education, as able or unable to take advantage of opportunities for improvement or innovation offered by the system. In the United States the context was one of expansion of 'elementary' and 'secondary' or 'high school' education which differed in many ways from state to state, and between public and private schools, but which developed on broadly similar structural lines from the pattern that emerged in the late nineteenth century. In Europe at different points the context was one of reorganization, to provide new types of school, or to replace parallel education tracks through the system with common stages of progression. In Britain the scholarship bridge between elementary and grammar schools was hotly contested as an adequate model for an education system throughout the decades up to the Second World War. The new Labour Party, other labour movement organizations, progressive educators and others (including the Hadow Committee's report, *The Education of the Adolescent*, in 1926) in various ways demanded 'secondary education for all'[9] and a reorganization that would eliminate 'elementary' education and produce an end-on system of primary and secondary schools. That was in fact the central provision of the Education Act of 1944, which required that secondary education be provided by all local education authorities –

> and the schools available for an area shall not be deemed to be
> sufficient unless they are sufficient in number, character, and
> equipment to afford for all pupils opportunities for education offering
> such variety of instruction and training as may be desirable in view of
> their different ages, abilities, and aptitudes.[10]

The 1944 Act was followed in subsequent decades by intense controversy over the nature of the provision of secondary education, controversy which overshadowed all other issues in education in the 1950s–1970s. The choice was between comprehensive schools (what the Americans had called common schools) and a division between secondary grammar, secondary technical and secondary modern schools. It is not necessary here to follow the complexities of the debates and the respective policies of the Conservative and Labour Parties when in government, but two aspects of the developments are of particular interest. The first is that the comprehensive school, gaining in numbers and authority in the 1950s and 1960s, depended to a large extent for its reputation with parents and others on comparisons of its examination results with those of the tripartite system. Early supporters of the comprehensive school argued strongly that boys and girls who would otherwise be deprived of an academic education by failure in the eleven-plus selection examination could more easily develop and be transferred into such work in the comprehensive school than between schools. This, they argued, at least partly accounted for the examination successes seen in early surveys.[11] The schools were at this stage being defended on a variety of grounds, including equity and the virtues of scale, but also on the basis of the academic criteria that had been strong features of the grammar school. Many inside the schools regretted this. The headmaster and his deputy at one comprehensive school voiced this latter position in 1958, beginning an article entitled 'External examinations and internal assessment':

> The educational achievements of the comprehensive school are likely
> to be judged publicly at three levels: by the number and quality of
> university and college entrants; by the number and degree of success
> of candidates in external examinations; and by the number of
> 'illiterates' that come from our schools. It is unfortunate, perhaps, that
> we cannot be judged by the degree to which our children are able to
> integrate themselves into society, at whatever level, since the purpose
> of education is to prepare the child for life.

The general public, they admitted, would assess these schools 'by some form of statistical analysis, and performance in public examination lends itself most readily to this method of investigation'. They concluded that the schools were using both external examinations and internal assessment 'with increasing effectiveness' to serve the needs and abilities of the pupils.[12] The problems of introducing new secondary structures, including comprehensive-type schools, were not unique to Britain, as France, Italy and other European countries also attempted to remodel their secondary education.

To reach both the secondary grammar and the secondary technical schools (the latter never proving popular with local authorities and government officials, and being established in relatively small numbers) children 'passed' the eleven-plus examination, and those who went to the secondary modern school were perceived as having 'failed'. This was not the official language, which in commission reports and government documents had argued in favour of diversity for children with diverse talents and needs. At the beginning of 1956 there were in England 1,357 secondary grammar schools of various kinds, and 3,636 secondary modern schools, and the latter were invariably seen by parents as the destination for failures. Reporting on the secondary modern schools in 1958 H. C. Dent found some where parents were supportive and involved in the life of the school, but more where the opposite was the case, where parents were apathetic, where standards were low, where it was recognized that the children had been consigned to the lowest rung in the educational hierarchy. Middle-class parents felt acutely the failure of their children to go on to the grammar school they had taken for granted. In the eyes of these and many other parents the secondary modern school was still the old elementary school, their children were stigmatized, and there were important social as well as educational consequences. The parents who were not disturbed by their children attending secondary modern schools tended to be ones 'who simply did not care, those who did not understand, those who were too ignorant or too unambitious to desire for their children anything more than they themselves had got

61

from the Elementary School, those who regarded school as an unavoidable but annoying postponement of wage-earning', and who would therefore know that there would be no resistance to their children leaving school at the earliest opportunity. Dent found the position to be changing, as the secondary modern schools were able to enter children for public examinations previously reserved for the grammar and technical schools, and as parents found the schools able to offer more for their children.[13]

The content of schooling not only changed during the first half of the century, but was also the subject of constant scrutiny by educators and by those who made and influenced policy. A joint committee of local authorities and teachers expressed the view in 1930 that members of local education committees had shown a growing interest in 'education itself', as distinct from the provision of schools, teachers and resources, since the 1902 Education Act. Such members had wanted to know more about the work 'actually done' in schools, not just to ensure that money was well spent, but also to supplement what they learned from inspectors' reports with evidence of 'the effectiveness of instruction in the area as a whole'.[14] Within this enhanced interest by the local controllers of public education, as at school and national levels also, was a direct interest in and debate about appropriate curricula. Discussion focused on the breadth of the curriculum and the style of teaching, on 'progressive methods, on range and choice in the secondary school. There was debate about the 'play way', open-air schools, discipline and much else. The 'grammar school' model established in the early century was eroded by pressure for an extension of the 'modern' content, and curricular traditions of all kinds were constantly under scrutiny. The 1931 Hadow Report, *The Primary School*, for instance, in its chapter on the curriculum, considered 'the traditional curriculum of the Public Elementary School', curriculum principles in relation to 'the complexity of modern industrial civilization', physical welfare and efficiency, language, manual skill, aesthetic subjects, literature, science, geography and history, the practice of treating the curriculum in terms of subjects, the desirability of new methods of constructing curricula, and the need for a thorough grounding in reading, writing and arithmetic.[15]

At the heart of such discussions of the curriculum internationally was a conception not only of what was to be learned but also of the learner and of the curriculum as an important representation of standards. If a 'good' school had a 'good' curriculum it was because it targeted the right characteristics of the individual child, as a 'whole person', as technically skilled, as academically well prepared, or whatever was appropriate for the new brand of school and its clientele. In the second half of the century curriculum development was to aim across wider frontiers and seek to develop widely applicable strategies for teaching science and mathematics, languages or other subjects that in the United States, Britain and elsewhere were the subject of major curriculum development projects. In the United States one important strand throughout the century was that of the nature and place of 'vocational education', a concept that had different resonances in Britain and other countries. The American version of vocational content, which satisfied many parents and repelled others, tended to be an alternative to the academic mainstream, as a lower-ability, often lower-class curriculum. In Britain in the first half of the century the vocational content of the elementary school curriculum often included similar components, including technical and craft subjects for boys and domestic training for girls, but the grammar schools were only marginally touched by this version of the vocational – with a minor corner of the curriculum reserved for manual skills. In another sense, however, all schools were perceived by their publics as broadly vocational, in preparing for something – either employment, the functions of one or another form of educational and social leadership or followership, or the attributes of a power elite. Not until the 1980s was there in Britain, unlike other industrialized countries of continental Europe for example, any serious, sustained attempt to identify the technological contribution to the concept of culture embodied in the educational system and its sectors of schooling.

The teachers in the early British comprehensive schools were right to see their public image as dependent on the statistical and comparative evidence resulting from external examinations and internal assessment. By mid-century perceptions of schooling had been influenced for decades by an increasing proliferation of forms of measurement claiming to make objective judgements about individual children and about their schools. The British system of public examinations had already a century of history. Since 1907 a system of examinations for places in grammar schools had become a major feature of the educational landscape. From the end of the nineteenth century the measurement of intelligence, pioneered in France, the United States and Britain, dominated educational research and increasingly the organization of school systems. These 'tests of educable capacity' became part of the selection procedure, and were presented as, if not infallible, at least the most reliable means of sorting children for entry to secondary, or to different types of secondary, education. The vocabulary of education expanded to embrace IQ tests, standardized tests of attainment, streaming, mental training. . . . A 1924 Consultative Committee Report, *Psychological Tests of Educable Capacity*, outlined a whole variety of uses for individual and group tests of intelligence, for entry to schools and within different types of school. It recommended experiments with the use of such tests in technical and other schools, and saw a particular use in girls' secondary schools, where the entrants had a great diversity of attainments because of their previous schooling: 'we think that the data obtained by the careful application of group tests of intelligence would in some instances be of real value as a partial check on the other data available. The tests might also be used as an aid in classifying entrants of the same attainments.'[16] Measurement had become more than the prominent phenomenon identified by the *Cornhill Magazine*; it had become an integral part of educational thinking, planning and provision, and this was especially true of a country where, like Britain, the provision of places in public 'secondary' education was limited, and some form of selection was inevitable. So in public education one major element – the clientele of a school – was apparently beyond comment, since 'scientific' procedures were used to determine what it should be.

An increasingly influential educational constituency was the expert, the professional, and new careers in testing, measurement, research and guidance opened up in Britain as in other countries. In educational research generally there was increasing emphasis on, and often dispute about, methodology. What needed to be known, how could it be known, what instruments had to be devised to make it known, on what scale should investigations be conducted, what constituted evidence? Surveys, case studies, observation and, particularly, instruments that permitted statistical answers to questions were part of the developing and often disputed territory of research, applied to children, child development, children's attainment; the prevalence, distribution and causes of backwardness; school administration and organization; the social distribution of educational success in tests, and almost all aspects of educational provision, practices and experience. While the report *Psychological Tests of Educable Capacity* recommended the use of tests within elementary schools about the age of seven in order to assist in 'preliminary classification' for entry to the upper school, the tests should only be applied when 'the services of a properly trained person are available'.[17] It is true, as the Hadow Committee on primary schools pointed out in 1931, that there were warnings about the possible distortion of curricula by training for tests and examinations, the dangers of comparing schools on the basis of lists of successes for places in grammar schools, and dissatisfaction with 'any external method of classifying pupils. . . . It arises from an exaggerated faith in examinations as a criterion of the efficiency of a school.'[18] It may be argued that the professionaliza-tion of educational procedures was part of the general professionalization of societies, with wider dependence on expert opinion in all aspects of life.[19] The scale, range and influence of the expert sub-professions of education in the first half of the twentieth century are an especially vivid example.

The growth of measurement and testing paralleled the growth of the progressive education movement in the early decades of the century, and though the former was to some extent a limiting condition for the latter, progressive education either managed to resist the pressures of measures, or accommodated it. For some progressive educationists psychological testing, for example, proved acceptable as a means of tailoring education to the needs of the individual child. For others progressive methods were merely an improved way of motivating children and enabling them to succeed in the world of examinations. For most progressives, however, examinations and testing were probably at best a necessary evil, and at worst inimical to their view of the development of the human personality. The progressive education movement was international in scope, as the influence of its supporters spread from country to country, and as international conferences, informal contacts and publications spread debates about progressive ideas and practices more fully internationally and intercontinentally than any educational movement had previously done. The growth of progressive education from the 1890s in particular raised new difficulties about identifying the characteristics of a good progressive school, and what was good about such a school by comparison with traditional schools. Judgements about progressive education were judgements about schools, methods and ideas. A school could be lauded or reviled precisely because it espoused a specific version of progressive ideology, or because it was courageously experimental or embarrassingly different.

The most common element in progressive schooling that affected judgements made of it was its ability to treat 'the whole child'. The basic critique of established education was that typified by John Dewey's early comment: 'the child's life is an integral, a total one . . . it is the child's own world. It has the unity and completeness of his own life. He goes to school, and various studies divide and fractionize the world for him.'[20] Most progressive thinking began with such a theory and its implications. The traditional curriculum was seen as in conflict with the experience of the child. The literature of progressivism consistently emphasized the need for the school to take account of the child's personality, the organic nature of growth. 'In the progressive philosophy,' as summarized in an encyclopaedia of research at mid-century, '*growth* and *learning* are synonymous'. Progressive schooling was postulated basically on a model of growth and teaching and learning quite different from the principles embodied in traditional curricula:

> biology, endocrinology, physiology, neurology, anthropology, psychology (including mental hygiene, psychiatry, and analysis), nutrition, medicine, and all other fields yielding information about the growth needs of the human individual have been tapped by progressive education for significant factors that should bear upon educational planning . . . The biologists' emphasis on the organic nature of experience gave root to the progressives' stress on taking all factors in child life into account when dealing with the child.[21]

There were, of course, widely varied interpretations of how to translate such an emphasis into an appropriate school organization. The progressive education movement was a collection of widely disparate interpretations with frequent controversies over such basic issues as the relationship between education and the needs of a democratic society, or the structure of the curriculum and the role of the teacher.

The modern progressive school movement in Britain began with the creation of Abbotsholme, the first of the independent schools to be established in opposition to the prevailing structures, aims and ethos of the public schools. Cecil Reddie described his new school as making an attempt 'to develop harmoniously all the powers of the boy – to train him in fact how to *live*, and become a rational member of society', and it was not relevant whether the boy was to go on to be a student or a practical man. He would be the better person for having had 'all the different sides of his nature well developed'. Reddie acknowledged the achievements of the public school, and believed that new schools should be based on the idea of the public school, but with considerable changes. The majority of public schoolboys wasted 'a large part of their school career in studying subjects, such as the dead languages, which only a few really require in after life'. The games they played were 'elaborate and artificial', and the boys were frequently herded together to watch 'gladiatorial shows till their conversation is narrowed down to mere athletic "shop"'. At Abbotsholme the training was to be 'physical and manual, artistic and imaginative, literary and intellectual, and moral and religious'.[22] J. H. Badley, establishing the second of the schools, Bedales, in 1893, also paid tribute to the public school tradition, and made the same criticisms of narrowness and the tendency for games to become an 'irksome and monotonous burden'. Bedales was innovative in being a coeducational boarding-school, and it emphasized a balance of academic, creative and social activities, including such leisure activities as those in literary, musical, scientific, engineering and social-work societies; it also provided a combination of prescribed studies and choice.

Crucial to the running of Bedales and other schools that followed was the involvement of the boys and girls in a school parliament. Badley described this in

1923 as having the power to frame and amend school rules, to debate any matters submitted to it, to consult the whole school on unresolved issues, to discuss grievances and put them right, and to provide a means by which 'the Staff and School may understand each other's point of view and learn the reasons why any particular measure is necessary'. The headmaster presided, and the parliament contained the housemaster and housemistress, the head of the school (a boy or girl who acted as secretary), and 24 elected representatives, two from each of the forms.[23] These attempts to transform the public school were not new, since other experiments in school and curriculum organization had taken place in the nineteenth century. The most relevant to the Bedales approach was that of the Hills' schools in the early nineteenth century, at which, in the words of one of the brothers, 'we endeavour to teach our pupils the arts of *self-government* and *self-education*. . . . The principle of our government is to leave, as much as possible, all power in the hands of the boys themselves.'[24] The difference in the twentieth century was that such ideas were to become part of a wider and more influential movement.

Democratizing school life in order to promote cooperative and responsible attitudes was one aspect of progressive education. Promoting greater individual liberty to develop was another, and to one extent or another this permeated progressive schools after the First World War – the most famous being Summerhill from 1921 with its attempt to permit children to grow without having decisions or ideas or action imposed on them by authority, a concept which A. S. Neill found unacceptable and which he did all he could to dismantle. Children were to be allowed to arrive at their own opinions as a preliminary to action.[25] Summerhill was popularly known as a 'do what you like' school. This aspect of the progressive movement had considerable influence in the creation of similar schools in the United States, and in countries in other continents. Neill's ideas of freedom and respect for the child were also an influential component of the spread of progressive ideas, in this case not in the creation of independent schools but in challenging the prevailing structures and procedures of school systems. His articulation of the philosophy and psychology of schooling joined the approaches of Froebel, Montessori, Dewey and the increasing number of progressive educators and educationists of the 1920s and 1930s in pressures to break down the rigidities of established school systems, at different levels, in different countries.

Other progressive innovations included, for example, the establishment of the King Alfred School Society in 1898, opening a coeducational day school which proclaimed its intention to 'give practical expression to the best theories of education extant'. King Alfred's approach had no basis in religion, and it was to be one of the first schools to put a range of principles of school reform into practice 'as a coherent plan of education for the whole of the child's school life'. The educational value of personal liberty was one of the principles. Such principles, however widely recognized they may have been, were 'at that time rarely adopted except for small children'.[26] Bedales, Bryanston and other independent schools were also to one extent or another to adopt the Dalton Plan, named from its origins in Dalton, Massachusetts. In this case Helen Parkhurst took a view at her school in some respects diametrically opposite to that of Neill, arguing against a freedom which meant licence and indiscipline: 'the child who "does as he likes" is not a free child. He is, on the contrary, apt to become the slave of bad habits, selfish, and quite unfit for community life'. Her Dalton Plan conceived freedom within the shared social responsibilities of the school. She dismantled the timetable, making it possible for teachers to act as subject advisers, and for the boys and girls to undertake 'contract work' emancipated from the tyranny of school clocks and bells. Work could be more collaborative amongst pupils at all levels, and classrooms could become subject laboratories. The intention was not to abandon 'subjects' but to increase pupil initiative and interest, strengthening motivation to sustain and complete the work schedules planned. The plan was capable of being applied 'as an efficiency measure' within established school arrangements, but she hoped that it would be used 'for the carrying out of a freer curriculum composed entirely of projects set by the pupils themselves'.[27] The plan, either 'pure' or combined in some way with a structured timetable, was attractive not only to some independent schools, but also to some local authority grammar schools. The County Secondary School for Girls, Streatham, was described in 1922 by its headmistress, Rosa Bassett (whose name the school was later to bear), as having tested the plan for the past year, and 'we feel it enlists, more than any other system does, the co-operation of the pupil in her education'. The school at this stage had class lessons for part of the week, but most of the school had half the week for 'free study' on the 'syllabuses of work' provided for each girl in each subject at the beginning of the month. What Rosa Bassett was discovering at this stage, however, as was to be the case in many schools developing along progressive lines, was the difficulty of applying commonly accepted means of assessing results. The plan, in her view, undoubtedly encouraged a girl to study more than before, 'though its effect many not be at once apparent, for naturally the ordinary testing devices cannot gauge the growth of the child's understanding. We are, in fact, but slowly finding out how to test intelligence.'[28]

The Dalton Plan was only one of the progressive methods of organizing school work, the classroom, the school day, pupil grouping, and teaching methods generally, that were experimented with and often sustained, especially in British elementary schools. Local authorities differed in their willingness to support schools in such experimentation, but British headteachers and their staff often enjoyed a considerable measure of latitude in how they organized and taught the curriculum. The state was not willing or able to reach down into the classroom and shape it, and there was a widespread view in any case that as long as schools performed their overall functions, the methods adopted need not be a cause for concern. The problems of making judgements in this connection were only part of the difficulty of making judgements within an educational system subject to competing ideas and pressures, and changing in a variety of ways. More than in other cases, the progressive schools and to some extent other schools partially using progressive or experimental methods within more traditional settings were difficult to judge on anything except their own terms, asking questions for example about the acceptability of coeducation and its implementation, or about the particular version of a pupil-centred curriculum. Clearly judgements about a school of this kind would also focus on its environment or the teachers' understanding of children as well as their academic qualifications. Was a school pursuing the same ends as other schools but by different means, or were the ends different and, if so, on what basis could the outcomes be judged? Even in 1972 a sympathetic American commentator discussing the evaluation of learning in British primary schools could begin: 'We would all be able to proceed much more sensibly if we had clearer notions of how to go about evaluating learning in informal settings.' Americans, with different school approaches in mind, would no doubt complain about the 'relative absence of measurable objectives' in British primary schools, and what might seem to be their 'romanticism'.[29]

What these diversities indicate is how much more complex the mosaic of judgements had become than even the nineteenth-century pattern. The range of research-based or expert contributions to the basis of progressive education was to a lesser extent true of education in general. Schooling was being pressed into taking account, for example, of the nature of child development, and in the later century the question of how to assess 'progress' was to assume increasing importance. By mid-century the American *Encyclopedia of Educational Research* included 'child development' as one of its most substantial entries, in fact a series of 16 entries by a variety of authors under different headings – including environmental factors, early infancy, physical growth, constitution types, language, locomotor and manipulatory control, moral concepts and conduct, and social development.[30] Special categories of children, including the 'backward', were being more systematically researched and discussed, and in Britain local authorities such as the London County Council developed a range of special schools for children with specific physical or mental disabilities. In Britain, the United States and other countries specialists in dealing with such categories of children were being included in administrative teams, setting up child guidance clinics and centres, and acting as advisers.

The development of research and a corpus of expert data or opinion did not necessarily affect schools, generally caught up in the routines of their particular traditions. The climate of expectation of what constituted good school management, organization and performance was, however, affected by the various challenges to established procedures. National and local inspection, for example, continued but was influenced by new developments, and in some cases influenced these in return. P. B. Ballard, an Inspector of Schools for the London County Council, found himself early in the century involved in mental measurement. His assistant on one occasion reported to him that the reading in one class of a girls' school was 'below the average'. Conducting his own inquiry he concluded that the girls were in fact 'above the average. What, then, was the average?' What was the average reading ability of girls of eight? He asked his assistant, his chief, his colleagues, the Board of Education inspectors, lecturers at training colleges, professors of education, medical men, psychologists, 'and from none of them could I get a clear and definite reply. They did not even know what was meant by average', whether it was a 'point' or a 'patch', a mathematical mark with half the measurements above and half below, or a range of marks around the middle: 'Here were we all glibly pronouncing school attainments to be above or below the average, and yet we had only the vaguest notion of what we were talking about.'

From this beginning he began devising standardized tests.[31] Since the purpose of any kind of assessment was to attempt to evaluate learning outcomes, new developments such as psychological measurement joined the established approaches through examinations and inspection of the nineteenth century. The 1930 Joint Advisory Committee Report, *Examinations in Public Elementary*

Schools, expressed the view that prevailed and was to continue to prevail: 'Inspection accompanied by judicious examination is, generally speaking, the best means of ascertaining the quality of the instruction.' Inspection on its own could result in superficial findings, and examinations alone could result in 'incorrect conclusions'.[32]

The ways of judging the quality of schooling had in the twentieth century become more associated with national or nationwide structures or procedures. The precursor of the American Educational Research Association was founded in 1915, and it became the AERA in 1922. British educational developments from the 1860s in particular but with great strength in the first half of the twentieth century, were connected with national commissions, national debate, national legislation, and the regulations and budgetary controls of central and local government. In many European countries state control of public education was firmly established at various points in the nineteenth century, and firmly entrenched in the twentieth century. Although educational initiatives and critiques came from many directions, the state was often the arbiter, and for research or pressure to be influential it was most likely to be directed at government agencies, parliaments or the national bodies which most powerfully articulated the bases of policy. Education publishing, of journals and books, increased considerably in the first half of the twentieth century, as did the number and scale of organizations of teachers and educationists. The literature of analysis and advice on good teaching, good administration, good assessment, accompanied a growing literature of comment on educational systems. The strands of educational psychology, philosophy, history and administration became particularly demarcated in the first half of the century, partly in relation to the expansion of teacher education in the colleges and universities. A kind of applied sociology of education was beginning to be developed, notably in Britain, in the 1920s and 1930s, but the place of sociology in the educational canon was not firmly established until the 1950s. The diverse threads of educational change were accompanied by a literature of educational theory, pointing most directly in all countries at definitions of the aims of education.

Aims were pursued at the level of national or ideological commitment, and in relation to particular areas of concern. In the Soviet Union, Germany, the United States and across Europe and other continents the relationship between education and national culture, national development, or the application of ideologies, produced a considerable literature. Of particular relevance here was the pursuit of aims in the context of attempts to defend or change policies directly affecting the public and private provision of education. Debate focused on the meaning of liberal and vocational education, citizenship, education for democracy and against Fascism, the purposes of schooling for specific age groups, or for children of particular ability or social groups, the education of girls, the social waste of selective systems, the difference between education and training. Over all of these and other cases controversy was as acute as over any other aspect of social policy, and in relation to the social barriers to grammar school education, perhaps more so. It was relatively easy to formulate general aims, but since these were always open to interpretation, neither recommended policies nor the means of evaluating educational practices was straightforward.

The difficulties in attempting to define the aims of education were generally recognized in the first half of the century, even as individuals and committees attempted to elaborate if not their definitions at least their priority aims. At the progressive end of the spectrum, T. Percy Nunn indicated the different purposes that were postulated for education, and underlined the difficulties inherent in defining purpose as in the case, for example, of forming character or preparing for sound living. These seemed satisfactory enough aims until, 'pursuing the matter farther, we ask what kind of character it is desirable to "form", what activities "complete living" includes. . . . ' Since every scheme of education was basically a 'practical philosophy', it

> necessarily touches life at every point. Hence any educational aims which are concrete enough to give definite guidance are correlative to ideals of life – and, as ideals of life are eternally at variance, their conflict will be reflected in educational theories . . . there can be no universal aim of education if that aim is to include the assertion of any particular ideal of life.

Educational efforts therefore had to be 'limited to securing for every one the conditions under which individuality is most completely developed'.[33] Nunn's views on education theories and the ideals of life always being at variance, contained in a book reprinted 22 times before 1938, were to be quoted approvingly by the Spens Committee in its discussion of influences on the curriculum in that year. The emphasis on varieties of 'ideals of life' was reflected in the 1920s even within the narrow compass of radical and reforming approaches to education. J. J. Findlay, a well-known professor of education, described a range of innovators' philosophies of schooling, with regard to the school's role in preparing children to 'function successfully' in the lives that lay before them. Some accepted the aim, some rejected it, some compromised somewhere around a concept such as 'social efficiency',[34] expressed in rather ambiguous terms.

Throughout the 1920s and 1930s, with education a crucial item on political agendas, educational theories tended, in Nunn's word, to be 'concrete', to be embodied as directly as possible in programmes and policies, in precise recommendations for changes to systems and schools. In his 1922 *Secondary Education for All*, Tawney's philosophy of education was often expressed in images, beginning with his view of the existing divided system of education as one in which 'slender hand-rails . . . have been built between the primary and the secondary school'. Secondary education was too often 'a landing without a staircase' and elementary education (or primary education, as the reformers wished it to be) was often 'a staircase without a landing'. For 90 per cent of children the primary school was like 'the rope which the Indian juggler throws into the air to end in vacancy'.[35] While some Labour and radical philosophies were already pointing towards the multilateral or comprehensive school, Tawney's view of adequate secondary school provision for all pointed towards variety: 'the greater the variety among secondary schools the better for education. . . . The demand of Labour for the democratising of secondary education implies no wish to sacrifice the peculiar excellence of particular institutions to a pedantic State-imposed uniformity.'[36] The influential Consultative Committee reports on education in the 1920s and 1930s similarly presented 'concrete theories', including perhaps the most famous pronouncement of any of them, that of the 1926 Hadow Report, *The Education of the Adolescent*, concerning 'a tide which begins to rise in the veins of youth at the age of eleven or twelve. It is called by the name of adolescence.' If that tide could be 'taken at the flood' it would 'move on to fortune'. The committee proposed, like Tawney and many others (Tawney was also a member of the Hadow Committee), that all children should be transferred at the age of 11 or 12 to some form of secondary education.[37]

A prominent aim of education was commonly expressed, particularly in the world situation of the 1930s, in terms of citizenship. The background to a small pamphlet published in 1935 is revealing. It was co-authored by Sir Ernest Simon, who was chairman of the Association for Education in Citizenship, and a former Parliamentary Secretary to the Ministry of Health. He considered that vocational and cultural aims expressed for education ignored 'a man's third great function in life: his membership of the community', and the aim of the pamphlet was to deal explicitly with education for citizenship. The aim of the Association, as presented on its membership form, was 'to advance the study of and training in citizenship, by which is meant training the moral qualities necessary for the citizens of a democracy'. A foreword to the pamphlet was written by the then Parliamentary Secretary to the Board of Education, who began: 'It will be generally agreed that fitness for citizenship is one of the objectives which the schools of this country should keep before them.' There was need for an open mind on some aspects of the proposals, but the Board of Education had the previous year discussed the issues raised in the pamphlet with elementary school teachers, and intended to do so again in 1935.[38] The president of the Association was Sir Henry Hadow, whose 1926 committee had acknowledged that 'the need for instruction in civics or citizenship has long been recognised', though opinion on how to provide it was divided.[39] Hadow, vice-chancellor of Sheffield University, had himself in 1923 published a book entitled *Citizenship*, in which a chapter on education amongst other things surveyed an already well established contemporary literature on schools and citizenship or civics.[40] The Spens Committee in 1938 singled out education for citizenship for special mention in the introduction to its report, underlining – as did other commentators – the difficulty of raising the issues involved with pupils below the age of 16, though the committee added that:

> We do not underestimate the value of imparting to pupils, even those under 16, information about national and international affairs and, not least, local government . . . what is most important is inculcating a habit of mind. This may be done by emphasising the serious character of the social and other problems which have to be faced, and at the same time by insisting that, while there is need for enthusiasm in causes which are felt to be vital, there is need also for study and judgment.[41]

The Spens view was also that of the committee that reported on curriculum and examinations in secondary schools. Headed by Sir Cyril Norwood, president of St John's College, Oxford, in 1941, it continued to have reservations about the age at which it was possible to introduce the subject. It considered education for an 'enlightened and instructed public opinion' to be important, recommended that lessons devoted to public affairs should be given to older boys and girls, but thought that 'by appropriate illustration and comment and digression' the topics could be raised within the standard school subjects, such as history, geography and English.[42]

The interest in citizenship as an aim of education disguised a range of assumptions, from those at the progressive end of educational thought, to ones at the conservative end. In the latter case Cyril Norwood, then headmaster of Harrow School, told a 1930 conference at his school that education to him 'shapes itself primarily as an education for citizenship'. By that he meant that education should be responsive to the needs of national life, and since that constantly changed, so should the content of education: 'we ought to be consciously striving to turn out servants of the community, and within that aim we ought to seek to develop individual character and individual gifts to the full, always with a social reference'. He pilloried the individualism of the progressive educators, and related his conception of citizenship training to the modern 'unrestricted democracy of both sexes', in which the majority were 'less than half-educated', the popular press appealed to 'low intelligence and utter thoughtlessness, triviality and prurience', and general elections were campaigns of 'rival mendacities, shameless advertisement, slogans, and quackeries'. Democracy would survive only if the standard of education for everyone was raised, 'if the democracy can be educated up to that point when it will contentedly accept the direction of those who know'. If Britain was not to become a Mussolini-type system the high intellectual standards of the civil service had to be encouraged, and respect for knowledge strengthened: 'The Great Britain of the future has not only to be saved in the schools: it has to be created there.'[43]

If schools were to be judged by how well they accomplished their particular aims, even an aim defined 'concretely' in terms of citizenship had to face a considerable degree of 'variance' in making the judgement. The variance was reflected in other aspects of educational emphasis and change in the decades preceding and following the Second World War. The Norwood Report sought to balance acknowledgement of differences between categories of pupils with the fact that all pupils 'have common needs and a common destiny; physical and spiritual and moral ideals are of vital concern to all alike, and secondary education, whatever form it may take, must regard as its chief aim the satisfaction of all the needs of the child, both as a human being and as a member of a community'.[44] Political and Economic Planning (PEP), reporting on 'the control of education' just before the war, pointed to the complexities in British education which resulted partly from the existence of geographical boundaries between local authorities for different types of education, but also from

> the survival up and down the country of schools dedicated to a particular religion or a particular social class. The ancient ideal of religious education and the later cult of the Old School Tie cut across the struggling new ideal of a national system designed to give all boys and girls, regardless of origin, the best education by which they are able to profit.

The result was waste deriving from religious or class barriers, such waste being acceptable to many people as 'a price well worth paying for independence and diversity'.[45] At every point in the educational landscape there were rival theories claiming attention, and established values – such as those of the public schools – under sympathetic or hostile scrutiny. After the war the position of the public schools, school reorganization under the terms of the 1944 Act, the raising of the school-leaving age, and especially the notion of the comprehensive school were to be similarly subjected to scrutiny and debate and often violent controversy, amongst the professionals, the politicians and the public.

Some of the emergent threads in educational research and discussion in pre-war Britain and in other countries were to become increasingly central from the 1950s. This was true, for example, of research in the 1920s and 1930s on the relationship between school 'failure' and poverty, and the 'social waste' resulting from the maldistribution of educational resources and opportunity. In this lay the beginnings of a systematic sociology of education. It was also true of the training, status and powers of teachers, and of the balance of involvement in schools of what the Spens Report described as 'the several parties whose interest in and influence upon the educational process need to be borne in mind' – the state (or the community imposing its 'form and pressure' also on schools not subject to state regulation), parents and teachers.[46] It was true of the structure and administration of education, the power of the media, the relationship between schools and further and higher education and employment, and the roles of the various kinds of assessment of pupils and the application of testing and measuring procedures to all aspects of educational systems, schools and their procedures. The *Encyclopedia of Educational Research* published in the United States in 1950 was a guide to what had been and what were going to be the priority concerns of educational systems, schools, professional educators and all concerned with judging schools – and not just in the United States. It contained, as we have seen, major articles on areas such as child development and the science of education. Its coverage extended to the organization and administration of elementary and secondary education, the range of examinations, testing and evaluation, the condition of educational psychology and other disciplines relevant to the field of education, pre-school education and progressive education, special schools and child guidance clinics, curriculum development and the literature of education, research bureaus and teacher education, and what was by now a vast range of discernible, researchable topics in the complexities of modern education. Contributors to the encyclopaedia found that curriculum development, for instance, had once been relatively simple but that recent research had undermined the simple faiths on which curricula had been built. Evaluation and testing now depended on the validity of a variety of instruments.[47] It was an encyclopaedia of mid-century complexities.

In Norwood's 'unrestricted democracy' – a concept that was to be increasingly contested in the later twentieth century – a 'good school' was open to interpretation not only from diverse constituencies and on diverse criteria, as it had been in the nineteenth century, but also from powerful political, professional and media forces shaping opinion and influencing the making or withholding of judgement. The term 'a good school' was often used in a snobbish sense of a socially desirable or expensive independent school. In relation to public education, and to church-related schools, however, the concept inevitably had elusive meanings. Those meanings had become more slippery amongst the competing values of classes and ideologies, power and aspiration, expertise and ignorance.

NOTES

1 P. B. Botsman and R. K. Browne [1977]. *Community Attitudes to Education in Queensland*. Australian College of Education, Vol. 1, pp. 72–3.

2 B. Othaniel Smith (1950). 'Science of education'. In Walter S. Monroe (ed.), *Encyclopedia of Educational Research*. New York: Macmillan, p. 114.

3 Lord Eustace Percy [1930]. *Education at the Crossroads*. London: Evans, pp. 54–5.

4 Ibid., pp. 10, 103–4.

5 W. H. Auden, 'Honours' [Gresham's School, Holt]', and E. Arnot Robinson, 'Potting shed of the English rose [Sherborne]'. In Graham Greene (ed.) (1984). *The Old School*. Oxford: Oxford University Press, pp. 1, 153–4; first published 1934.

6 A. D. Provand (1901). 'Industrial needs'. In Laurie Magnus (ed.), *National Education: Essays towards a Constructive Policy*. London: John Murray, p. 129.

7 Bertrand Russell (1934). *Freedom and Organization: 1814–1914*. London: Allen & Unwin, p. 136.

8 David Tyack *et al.* (1987). *Law and the Shaping of Public Education, 1785–1954*. Madison: University of Wisconsin Press, p. 53.

9 The phrase was the title of R. H. Tawney (1922). *Secondary Education for All: A Policy for Labour*. London: Allen & Unwin.

10 Education Act, 1944, section 8 (1).

11 See Robin Pedley *et al.* [1955]. *Comprehensive Schools To-day*. London: Councils and Education Press (including articles by comprehensive school critics); Robin Pedley (1963). *The Comprehensive School*. Harmondsworth: Penguin.

12 N. C. P. Tyack and C. D. Poster (1958). 'External examinations and internal assessment'. In National Union of Teachers (ed.), *Inside the Comprehensive School*. London: Schoolmaster Publishing Co., pp. 61, 66.

13 H. C. Dent (1958). *Secondary Modern Schools: An Interim Report*. London: Routledge & Kegan Paul, pp. 70, 75–6, 157–9, 163–6.

14 Joint Advisory Committee of the Association of Education Committees and the National Union of Teachers [1930]. *Examinations in Public Elementary Schools*. London: *Education* and *The Schoolmaster*, p. 21.

15 Board of Education (1931). *Report of the Consultative Committee on the Primary School* (Hadow Report). London: HMSO, pp. ix–x.

16 Board of Education (1924). *Report of the Consultative Committee on Psychological Tests of Educable Capacity and Their Possible Use in the Public System of Education*. London: HMSO, pp. 127–8.

17 Ibid., p. 125.

18 *The Primary School* (Hadow Report), pp. 123, 131–2.

19 See Burton J. Bledstein (1976). *The Culture of Professionalism: The Middle Class and the Development of Higher Education in America*. New York: Norton; Harold Perkin (1989). *The Rise of Professional Society in England since 1880*. London: Routledge.

20 John Dewey (1902). *The Child and the Curriculum*. Chicago: University of Chicago Press, pp. 5–6.

21 Alice V. Keliher (1950), 'Progressive education'. In Walter S. Monroe, *Encyclopedia of Educational Research*. New York: Macmillan, p. 894.

22 Cecil Reddie (1900). *Abbotsholme*. London: George Allen, pp. 21–4.

23 J. H. Badley (1923). *Bedales: A Pioneer School*. London: Methuen, pp. 1–4, 99, 127–8, 154–5.

24 Matthew Davenport Hill (1822). *Plans for the Government and Liberal Instruction of Boys, in Large Numbers; Drawn from Experience*. London: Whittaker, pp. ix, 1. See also W. A. C. Stewart and W. P. McCann (1967). *The Educational Innovators 1750–1880*. London: Macmillan, ch. 6.

25 See, for example, A. S. Neill (1960). *Summerhill: A Radical Approach to Child Rearing*. New York: Hart.

26 B. H. Montgomery and Audrey Paul Jones [n.d.]. *King Alfred*. London: The School, p. 1.

27 Helen Parkhurst (1922). *Education on the Dalton Plan*. London: Bell, pp. 15–16, 33, 37.

28 Rosa Bassett, 'A year's experience in an English secondary school'. Ibid., pp. 125–6.

29 Joseph Featherstone (1972). 'Evaluating learning in informal settings'. In Schools Council, *British Primary Schools Today 2*. Basingstoke: Macmillan, pp. 44–5.

30 Monroe, *Encyclopedia of Educational Research*, pp. 137–97.

31 Philip Boswood Ballard (1937). *Things I Cannot Forget*. London: University of London Press, pp. 198–200.

32 Joint Advisory Committee, *Examinations in Public Elementary Schools*, p. 62.

33 T. Percy Nunn (1920). *Education: Its Data and First Principles*. London: Edward Arnold pp. 1–5.

34 J. J. Findlay (1927). *The Foundations of Education: A Survey of Principles and Practice*. Vol. 2: *The Practice of Education*. London: University of London Press, pp. 152–3.

35 Tawney, *Secondary Education for All*, pp. 25–6.

36 Ibid., p. 30.

37 Board of Education (1926). *Report of the Consultative Committee on the Education of the Adolescent* (Hadow Report). London: HMSO, p. xix.

38 Sir Ernest Simon (1935). 'The case for a training for citizenship in a democratic state', and H. Ramsbotham, 'Foreword'. In Sir Ernest Simon and Eva M. Hubback (eds), *Training for Citizenship*. London: Oxford University Press, pp. 3, 7; Association for Education in Citizenship [n.d.], leaflet.

39 *The Education of the Adolescent* (Hadow Report), p. 196.

40 W. H. Hadow (1923). *Citizenship*. Oxford: Clarendon Press, ch. 9.

41 Board of Education (1938). *Report of the Consultative Committee on Secondary Education with Special Reference to Grammar Schools and Technical High Schools* (Spens Report). London: HMSO, pp. xxxvii–xxxviii.

42 Board of Education (1941). *Curriculum and Examinations in Secondary Schools* (Norwood Report). London: HMSO, pp. 57–9.

43 Cyril Norwood (1931). 'Unity and purpose in education'. In T. F. Coade (ed.), *Harrow Lectures on Education*. London: Cambridge University Press, pp. 5, 8.

44 *Curriculum and Examinations* (Norwood Report), pp. 4–5.

45 PEP (1939). *Planning*, **141** (21 February), 1–2.

46 *Secondary Education* (Spens Report), pp. 147–9.

47 Monroe, *Encyclopedia of Educational Research*, pp. 307, 403–4 and *passim*.

Chapter 6

'Effective Schools': A Research Movement

This nineteenth- and twentieth-century history of plural values, theories, practices and judgements, mainly in Britain, could be paralleled, with different features relating to class and culture, and the structures and content of schooling, public and private, and different methods of assessing students and evaluating schools, in other countries. The elements of pluralism may have varied and been combined differently, but similar blends of complexities of schools and constituencies would be evident. In the United States the account would have contained other elements, relating to non-federal control of education, the long history of racial discrimination and oppression, a different pattern of church-related and private education, and other interpretations of the goals of schooling. In the nineteenth and twentieth centuries the dominant values in American society have frequently been different from those governing policy elsewhere. Given the particular, disaggregated pattern of American education, its scale, diversity and the relatively weak role of federal departments and agencies in shaping and monitoring education, answers to some of the questions we have considered have been sought in characteristically American ways. In this century the United States has seen a proliferation of state research units and privately funded research organizations, as well as university and independent evaluation centres, and a whole range of permanent and transitory policy-directed institutes, task forces, and other units concerned with the collection of educational data, and offering expertise and advice.[1] The international development of evaluation strategies was an outcrop particularly of the educational programmes of President Johnson's 'war on poverty'. International research networks have to a large extent depended on the opportunities provided by the American Educational Research Association and the research connections developed by American universities and other organizations. Consideration of ways of judging the quality of schooling from the 1960s does not mean abandoning the specific issues and developments shaping schools and judgements of schools in Britain and other countries. It does, however, mean taking account directly of the research-based approach to 'effective schools' which was a response to aspects of the educational 'war on poverty', but which was also a response that stemmed from the by then strong American tradition of wide-ranging educational research. The effective schools research and its impact in the United States and to some extent internationally formed one of the most important and influential developments of the second half of the twentieth century with regard to ways of making judgements of schools.

The important educational staging posts towards a research-based interest in 'effective schools' were the emergence to prominence of the sociology of education in the late 1950s in Britain, and the 'discovery of poverty' in the United States in the early 1960s. The American rediscovery of the existence not only of pockets of poverty but of widespread and increasing poverty that post-war affluence had failed to eradicate, and the beginnings of resultant policies under President Kennedy, came rapidly to the forefront of the federal agenda when President Johnson succeeded him. The range of new policies implemented from 1964 under the Johnson presidency included civil rights legislation, and a large number of health, welfare and education measures. In the period 1964–7 the United States adopted in particular a body of legislation relating to education at all levels, notably the Economic Opportunity Act of 1964, which produced the Head Start pre-school programme, and Title I of the Elementary and Secondary Education Act (ESEA), aimed explicitly at combating poverty.[2] One of the actors involved later reflected that the ESEA was 'without question one of the most significant educational measures ever enacted'.[3] Other countries also fought an 'educational war on poverty', though not in such a major and sustained way. Considerable federal funds were devoted to the improvement of schooling for the children of the poor under this Act, directing resources to special programmes and strategies of support. A focus on pre-school provision, mainly through Head Start and parallel state and private programmes, was the component of the burst of educational energies that was most confidently developed as a basis for the improved education of the children of disadvantaged poor and minority families. The programme resulted from a marriage of politics and the research on early childhood development that had been developing particularly rapidly since the beginning of the decade, and had begun to suggest the possibility of accelerating disadvantaged children's learning at this stage as a basis for improved later school performance. The 'war on poverty' programmes were not without controversy. In some cases they were seen not as a contribution to but as a diversion from the political needs of the American poor, especially the black Americans who had found their voice in the civil rights movement. Head Start, however, was one of the most popular products of the Economic Opportunity Act, and education was for a period at the heart of policy-making for social change.

In different circumstances, the sociology of education in Britain also pointed towards barriers to social justice and the means of surmounting them. In the British situation of national policy-making for the education system, and in the light of developments following the 1944 Education Act, the research demonstrated that 'secondary education for all' had not solved the basic injustices of the educational system. The continued existence of selection for the grammar school was seen to uphold the same class-based divisions as those of the late nineteenth century. A key text was Floud, Halsey and Martin's *Social Class and Educational Opportunity* in 1956, which clearly demarcated the sociological territory that had begun to take shape in the pre-war accounts of the relationship between social class and access to education. *Social Class and Educational Opportunity* was followed by a considerable literature which analysed the nature of existing secondary school provision, the factors militating against working-class children gaining access to and succeeding in grammar school education, and pointed to the solution that was gaining political and educational ground – the comprehensive secondary school. Floud and Halsey commented in 1957 that the 'social waste' involved in able children failing to find grammar school places was 'difficult to avoid so long as grammar school provision takes the relatively inflexible form of places in separately organized and housed schools, entrants to which are selected by competitive examination'.[4] Another well-known study, Jackson and Marsden's *Education and the Working Class* in 1962, concluded that any real equality was impossible in the present educational system and that 'the first practical step is to abandon selection at 11, and accept the comprehensive principle'.[5] The central thrust of the comprehensive school movement that relied not only but substantially on the evidence produced by the sociologists, was – unlike the American developments – targeted on a change in the *system*, with a more equitable secondary education as the main target.

In their different ways the British and American research emphases by the mid-1960s were on the importance of taking social background into account in determining educational policy, together with an expression of confidence in the role of the schools if adapted to meet the particular needs of poor, minority or working-class children. The implied reforms were directed at structural change (as in the case of the British comprehensive school), pre-school provision (as with the American Head Start programme), identifying and helping 'at risk' children (as with a project mounted from 1967 at University College Swansea), the development of 'educational priority areas' (recommended by the Plowden Committee on primary schools in 1967 and implemented the following year), and other changes in curriculum and teaching strategies, and associated health and environmental policies. The policies were different according to the particular educational system, and to the conceptual basis in social class or poverty. The former tended to underline structural changes and the latter area action programmes and some form of compensatory education.

The internationally important development from the point of within-school strategies was the cluster of American programmes aimed at the pre-school and the early grades of elementary school. Initial internal evaluations of Head Start were positive, mainly reflecting the enthusiasm of participants. As external evaluations began to be conducted, the outcomes appeared less clear-cut. The first publicized evaluation of Head Start in 1967 suggested that immediate gains were registered by the Head Start children, but that several months later, in kindergarten, the gains had 'washed out' and there was no significant difference in the scores of Head Start and non-Head Start children.[6] Of crucial importance to subsequent developments, including the developing importance of evaluation studies, was the Coleman Report of 1966, *Equality of Educational Opportunity*.[7] The report arose from a congressionally mandated study of the educational opportunities available to different racial and ethnic groups. The data collected from over 4,000 schools and the administration of standardized tests of ability and achievement to 645,000 pupils were used to relate school resources to pupil achievement. The conclusions were dramatic, and one account summarized their message in these terms:

> A study which had set out to document for Congress inequalities in
> school resources and facilities, so that remedial legislation could be
> drafted, ended up by concluding not only that resources and facility
> differences between black and white schools within geographic
> regions were not large, but further that resources and facilities didn't

appear to make much difference to student achievement once home background factors were taken into account.[8]

The essential Coleman message was that school differences accounted for only a small percentage of differences in pupils' attainment, but this was generally interpreted in the press and elsewhere to mean that school made no difference, that teaching was unimportant. Children seemed locked into patterns of attainment determined massively by their families and environment. Coleman in the United States was offering a stronger message than had derived from a decade of British sociological work on education and social class, and than the Plowden Committee in Britain were to suggest in 1967 on the basis of research findings regarding the influence of parents' attitudes on primary school children's performance. The Coleman Report became central to consideration of the relevance of school resources, school effects, the value of strategies for changing the educational system or individual schools or for affecting the value systems of educators or society. The report was the subject of widespread international comment, including critiques of the report's data and methodology, weaknesses in the assumptions and parameters of the research, and the difficulty of making deductions from research conducted before the compensatory policies being studied had been seriously implemented. In this and in other connections the debate was frequently to focus on whether the strategy studied had been really tried, whether to give up or do better. Interpreting and knowing where to go from Coleman became a challenge to education and social science in the United States and internationally. What the report clearly did was refocus attention, in any discussion of educational opportunity and the role of the schools, on results. Whatever its other implications, it was what has been described as 'the beginning of the intellectual disillusion with education'.[9] Unlike the work of the British sociologists, the report seemed to suggest not that schools should change, but that there was little they could do.

A second study, published in 1972, pointed in the same direction. Christopher Jencks and colleagues, reworking the data in their book *Inequality*, came to a similarly disturbing set of conclusions. They deduced that the equalization of school resources would not make students 'appreciably more equal after they finish school'; the most important determinant of educational attainment was family background, the main purpose of schools was to get children to behave as administrators wanted, and the egalitarian trend in education had not materially affected the distribution of incomes over the previous 25 years.[10] Again, critics attacked the report as excessively narrow in its use of quantitative data and standardized test scores as a basis of judgement, or saw in the approach a naive and historically unacceptable view of political and social approaches to equalization. By focusing exclusively on equalizing economic status Jencks was held to have dealt with only one, and not necessarily the most important, outcome of education in changing people and their lives.[11] Like the Coleman Report, however, what the Jencks study did was focus attention sharply on the relationship between school and outcomes. It also reflected and strengthened the growth of the evaluation movement in education. By the time the educational anti-poverty policies in the United States were becoming international currency they were being accompanied by strong negative messages not only about those policies but about education in general.

The effective schools movement which emerged in the 1970s arose largely out of attempts to review and to counter the negative messages about education associated with the early evaluations of the 1960s programmes, particularly the Coleman Report, together with responses to public criticism of the schools. In the United States the origins of the movement were roughly the same as the origins of the 'war on poverty' programmes – a search for school improvements that would provide an effective education for all children, and specifically for 'educationally deprived' or disadvantaged children from poor or minority backgrounds. The motives were similar, the approaches radically different.

The underlying question addressed by those interested in the idea of 'effective schools' found increasing expression in the 1970s, and had to do with differences between schools. Coleman had denied any predominant role for schools in determining educational attainment, yet puzzling questions remained. Did the attainment levels of *similar* schools not sometimes differ? How could these be accounted for? How useful were past attempts to trace the differential impacts of teachers and school organization? On a number of possible measures could outcomes not be identified and explained by factors other than the students' home backgrounds? Although large-scale surveys of the Coleman type did not reveal such differences, research in the United States and in Britain began to suggest greater variation amongst schools than was identifiable on the larger scale. From these early analyses grew an American, British and international research effort to identify and account for relationships between school characteristics on the one hand and levels of student attainment on the other. What, in other words, were the differences between an effective and an ineffective school, and what accounted for them? Schools had, of course, been studied, analysed and evaluated in many ways before the 1970s, regarding, for example, the respective merits of large and small schools.[12] The 'planned variation' studies incorporated in the Head Start and Follow Through programmes, for example, had been designed to identify approaches which characterized programmes that were successful in achieving specific aims. The effective schools research, however, was the first time that schools had been researched with the precise purpose of identifying the major characteristics that could explain their differential effects, within and especially between schools. The first of the American projects to go in this direction, by George Weber in the school year 1970–1, explicitly rejected an approach that focused on the effective teacher and the single class, or one that focused on the system, choosing the school as the unit of study.[13] Coleman and later Jencks highlighted the importance of considering the outcomes of schooling, and although the effective schools research took that message, it did not adopt their methodology or arrive at the same conclusions.

Weber's study, *Inner-City Children Can Be Taught to Read*, published in 1971, was to be influential in defining the direction of research. Weber knew that low reading attainment in the early grades of inner-city schools was a reality, and that most school people expected no more. Yet he had himself seen one inner-city school, and had read of others, where 'reading achievement was *not* relatively low', and where it was about or above the national average. His enquiries focused on non-selective public schools in the centres of large cities and attended by very poor children. He located four schools that could be considered successful, two in New York, one in Kansas City and one in Los Angeles, and examined them in some detail. He found his hypothesis, that such schools *could* be successful in teaching reading to such children, to be proven:

> At least four inner-city public schools exist in the United States where reading achievement in the early grades is far higher than in most inner-city schools . . . during the second half of the school year 1970–71 all four schools had reading achievement medians in third grade which equalled or exceeded the national norm and a percentage of non-readers unusually low for such schools.

Having demonstrated this to be the case, Weber asked: 'How do they do it? What are the secrets of success?' He knew the answers were difficult, because schools were complex institutions, and did things differently. But *something* in their practice differentiated them from unsuccessful schools: 'it seems reasonable to assume . . . that practice has something to do with their success'. He located what he took to be eight factors 'usually not present in successful inner-city schools', and these were: 'strong leadership, high expectations, good atmosphere, strong emphasis on reading, additional reading personnel, use of phonics, individualization, and careful evaluation of pupil progress'.[14]

Throughout the 1970s studies were published developing a similar kind of focus, and others circulated as reports. Some were state-sponsored or Washington-funded or foundation-supported projects, focusing on a small number of schools – what were frequently described as 'exemplary schools', 'unusually effective schools', or simply 'effective schools'.[15] A number of states also conducted studies of various kinds of their own 'exceptional schools', or especially what the researchers called 'outlier schools'. Four such studies completed before 1979, in New York, Pennsylvania, Delaware and Maryland, echoed and extended Weber's findings, summarized in factors characteristic of the group of schools as a whole, but not necessarily present in each school in the studies. The factors included: strong principal leadership and principal participation in the classroom; higher expectations on the part of the principal of student and teacher performance; greater and 'more pertinent' experience on the part of the principal and teachers; teachers rated as warmer, more responsive, placing more emphasis on cognitive development, with opportunities to experiment, and having higher expectations of students to graduate and go on to college; and more satisfactory parent–teacher relationships.[16] These kinds of factor were prominent in the early effective schools research literature of the 1970s and were to remain so in the research. Some other factors, including longer school day, and assessment by tests developed by the teachers themselves, were to be less prominent. The research in the early and mid-1970s tended to be centred, as in these studies, on the 'outlier' schools, highlighting variations between the highest- and lowest-achieving schools. The small scale of the research and this emphasis on 'outliers' limited its impact and credibility, but a momentum of interest was being established within the research community from the early 1970s and it was beginning to have echoes in the policy machinery of some states.

Educational and political attention was captured in 1972 by the Jencks study, *Inequality*, further strengthening the view that educational achievement had more to do with social class, family background and luck than with schooling, and that the life chances of the disadvantaged could be improved only by political and economic, not educational, change. Popular confidence in the hoped-for impacts of Head Start, Title I and other targeted anti-poverty educational strategies had at the same time been undermined by the early evaluations. The education research community, with the exception of the rapid growth of the new professional interest in evaluation, had lost some of the sense of purpose and direction generated in the mid-1960s. In these conditions and, as the 1970s wore on, with intensified criticism of public schools, an American research focus on the internal working of the schools increasingly seemed necessary. Weber saw his research as countering the dominant view, represented by the Coleman Report, that the performance of children in schools could be almost entirely explained in terms of the effects of socioeconomic status and its relationship to the outcomes of schooling. What happened between the input and the output was what was beginning to engage research interest.

This interest took a limited number of forms and derived energy from a limited number of directions. The 'outlier' studies, for example, derived from 'commonsense' perceptions of school differences and pointed towards techniques for identifying schools at the end of a spectrum of effectiveness. Sarason's 1971 study *The Culture of the School and the Problem of Change* provided impetus for some educationists to consider the internal life of schools and its influence on students' experience and attainments.[17] While some researchers were beginning to search for the exceptional or 'overachieving' school,[18] and the factors explaining its success, others were focusing on specific aspects of the process. Good, Biddle and Brophy, following earlier work in the 1970s by all three authors on aspects of classrooms and teacher effectiveness, in 1975 published a study entitled *Teachers Make a Difference*, which, unlike the Weber analysis, made teachers the focus of a discussion of effectiveness. In particular, they pointed to the fact that the Coleman research had indeed found relationships between school quality and pupil achievement, but that these had disappeared in the research design:

> when controls were imposed for community and pupil characteristics,
> a finding which the authors interpreted as indicating that pupil
> achievement was controlled by pupil characteristics rather than by
> the school. But the same findings might also be taken to indicate that
> school quality does affect pupil achievement, but that school quality is
> so tied up with community and pupil characteristics that an
> independent measure of it cannot be obtained.

They accepted Featherstone's view that the Coleman research had not shown that schools make no difference, but that by certain 'crude measures' it had shown them to be similar. Given that schools and teachers had a variety of goals it was important to focus on specific ones, and by doing so teachers could be shown to 'vary in their influence on students'.[19]

The early 1970s research surfaced in publications around the middle of the decade containing other elements which might explain differences in school and student performance, and alternative methodologies for doing so were being explored. Published in 1975, for example, was a report on a study of 104 school districts in Colorado, addressing the relationship between school district organization and student achievement. Bidwell and Kasarda began this account in the *American Sociological Review* (acknowledging advice from Coleman and Jencks) with the question, 'What makes an organization effective?' Building on 1960s research on organizations, which had not been specifically school-related, they turned attention to the need for empirical research in school settings that would explore the links between inputs and outputs, bringing organizational analysis into the educational sphere and, in their case, investigating whether and how attributes of school district organization affect the transformation of environmental inputs into 'students' aggregate levels of academic achievement'. They criticized the Coleman *Equality of Educational Opportunity* findings for failing to allow for differences in school and school district structures, curricula, and the influences of forms of organization, teaching activities, and control, on student achievement. They suggested that the school might not be 'the most appropriate unit' for estimating effects on student achievement, and thought that the classroom and the school district might be more revealing. Just as Sarason and others were turning attention to the internal life and culture of the school, Bidwell and Kasarda were considering how school organization and its wider setting might intervene between the social, resource and other inputs to schooling, and its outcomes. From their analysis of school district size, organization, staffing, professional staff support, fiscal resources and other elements they concluded tentatively that variations at the school district level bore a significant relationship to achievement.[20] What the authors were essentially emphasizing, however, was not possibly conclusive findings, but sources of explanation contained in types of variation that had been ignored in the earlier research.

Following the path of some of the 'war on poverty' attempts to evaluate which programmes worked better than others, researchers were now also searching not only for 'successful' schools but also for acceptable ways of identifying them. Dyer in 1972 suggested a model that was to be used or developed for the next couple of decades, comparing predicted with actual performance by the schools' students. The prediction was based on the input conditions at the moment of calculation (characteristics of the students, homes and community) and the variable – the students' level of performance at that point. From these a prediction was made of the students' likely performance (the 'output') at a later point in time. The difference between the two was an indicator of the school's relative effectiveness.[21] On the basis of such estimates it was possible to select the schools (especially the 'outlier' schools) whose characteristics would be worth investigation. The general trend of these various approaches to research was to move away from the large scale, the average, to the smaller sample, the unit, the case study, detailed study of organization and activity, observation and other evidence of the interactive working of schools, their sub-units, and specific contexts. Researchers, in one description, had moved from the study of 'relatively static characteristics' to the examination of 'more complex and dynamic *processes* in schools and classrooms'.

As a result,

> researchers have come to rely increasingly on first-hand observation
> and concrete descriptions of educational practices. They are more
> likely to conduct indepth interviews with teachers, principals, and
> students, rather then rely exclusively on survey questionnaires
> typically administered in large groups or through the mails.[22]

A research 'movement' was now taking shape, in the limited sense of the
adoption by a community of researchers – albeit a relatively small one and
alongside researchers heading in other directions – of a changed set of objectives.
Ascertaining and accounting for school differences in the United States inevitably
meant local studies, often published in journals not necessarily central to the
concerns of the educational research or policy communities, and with ripple effects
not easy to judge. This was true of the Bidwell and Kasarda study, and it is true, for
example, of a study by Summers and Wolfe entitled 'Do schools make a difference?',
published in the *American Economic Review* in 1977. Their findings, based on a
'microeconomic examination' of Philadelphia School District data, suggested four
conclusions:

> 1) that when there are extensive pupil-specific data available, more
> impact from school inputs is revealed; 2) that when the effects of
> school inputs are examined differentially, more impact and insight
> emerge; 3) that most of the effects of family income and race can be
> tagged to specific school inputs; and 4) that the low achiever, the low-
> income student, and the black student do respond in terms of
> achievement growth to some school inputs.

They emphasized what they called the most interesting finding, one with serious
policy implications – that 'there appear to be school inputs which help the
disadvantaged do better', and these findings emerged only when 'pupil-specific data
were used and examined in relation to student characteristics'.[23] From this point
and into the 1980s this theme was to be elaborated in a number of influential studies,
inaugurating a new phase of debate and policy-making based on the growing
conviction that schools can and do make a difference, and that 'pupil-specific' and
'school-specific' data could offer the necessary explanations of how they do so. The
research was concerned with interpreting school-related data, school organization,
administration and culture, and the many elements of school structures and processes that could account for the differences. It was either directly or by implication returning responsibility for educational attainment to the school. The new
generation of research was described in 1986 by one active participant as rejecting

> conclusions about the seemingly unalterable nature of the influence of
> family background on student achievement stemming from the
> *Equality of Educational Opportunity* study. . . . The study's major
> and longest lasting finding was that family background was the most
> important variable affecting children's learning and that schools had
> little effect. . . . A substantial and ever-growing research base for how
> schools can improve, how administrators can become effective

leaders and how teachers can help all children become effective learners has emerged over the past decade.[24]

A sustained attempt was being made to inter the central message of the Coleman and Jencks research.

By the mid-1970s some of the research was comparing pairs of schools, matched as high-achieving and low-achieving. A study published by the state of New York in 1974, for example, compared two inner-city schools, and identified administrative and curriculum planning factors among those accounting for differences in reading achievement. Two years later a more extended study was published of 21 pairs of California elementary schools matched on the basis of student characteristics and performance. Important factors affecting achievement appeared to include strong support by principals, a more supportive atmosphere, the presence of adult volunteers to help with mathematics, a higher level of support by the district administration, and more effective classroom organization and practices.[25] The focus then moved to Michigan, where the Department of Education had established an annual test for all grade 4 and grade 7 students in public schools, and the data were used as a basis for identifying schools with consistently higher and lower levels of achievement. A number of researchers became engaged in studying the characteristics of these schools, and in various combinations over the second half of the decade published reports, for example, of 'school climate', 'school social systems' and 'changes in school characteristics coincident with changes in student achievement'. Accounts, soon to be well known, came out of these studies in Detroit and elsewhere, including a 'Search for Effective Schools' project.[26] Brookover and Lezotte categorized pairs of 'improving schools' and 'declining schools', emphasizing among other things the importance of basic objectives in reading and mathematics, high expectations on the part of teachers and principals, leadership by the latter, and less complacency.[27] A substantial study by Brookover and a group of researchers in 1979, *School Social Systems and Student Achievement* had the subtitle *Schools Can Make a Difference*. This study of a random sample of Michigan elementary schools, including an observational study of four of them, concluded that 'school social systems' could offer 'a potent source of explanation for school level differences in achievement'. It aimed explicitly to go beyond the Coleman and other emphases on socioeconomic and racial composition as explanations of school variance, considering them to be important but not sufficient explanations. 'What else about schools', they asked, 'may explain the difference in outcomes?' The researchers looked for specific features of the schools' social structure, rather than assuming that social composition was the only applicable measure. Alongside the latter, the study considered such characteristics as school size, attendance rates, the personnel:student ratio, teachers' qualifications and training, and others. The social interactions that took place within this school system had not been considered in the Jencks study, and reliance on pupils' social background as the only input variable had led some researchers to conclude 'that nothing about the school social system can affect the learning which occurs in the social unit. This study rejects that conclusion.' It looked, in addition to the structure, at the school's operational aspects, and at perceptions of these by students and teachers. Two conclusions indicated the strength of the conviction that was emerging from such research. First, the combination of 'social system variables' (social composition and personnel inputs, social structure of the school, and its social climate) accounted for 'more than 85 per cent of the between-school variance in mean reading and math achievement'. Secondly, the fact that some schools with predominantly lower socioeconomic white or black students

> do demonstrate a high level of academic achievement suggests that
> the socioeconomic and racial variables are not directly causal forces
> in the school social system. We, therefore, conclude that the school
> social climate and the instruction behaviors associated with it are
> more direct causal links in the production of achievement behavior in
> reading and mathematics.[28]

Two important elements in such research and its conclusions were to stand out – the bypassing of social background and race as direct explanations of student performance, and the search for combinations of factors that would explain the levels of school performance. The Michigan research projected these elements most securely into the policy domain, and one of those directly involved in Michigan and New York was Ronald Edmonds, who was to do most to turn pieces of effective schools research into a movement.

In the mid- and late 1970s Edmonds wrote, alone and with others, a number of papers relating to effective schools or school effectiveness. A report by Edmonds and John R. Frederiksen in 1979 looked at the identification and analysis of city schools that were 'instructionally effective' for poor children. Desegregation by busing was not proving an adequate remedy to segregation, partly because of the schools' 'seeming inability to effectively educate desegregated children who are poor'. There was also, however, a body of recent social science literature, including some by Coleman and Jencks, which could be said 'to virtually repudiate urban school reform as an instrument of social equity'. Edmonds and Frederiksen postulated that there were schools that were effective for poor and/or minority children. A 1973 study of a group of 20 Detroit inner-city elementary schools had shown eight to be above the city average in mathematics, nine in reading and five in both. Comparisons between schools matched for economic status, racial and other characteristics produced performance differences 'independent of family background'. The authors criticized the methodology of the Coleman research in particular, on the basis of a rerun of the Coleman research data, which they considered not to substantiate its main conclusions. Central to their own findings was the rejection of what they considered the prevalent myth:

> A very great proportion of the American people believe that family
> background and home environment are principal causes of the quality
> of pupil performance. In fact, no notion about schooling is more
> widely held than the belief that the family is somehow principal
> determinant of whether or not a child will do well in school. . . . Such
> a belief has the effect of absolving educators of their professional
> responsibility to be instructionally effective for all pupils.

The social scientists, they contended, were partly to blame. The authors acknowledged the importance of family background, but could 'not overemphasize our rejection of the notion that a school is relieved of its instructional obligations when teaching the children of the poor. We reject such a notion partly because we recognize the existence of schools that successfully teach basic school skills to all children.' Such schools served their pupils by modifying curricular design, text selection and teaching strategy to respond to pupil differences.[29] The same basic premise emerged from the work of Brookover, Lezotte, Frederiksen, Edmonds and others in detailed work on Michigan schools in particular. It was central to this early work that it saw itself as having picked up, from a very different starting point from that of the 1960s, the challenge of directing education towards a solution of problems associated with poverty and race. A good school for these researchers was one which adopted the strategies, made the adaptations and accepted the responsibilities of proving 'instructionally effective' for all children.

It was Edmonds's formulations of what he saw as 'the most tangible and indispensable characteristics of effective schools' in 1979 that were to have the most far-reaching influence with both researchers and policy-makers. His was to be one of the unusual instances of a research-based activity that was to reach directly into the vocabularies and decision-making of American states, and then into congressional policy-making. In his paper 'Effective schools for the urban poor' Edmonds traced the origins of the movement in Weber and elsewhere, and outlined the reanalysis of the Coleman data that had emerged from the 'Search for Effective Schools' project, and presented, among other places, in his joint report with Frederiksen. He repeated the conclusion that differences in performance between effective and ineffective schools could not be attributed to differences in the social class and family background of pupils. He also repeated the charge that many social scientists and opinion-makers had perpetuated beliefs which absolved educators of their responsibilities. He began his argument from the starting-point of equity: 'I measure our progress as a social order by our willingness to advance the equity interests of the least among us'. The argument then proceeded through a formulation that was to become widely adopted:

> I require that an effective school bring the children of the poor to
> those minimal masteries of basic school skills that now describe
> minimally successful pupil performance for the children of the middle
> class.

He clearly drew energy from the concerns of the war on poverty, and his emphasis on equity for the children of the poor derived explicitly from political considerations. The educational solutions, however, lay not in targeting the children of the poor as a separate constituency, but in applying to public schools the conclusions from the new wave of research. It was for the *schools* to set and reach standards for all children, and thus to remedy their failure adequately to teach the children of the poor. Edmonds built his argument out of equity concerns, minimum competency emphases and school accountability. From this amalgam stemmed his formulation of what distinguishes effective schools, a formulation in six points that were to be telescoped, expanded, revised and amended by other analysts and researchers in various ways, but maintaining the same central elements. His formulation represented the clearest and most firmly based expression to date of the effective schools research and movement, and was to be picked up at various policy-making levels. He summarized the essential characteristics of 'effective' or 'good' schools:

> (a) They have strong administrative leadership without which the disparate elements of good schooling can neither be brought together nor kept together; (b) Schools that are instructionally effective for poor children have a climate of expectation in which no children are permitted to fall below minimum but efficacious levels of achievement; (c) The school's atmosphere is orderly without being rigid, quiet without being oppressive, and generally conducive to the instructional business at hand; (d) Effective schools get that way partly by making it clear that pupil acquisition of basic school skills takes precedence over all other school activities; (e) When necessary, school energy and resources can be diverted from other business in furtherance of the fundamental objectives; and (f) There must be some means by which pupil progress can be frequently monitored . . . some means must exist in the school by which the principal and the teachers remain constantly aware of pupil progress in relationship to instructional objectives.[30]

There was in this an underlying assumption, not necessarily as explicit, that was to remain in further consideration of the nature of effective schools. It was in the identifiable characteristics of the effective school and the schools' accountability for implementing them, that the satisfactory education of the children of the poor, as of all children, was to be found.

We shall return to the way in which the American research, analysis and argument penetrated the policy arena and the work of schools, but it is important at this point to underline the development of a parallel, and partially related, British version of this research. With regard to educational strategies against poverty the British versions of the 1960s American educational concern with and programmes relating to poverty had followed their American counterparts. This was not the case with effective schools concerns. The beginnings of the British research lie, as in the American case, in the mid-1960s. The Coleman findings of 1966 were confusedly pondered over in Britain just as the first intimations of the 'war on poverty' programmes themselves were being heard. British research on the comprehensive secondary school in the late 1950s and 1960s had included a strong component of concern about whether such schools could minimize social class differences.[31] Within-school factors other than 'streaming' received little or no attention by comparison with the wider political and educational concern with equity in the education system and generally. The Coleman findings were puzzling to British educationists, but they seemed marginal to these dominant British issues. The 1967 Plowden Report, *Children and Their Primary Schools*, while very different from the Coleman research in most respects, in one critical way conveyed the same message. Apart from its focus on progressive teaching methods, the curriculum, relationships with parents, and other aspects of primary schooling and transition to secondary education, the report addressed the issue of home and school influence on pupil attainment, suggesting that social class accounted for attainment less than might previously have been thought, but heavily emphasized the importance of parental attitude. The emphasis on the significance of parental attitude in determining children's school performance, its focus on 'educational priority areas' as a solution to educational and social disadvantage, and its picture of environmental handicaps reinforced the picture of 'education in the slums' in the 1963 Newsom Report on *Half Our Future*. The Plowden Report conveyed more ambiguous messages about the roles of schools than did the Coleman Report in the United States. Whatever else, the Plowden Report directed attention away from social class and the educational system towards poverty, disadvantage and primary schools. It emphasized the importance of good primary schools in general, and combined socioeconomic explanations of the poverty of schooling where it occurred with a commitment to a broadly progressive approach to teaching and the classroom, and to the health and development of the child. The Plowden research had mainly to do with environmental and family relationships to educational performance, but the report was additionally concerned with pedagogy, curriculum and organization. The underlying messages were of the need for improved, progressive teaching methods in general, and the need for economic assistance in areas of social deprivation.[32] Chapters on 'How primary schools are organised', 'The staffing of schools', or 'The deployment of staff' were concerned with team teaching, size and composition of classes, and the details of staffing numbers or recruitment – not with between-school differences. Differences in education generally were seen in terms of social disparities, not the organization or culture of schools. Although there was in British teacher education, particularly at in-service levels, a growing interest in aspects of school administration, this was largely a concern with the organization and control of the education system and its schools, and the roles of the participants. An article in *New Society* in late 1967 began to suggest, stumblingly but crucially, a different direction of attention and research.

Michael Power's article on 'Delinquent schools' indicated significant differences in the delinquency rates he discovered in secondary schools in the same area – the London district of Tower Hamlets. The study was unable to explain the differences by reference to pupils' social background, and the question Power raised was whether a school's better or worse delinquency record resulted from factors in the schools themselves.[33] The Inner London Education Authority and the teachers' unions concerned refused Power permission to continue the research within the schools in order to pursue the answer to that sensitive question. Answers came from other directions in the middle of the 1970s at almost exactly the same time as the work on school differences in the United States. British 'school differences research' met with something of a hostile reception in the British research community.[34] David Reynolds and colleagues published an article in *New Society* in 1976 with the title 'Schools do make a difference', presented as a preliminary account of a study 'attempting to find out whether the individual school does make a difference to the sort of adolescents that its pupils become; and if it does, what it is about the schools that makes the difference'. The study was conducted in a relatively homogeneous working-class area so that differences by late adolescence were likely to reflect differences in schools and less likely to reflect differences amongst pupils at the point of entry to them. The data related to nine secondary schools between 1966–7 and 1972–3, and differences were assessed on three measures – school attendance, academic success defined as going on to post-secondary education at the local technical college, and delinquency. The core of the data showed that:

> On attendance, the school with the top rate was getting 89.1 per cent attendance, and the bottom school 77.2 per cent, over these years. One school sent over half its pupils into the local tech (which is regarded locally as the key to obtaining an apprenticeship or craft), and another got only 8.4 per cent into the tech per year. The school with the highest delinquency rate had 10.5 per cent of its boys recorded as officially delinquent each school year. The bottom-rate school averaged only 3.8 per cent delinquent per year.

The results were consistent, over the years and with each other. Schools with a high delinquency rate had low academic attainment and low attendance rates. The differences could not be explained by social class composition or some schools acquiring more 'problem-prone' intakes. The research was attempting to determine what, in the schools' 'independent effect', influenced pupils' academic and social development so dramatically.[35]

In the same year as this article Neville Bennett and colleagues published what was probably the most talked-about educational book of the decade in Britain, *Teaching Styles and Pupil Progress*. Although describing a very different kind of research, and looking for very different explanations of school experience, the book did focus attention on classroom differences, and particularly on the 'effectiveness' of different teaching approaches. This was not 'effective schools' research, but in categorizing teaching styles and their impact it further directed attention away from broad social class explanations of pupil progress towards the realities of classroom interaction. The central message of the book as heard by the public (mediated through considerable media attention) was that 'progressive' methods didn't work, and in fact the book's general conclusion was that progressive 'open' teaching methods were unsuccessful when practised by teachers insufficiently prepared or ill-suited to use them. The findings, which Bennett knew would be 'disturbing to many teachers and parents', were statistically and educationally significant in all the attainment areas tested in the research. The researchers found that in reading, the pupils of what their typology called 'formal' and 'mixed' teachers progressed more than those of 'informal' teachers, there being some three to five months' difference in performance. In mathematics 'formally' taught pupils were superior to the other two kinds, the difference being four to five months. In English the 'formally' taught out-performed both of the others, the difference being between three and five months. The findings would be 'disturbing' because they indicated that 'the teaching approaches advocated by the Plowden Report, and many of the educational advisory staff and college lecturers, often result in poorer academic progress, particularly among high ability children'.[36] A project conducted at the University of Leicester contested Bennett's findings. It concluded that the individualized work and attention recommended by Plowden raised serious classroom management problems for teachers when classes averaged 30 in size. Big changes had, of course, taken place, and many schools had adopted flexible forms of classroom organization. While the Leicester researchers found that 'in general, good order and effective classroom management prevail in this new situation, one thing that does seem clear is that "progressive" teaching, if by this is meant teaching having the characteristics defined by the Plowden Report, hardly exists in practice'. A reanalysis of the *Teaching Styles and Pupil Progress* data several years later found weaknesses in the methods used, including the way different teacher characteristics were clustered into the small number used.[37]

The prevailing interests in the British research community had changed markedly by the second half of the 1970s. Economic stringency, inflation and poor industrial performance contributed massively to the emergence of accountability and standards as central themes of policy discourse, and to an accelerating search for a 'common' or 'core' curriculum. By 1979, the end of the period of Labour government in which this was happening, a research emphasis on the 'assessment of performance' and testing was strong, including controversy over the nature and role of evaluation, narrow versions of all of which were described by Barry MacDonald in 1978 as gaining in strength, and serving as 'tunnels to dystopia'.[38] These preoccupations were to be important in the new policy climate created by the Conservative government in the 1980s.

The British research literature on school differences surfaced most clearly in two publications in 1978-9. The first, which had surprisingly little impact, was entitled *Sources of Difference in School Achievement*, a National Foundation for Educational Research (NFER) study by Alan Brimer and colleagues. Tracing the interest of government agencies in 'effectiveness' and reform to the Plowden and Coleman studies – and to the latter's predecessors and successors – the book highlighted the methodological problems of measuring effectiveness and the failure of large-scale surveys to indicate whether children benefit from school, the relative importance of home and school, and the differential impact of schools. The NFER research had used public examination results to analyse the relationship between the characteristics of pupils and schools on the one hand, and pupil achievement on the other. It indicated larger school differences than could be derived from the Coleman study: 'between school variance is a larger proportion of total variance than the findings [of the Coleman research] would have led us to expect'. The specifically *school* contribution to explaining variance was greater than Coleman suggested.[39] Brimer's study, together with a number of other studies pointing in the same direction,[40] indicated how closely some British research resembled the American research interest and acknowledged their common academic ancestry. The work of Michael Rutter and colleagues, published in 1979, was to make the transatlantic nature of the research movement even clearer, given the immediate widespread interest it provoked in the American education research community.

The Rutter team's study, *Fifteen Thousand Hours: Secondary Schools and Their Effects on Children*, investigated 12 London secondary schools, and again rejected research findings such as those of Coleman and Jencks, since they had ignored the internal life of schools. This research also went beyond those studies which had attempted to describe such features as amount of teaching, size, organization of groups, teacher expectations, class management and school climate. Like the American work of the same period it was concerned with the relationships between school features and outcomes. It used four measures of outcome – attendance, behaviour, examination successes and delinquency. It analysed organizational and process variables, including status, sex composition, size and space, age of buildings and number of sites, staffing and class size, and aspects of the internal organization of the school, and investigated the association between school features on the one hand and school processes on the other. The main conclusions of the study derived from the marked differences observed in the behaviour and attainments of pupils in the schools studied. Differences in the proportion of 'behaviourally difficult or low achieving children they admitted' did not wholly account for later behaviour and attainment differences. As Reynolds had found, outcome variations were consistent with each other and over time. Size of school, age of buildings and other physical factors did not explain the outcome differences, which were, however, 'systematically related to their characteristics as social institutions':

> Factors as varied as the degree of academic emphasis, teacher actions
> in lessons, the availability of incentives and rewards, good conditions
> for pupils, and the extent to which children were able to take
> responsibility were all significantly associated with outcome
> differences between schools. All of these factors were open to
> modification by the staff, rather than fixed by external constraints.

The research concluded, with some caution, that there was a 'strong probability that the associations between school process and outcome reflect in part a *causal* process'. Perhaps more emphatically than Brookover and colleagues in the United States, however, examining the same phenomena in the same year, the research pointed to the cumulative impact of particular school characteristics:

> the association between the *combined* measure of overall school
> process and each of the measures of outcome was much stronger
> than any of the associations with individual process variables. This
> suggests that the *cumulative* effect of these various social factors was
> considerably greater than the effect of any of the individual factors on
> their own. The implication is that the individual actions or measures
> may combine to create a particular *ethos*, or set of values, attitudes
> and behaviours which will become characteristic of the school as a
> whole . . . to an appreciable extent children's behaviour and attitudes
> are shaped and influenced by their experiences at school and, in
> particular, by the qualities of the school as a social institution.[41]

Fifteen Thousand Hours was the subject of widespread critical comment regarding its methodology and what some commentators saw as a narrowing of focus, the omission of significant factors affecting school and pupil performance. Burgess, for example, accused it of 'diverting attention from questions which we should be asking about inner-city schools . . . the focus of *Fifteen Thousand Hours* is almost exclusively managerial'. He considered the study to have mistakenly taken public examinations as 'the single, measured outcome of academic achievement'. It ignored curriculum and pedagogy, and had no 'sense of history, both a broad and more local framework within which the achievement of these schools can be placed and evaluated', and it had no sense of the 'actual texture' of the schools.[42] Rutter and his colleagues, however, continued to emphasize the probable effects of the phenomena they studied, agreeing that other aspects of schooling were important parallel strands in understanding pupils' attainment.[43]

While a momentum of British effective schools research was maintained into the 1980s, the policy environment of British education was such that the dominant issues for debate and investigation severely limited the scope and impact of such research. The questions had been set out by Power, Reynolds, Brimer, Rutter and other research – as well as British interest in the main American research reports – relating to school intakes, characteristics, 'ethos' and their relationship to outcomes, but new policy pressures pointed much research towards such targets as the evaluation of curriculum changes, and eventually the National Curriculum and other features of the 1988 Education Reform Act and other initiatives of Conservative educational policy. The British and American effective schools studies to a large extent represented a single 'research movement', with the main literature in each country becoming well known in research circles internationally. From the end of the 1970s, however, the dynamic of such research, and particularly of its integration into the policy process, became fundamentally different in Britain and the United States.

In the 1980s effective schools research became relatively marginalized in Britain, and by the end of the decade existed to any serious extent in only one location in Scotland. The important exception in England was the work that resulted in 1988 in *School Matters*, a study of junior schools in London by Peter Mortimore and colleagues, attempting for the age range 7–11 what Rutter and colleagues (including Mortimore) had done for secondary schools. The study focused on pupil intakes, school environment and educational outcomes. The research looked in detail at extensive components of the schools, headteachers and their deputies, the teacher in the classroom, the curriculum, pupils' progress on cognitive and non-cognitive measures, teacher expectations and pupil grouping, and related the findings to an extended discussion of factors which influenced effectiveness and its interpretation. The firm conclusion was that an effective school raises the performance of all pupils: 'by attending a more effective school all pupils will benefit'. The study was innovative in classifying the factors that could contribute to positive effects in four broad categories of variables: at the school level, 'given' (buildings, resources, intake . . .) and policy (style of leadership, organization, staff, curriculum, relations with parents, equal opportunities . . .); at the classroom level, 'given' (class and teacher characteristics) and policy (teachers' aims and strategies, atmosphere . . .). From these the research produced a 'portrait' of an effective class and school, not as a recipe but as a framework, and it suggested the implications for all the partners of moves towards more effective schooling. When each of these makes a positive contribution, 'the result can be an increase in the school's effectiveness'.[44] The Rutter and Mortimore work was directed, like the equivalent American research, towards making schools more successful with all children. In that respect they were unlike the 'war on poverty' programmes or the educational priority areas which followed the Plowden Report, both of which specifically targeted the socially and educationally disadvantaged.

Earlier in the 1980s a School Differences Research Group had been meeting in Britain, and in 1985 Reynolds edited for the group a collection of papers called *Studying School Effectiveness*. In the mid-1980s there was still enough attention to this kind of research to pull together such a collection of approaches to topics including outcome measures, school climate, curriculum differences, quantitative and qualitative approaches to teacher and school effectiveness, and the theoretical considerations involved. Reynolds drew attention to previous neglect of 'the study of schools as institutions for learning.'[45] In 1987 Reid, Hopkins and Holly brought together in *Towards the Effective School*[46] the main outcomes to date of the range of British, American and other research, and offered guidance on their application. Other, differently focused, research went on from the existing evidence on school differences and their effect on pupil attainment, as in the case of David Smith and Sally Tomlinson's work on multi-racial comprehensive schools, and a local study of small rural secondary schools by John Tomlinson.[47] Smith and Tomlinson also re-emphasized that educational policies had little effect on individual differences, and that this finding had been initially misunderstood. That schooling did not eliminate social inequality did not mean that schools had little effect on whether children could learn to read, write and do arithmetic: 'the results of the present study show that there are very important differences between urban comprehensive schools in these terms. The level of achievement is radically higher in some schools than in others.'[48] By the end of the decade the effective schools research momentum had been largely lost, at least in England. In Scotland, the Centre for Educational Sociology at the University of Edinburgh sustained throughout the 1980s a vigorous research interest in effective schooling and the contexts of family and neighbourhood backgrounds.

A study in Scotland, *Reconstructions of Secondary Education*, conducted from the Centre and published in 1983, contained a chapter on 'school differences and school effects'. It emphasized the importance of understanding schools' history and local context, and the interaction of the two. Education was not, however, the authors pointed out, 'the irrevocable prisoner of tradition and past practice', and although the study thought that the question of school effectiveness was 'unresolved', it underlined that there were school differences within the teachers' control. The effectiveness studies, these authors yet again stressed, were combating a weakness in the Coleman and Jencks studies, which were cross-sectional and 'lacked information on how schools have changed their pupils over time'.[49] Other research which followed found 'significant variations in schooling outcomes between secondary schools . . . even after controlling for family background characteristics and pupil ability prior to entering secondary school.'[50] Even after more or less advantaged or disadvantaged backgrounds had been taken into account:

- there are educationally significant differences between educational authorities and between schools and their effectiveness. This variation in effectiveness relates to both the quality and equity of pupil-level outcomes associated with schools and educational authorities.
- educationally significant variation in *performance* is also found between sectors: non-denominational and Catholic, old and new.
- even within the cognitive domain, pupil outcomes (as measured by examination results) are multi-dimensional, ie. schools do not

necessarily have similar levels of performance across different curricular subjects.[51]

These and other studies from the Edinburgh Centre were important in sustaining a combined interest in school effectiveness and the neighbourhood and other social factors involved in targeting issues of disadvantage. Since this work was concerned predominantly with secondary education, and much of it was financially supported by the Scottish Education Department, it is intriguing that *Effective Secondary Schools*, a report produced by HM Inspectors of Schools and published by the Scottish Education Department in 1988, made no reference to any of the Centre's published or other findings, covered a variety of topics including effective learning and teaching, the conditions for effective learning, and a number of aspects of school management, and included a bibliography only one item of which (Reid *et al.*) was a product of the effective schools movement.[52] We shall return to some questions of the relationship between schools research and official attitudes and policy-making.

The British, like the American, research meshed with both an emerging literature of 'school improvement' and international activity of various kinds. The economic and policy contexts of all countries were changing in the 1980s, and under different pressures new aims or strategies were being formulated, in many cases with governments becoming more interventionist, planning and implementing measures of restructuring or reform, as part of their attempts to combat recession and promote economic growth. The American effective schools research in the late 1980s was having direct effects not visible elsewhere. In its less centralized system American education embraced a diversity of policy directions and implementation for different ways of solving common problems in the different states. The effective schools movement competed in these arenas for influence on local policy and practice, with impact that we shall later consider. A vital element in American educational policy debate and formation in the 1980s was the rapid crystallization of a 'reform' movement following the publication of a large number of anguished reports from 1983. *A Nation at Risk* in that year was only one – if the most sharply phrased and most widely cited and discussed – of the indictments of education's part in the industrial and economic crisis of the United States.[53] The crisis had the same causes and effects as that in the United Kingdom, but given the lack of central government controls the American solutions had to be fought over more widely, at a time when criticism of schools' performance was also running deep. The schools then, as frequently, were being held accountable for salient social problems, or at least for failing to counteract them. Concern about drugs, teenage pregnancy, adult illiteracy, vandalism and crime – and now international economic performance – pointed towards school inadequacies. The 'excellence' movement 'left the poor and minority behind'.[54] As in Britain, shaped in different forums and policy environments, the contexts in which the effective schools research was born had been rapidly remodelled. In the less unitary American structure, however, the effective schools research and models could more readily compete for attention than in the British situation, where choices were constrained by determined government policy.

In spite of, and to some extent because of, the changing American context, the effective schools case was presented with confidence and was in some states listened to with interest. Edmonds's research had received support from the National Institute of Education, where supervision of his work was the responsibility of Michael Cohen. In 1982 Cohen wrote an article entitled 'Effective schools: accumulating research findings', as the first in a series of articles based on the findings of 'research on effective schools and effective classrooms'. These were intended to cover classroom management, teacher expectations, principals' effective instructional leadership, testing, and effective staff development. Like Edmonds and others in the earlier period of the movement, Cohen emphasized the importance of the research in identifying practices 'particularly effective at improving the achievement levels of students from poor and minority backgrounds', and he offered a five-item version of the factors affecting school differences – strong administrative leadership, a school climate conducive to learning, emphasis on basic skills, teacher expectation that pupils 'can reach high levels of achievement' regardless of their background, and assessment of pupil performance. It was important that researchers were increasingly 'collaborating with practicing educators in conducting their research'.[55] The issues were being tackled from a variety of directions, and for a variety of audiences. A book entitled *Looking at Schools: Good, Bad and Indifferent* in 1980, with no reference to the effective schools movement and its work, looked at aspects of 'school tone' and organization as accounting for school differences, and the following year Joan Shoemaker, active in the movement in Connecticut and nationally, shared authorship of an article in an education journal on 'What principals can do', particularly stressing the connection between expectation and achievement.[56] The relationship between effective schools research and evaluation, including a detailed typology of effective schools literature, was the subject of an article in a journal addressing accreditation issues, and one 'practitioners' guide to school improvement' drew on the effective schools work and related it to the demand for 'excellence'.[57] The movement could be said to have 'arrived' in the American landscape when, in 1985, the National Institute of Education published a large 'effective schools sourcebook', including a 300-item bibliography. The volume explored aspects of elementary and secondary schools in relation to 'effectiveness', interpreted to include a wide range of school processes, organization and management, programmes and assessment, as well as district- and state-level policies. It described 39 effective school programmes in 20 of the American states. The whole volume was dedicated to explaining the implications of key areas of research for educational practice. Policy-makers, the editor claimed, were turning to research for guidance.[58]

As elsewhere the American movement was establishing links between the 'pure' effective schools research, and research and analysis coming from other directions, notably that concerned with educational change and school improvement strategies. The 'ecology of schooling' received attention, and there was continued interest in the concept of 'school culture' as a way into understanding school effects.[59] One book in 1988 attempted a synthesis of all of these approaches, in the framework of the 'multitude of goals' that schools have, and a 'multifaceted' definition of effectiveness.[60] David L. Clark and colleagues published a comparative analysis of effective schools and school improvement as 'two lines of enquiry', illustrating perhaps more than anything how many questions about school characteristics, and why effective schools exist, remained unanswered.[61] Discussions of effectiveness in the 1980s ranged from its research base and values to the elaboration of operational models and the relevance of strategies derived from management theory and business. Although attention was increasingly being directed towards interpretation and implementation, researchers were continuing to pursue the realities of the effective school. Some were elaborating more sophisticated models for studying school effects, others were exploring correlations between effective schools criteria and the socioeconomic status of the pupils.[62] Others looked at specific projects and schools, and drew conclusions, including the possible effectiveness of 'direct instruction' on improving pupil performance.

Within these studies of schools lurked the same controversy that existed in all the school developments of the nineteenth and twentieth centuries that we have considered – that between less formal methods and the more formal approach to 'direct instruction'. Eubanks and Levine, looking at effective elementary schools in New York City and Milwaukee in the early 1980s, suggested that amidst all the difficulties faced by inner-city schools the projects investigated had emphasized direct instruction for improving academic achievement. If properly implemented direct instruction could help to establish a coherent programme for the school and to improve the monitoring, evaluation and design of instructional arrangements. Experience in the two cities had suggested that 'intelligent implementation of direct instruction can result in substantial immediate improvement in student learning', but that these gains could 'level off' unless emphasis were placed on the development of 'higher order cognitive skills', which were currently being explored in the projects concerned.[63] Such research possibly remembered that Edmonds had emphasized that 'no one model explains school effectiveness for the poor or any other social class subset. Fortunately, children know how to learn in more ways than we know how to teach, thus permitting great latitude in choosing instructional strategy.'[64] A National Center for Effective Schools Research and Development was established in Michigan, publishing a considerable literature on the research, specific school and policy developments, and running workshop and other training devices. By the end of the 1980s the effective schools research, literature and movement had become an element in state and national debate and policy-making.

One criticism of the direction the movement had taken in the United States was of the way the research had been translated into forms of discourse that had 'captured the educators' and the public's fancy by reducing a disparate literature to simple recipes for school improvement'.[65] The effective schools researchers to some extent faced the same problem as that of the researchers whose work was used as a basis for the pre-school developments of the war on poverty: it could easily be simplified, and could be seen by policy-makers as a panacea. What critics of the effective schools research in fact most frequently pointed out was that descriptions of effective schools or their components could not easily be translated into 'recipes'. Purkey and Smith, in one of the earliest and fairest accounts and critiques of the accumulated research, adopted what they described as a 'skeptical' approach. They criticized or were cautious about research based on small samples, errors in the identification of schools, inappropriate comparisons, and often subjective criteria for determining success. They were also clear that more longitudinal research was needed to substantiate the claims of the research, and in addition they pointed out that adoption of the characteristics it had emphasized 'is unlikely to work in all schools, may not work as expected in many schools, and may in fact be counterproductive in some schools'. The ingredients suggested by different researchers had been 'divergent', and they had not provided guidance on how to develop effective schools. For that they turned to the literature on 'school culture'.[66] Other, often sympathetic, critics stressed the same difficulty of moving from the research on what is to what could be. Larry Cuban wrote a 'friendly but cautionary note' pointing to some of the weaknesses of the research, including the fact that 'the language is fuzzy'. He pointed out that a half dozen definitions of effectiveness 'dot the studies', that the concept was 'constricted' by being tied to test results, that most of the studies were of elementary schools, and that 'no one knows how to create effective schools':

> None of the highly detailed, lovingly written descriptions of effective
> schools can point to a blueprint of what a teacher, principal, or
> superintendent should *do* in order to improve academic achievement.
> Who knows with predictable precision how to construct a positive,
> enduring school climate? Exactly what do principals do to shape
> teacher expectations and instructional practices in ways that improve
> student performance?

The following year Cuban published a more extended discussion of the research entitled 'Transforming the frog into a prince'. This time he removed the question marks: 'No one knows how to grow effective schools.'[67] Ann Lieberman continued the theme in 1986:

> these 'Effective Schools and Effective Classrooms' findings are far
> easier to describe than to implement in schools and classrooms. They
> have an intuitive logic to them that makes them attractive but must
> not be sold as recipes. . . . We need not only good descriptions of
> good schools, but organizational strategies to get there.[68]

The effective schools researchers were not unaware of the criticisms and the difficulties. They were engaged in controversy, one important one being that with Lawrence Stedman, who began an appraisal of the effective schools work while he was a graduate student in policy at the University of Wisconsin, and then in the Office of Research and Evaluation in one of the Virginia public school districts. His critique stemmed from a belief that 'effectiveness' as described and advocated in the literature had been achieved by focusing narrowly on tests and curriculum objectives. The research had indeed shown that schools can make a difference and that poverty 'does not preclude academic success'. A broader view was needed, one that involved the students in their own learning in a 'well-rounded academic program.'[69] Working over the same ground as the original effective schools research, Stedman found that successful schools 'actively developed students' racial and ethnic identities and paid more individual attention to students. Their emphasis on cultural pluralism was strong.' The need now, however, was to move on from the demonstration that children are imprisoned in their impoverished backgrounds to 'alternative measures' of effectiveness. Stedman's article, which stimulated a controversy with Wilbur Brookover, was entitled 'It's time we changed the effective schools formula'.[70]

The focus on test results was not, of course, unusual in the United States, where judgement by tests was a strong feature of the educational system. Reynolds in Britain underlined the extent of the American research and willingness to discuss good and bad schools, but thought the effective schools bandwagon in the mid-1980s was rolling 'with great, perhaps excessive, speed'. He found some of the American enthusiasm worrying:

> there is an absence of any philosophical discussion of what schools
> ought to be doing and an uncritical acceptance of high achievement
> test scores as the educational system's only goal. . . . Some of the
> leaders of the movement also have a messianic certainty about what
> should be done to schools and to children.[71]

Both the American and the British research, different though they were in many ways, were accused of being narrow and evading some of the crucial social and cultural features of schools. Burgess, as we have seen, accused *Fifteen Thousand Hours* of having no sense of history or of the 'actual texture of the schools themselves': it was 'almost exclusively managerial'.[72] For Stephen Ball this was a fundamental criticism of all the effective schools research. He considered management to be a form of organization which 'reduces the autonomy of teachers and attempts to minimize their influence over policy making; it is also couched in an ideology of neutrality'. For these reasons he believed the 'school effectiveness movement' to have been 'thoroughly implicated in the formation of and establishing of the conditions for the discourse of management'.[73] For Michael Young the Rutter research evaded questions of inequality in and outside the schools, and encouraged more centralized forms of administration.[74]

The effective schools researchers were in fact drawing on an international literature of organizational behaviour and change, which also supported what was seen as a related emphasis on the mechanisms of school improvement; this embraced curriculum development, strengthening school organization, and changes in the teaching and learning process and teaching styles: 'it is content and process oriented.'[75] In Britain it involved a planning process that rested on some experience of school review procedures from the 1970s. The effective schools movement, to some extent linked with the school improvement work, took formal international shape in the 1980s. An international effective schools organization came into existence and held conferences in Holland, Israel, Wales and elsewhere from 1988. The annual proceedings from 1988 not only covered a wide variety of countries, and registered the impacts of Edmonds, Rutter and others, but also discussed the limitations of the early research and reported on new, different and more developed forms of research from Louisiana or Israel, the Netherlands or Scotland.[76] An international journal, *School Effectiveness and School Improvement*, was launched in 1990, with joint editors in Wales and the Netherlands, an editorial board also covering Australia, Canada and the United States, and an advisory board with members from these and five other countries in Scandinavia, Western Europe and Eastern Europe. The American Educational Research Association was a forum for hearing some of the international research and debate, and Peter Mortimore, for example, was a frequent speaker in the United States. Another new journal, *Qualitative Studies in Education*, in 1988, contained articles on effective schools developments in Europe, the United States, New Zealand and Canada.

The American, European and other effective schools interests were not identical, but they shared an international energy. The movement was partly eclipsed by other reform movements and aims, but in the United States particularly it retained an important foothold among the alternatives available. In Britain the dominant alternative was different, but as in previous centuries British, like wider European, American and other attempts to make schools effective in one way or another, raised sharp questions about the goals of education. As at many points in the history of schooling, however, the conditions became conducive to short-term pressures and policies, not to any longer-term reassessment of the goals of education. Reynolds had been right in the mid-1980s to point to the absence of philosophical discussion in the United States about what schools ought to be doing. The changed conditions of the 1980s and 1990s made that more difficult. The traditional emphases on good schools as serving a variety of values relating to the family, employment, social justice or creative citizenship did not disappear. Nor did basic differences between types, levels or sectors of schooling, and between the power and authority to define desirable school outcomes. What countries round the world were experiencing in the 1980s was the kind of change in economic conditions and policy directions that made 'philosophical discussion' marginal to urgent pressures to respond to economic competition and decline. The mounting concern of the British Conservative government in the 1980s with a nationally mandated curriculum and testing, with new forms of school finance and control, was paralleled, with differences according to national systems, in the United States, Canada, New Zealand and other countries. The question of what was wanted from schools became overlaid with anxieties about, for example, unemployment and delinquency. Conservative orthodoxies also aimed at retrieving schools for what were seen as the 'traditional values' that had been undermined in part by the progressive educational ideas of the 1960s and earlier.

The effective schools movement contained its own divisions, pointing variously towards managerial efficiency, better working environments or higher teacher expectations, classroom organization or teacher behaviour, forms of evaluation and assessment or gains for equity, or some mixture of these and others. In the changed conditions there were gains, to some of which we shall return, but one loss was in weakening the early emphasis of the effective schools movement on education and equity, while maintaining the message of the relationship between school differences and school outcomes. The voices of regret that concern about 'good' schools had been diminished were difficult to hear, but not entirely silent. In Britain the organizations of teachers, parents and others concerned with education were in the 1980s overridden by the certainties of central government. The National Association for Primary Education heard Professor Philip Gammage deliver an address in 1985 applauding the post-Coleman research that had reinstated the belief that schools mattered and affected children, and even if the effects were relatively small by comparison with those of the home, schools' contribution could be crucial. At the same time Gammage underlined the difficult time schools were having throughout the western world. In all of this, he asked – and this was the title of his address – 'What is a good school?' He accepted many of the elements identified by official commissions, the school inspectorate, and researchers such as Reynolds and Rutter using effectiveness measures. A 'good' school, however, had an informal culture of human relations to support such aims and measures:

> When we talk of the ethos or climate of a school, we must be aware of the disciplinary context, the relational, non-codified aspects of school life, the ambiance of transactions. In a good school, we would expect this 'hidden curriculum' to be supportive, perhaps warm, even kindly: a humanizing force in itself.

Some of those qualities would be powerfully affected by the head of the school, and curricular balance would be an important ingredient. Gammage saw targets beyond those elements:

> Most schools, however, are deemed good if they promote allegiance, broad cultural norms, and (above all) achievement. The 'good' school aims to motivate all of its pupils to achieve – a task of formidable, if not impossible, proportions. . . . Perhaps therefore the good school is that which most successfully matches its curricular organisation and ethos to an expectation of high commitment by children . . . a good school is 'good', not so much because of the specific nature of what is taught (though that is important) but through the manner in which a positive, supportive, richly and frequently interactive atmosphere is developed.

Research in the United States and Britain had emphasized the importance of factors of partnership between parent, child and school: '*Partnership* is in fact another of the few factors to emerge and re-emerge from research as the "sine qua non" of a good school on both sides of the Atlantic.'[77] Some of these constituent parts of what constitutes a good school would have been accepted by British policy-makers in the 1980s and early 1990s, but their combination and emphasis would have been very different. Unlike Gammage's portrait, that of the National Curriculum focused on the specifics of what is taught, with less and less being left for the school to decide in terms of matching and the ways in which it articulates its expectations. A good school in that respect, unlike Gammage's, was one which matched its work closely to nationally set goals. The dominant definitions of good schools in Britain, particularly since the late 1980s, have not only been a long way from considerations of warmth, kindliness and humanity, however hard the schools might work to keep these alive. The dominant definitions are also some way from the research-based attempts to identify what made schools effective.

In 1987 an American professor at the University of Georgia wrote an article entitled 'Good and/or effective schools: what do we want?' A mother had telephoned from another state to describe an effective schools programme, which had resulted, amongst other things, in more teacher-centred, whole-group instruction, greater reliance on textbooks and mimeographed drill sheets, the curtailment of individual and small-group projects, and the cancellation of field trips and free time. Her child had commented that 'school isn't fun any more'. Test scores had, in fact, risen, yet this mother and some other parents felt that the school was effective but 'isn't good' any more. Other incidents had caused this professor to reflect on the question of the difference between a school being 'effective' and being 'good'. In essence Carl Glickman was protesting at the narrow implementation of effective school and other reform efforts, those who argued for narrowing the curriculum focus, more frequent testing, measurable objectives, and a prescribed teaching approach with large groups. The research on effective schools was being treated as 'laws of science that apply to *all* teachers and *all* schools'. It was too often equated with what was desirable or good:

> By failing to distinguish between *effectiveness* and *goodness*, we have avoided two central questions in education. The first question with which schools and school systems must deal is, What is good? Only after that question has been answered should they deal with the second question, How do we become effective? . . . Effective schools can be good schools, and good schools must be effective schools – but the two are not necessarily the same.[78]

Barry Holtz, a researcher at the Jewish Theological Seminary of America, reviewed Rutter's *Fifteen Thousand Hours* in 1981. He broadly welcomed it, including the way it worked for the reduction of teachers' 'sense of powerlessness in the face of debilitating realities beyond their control'. And yet he felt something was missing, something of the 'vision' that was often overstated and romanticized in the 1960s, but which saw education as 'something bigger than improved reading scores and behavior'. Holtz concluded:

> As we acknowledge the important contribution of *Fifteen Thousand Hours* and other recent research of its kind, it may be worth our while to remember that we once hoped that schools would create new models of community, encourage new commitments toward meaningful vocations, end racial discrimination, and open up new avenues out of poverty and unhappiness. Right now, it seems, we rejoice if children can be taught to read.[79]

The effective schools movement did not replace the ways previous judgements about schools had been made, it added another complex ingredient to them.

NOTES

1 See James A. Smith (1991). *The Idea Brokers: Think Tanks and the Rise of the New Policy Elite*. New York: The Free Press.

2 These and other aspects of the educational policies of the Johnson era are discussed in Harold and Pamela Silver (1991). *An Educational War on Poverty: American and British Policy-Making 1960–1980*. Cambridge: Cambridge University Press.

3 John Brademas (1987). *The Politics of Education: Conflict and Consensus on Capitol Hill*. Norman: University of Oklahoma Press, p. 15.

4 Jean Floud and A. H. Halsey (1957). 'Intelligence tests, social class, and selection for secondary schools', *British Journal of Sociology*, **8**, reprinted in A. H. Halsey, Jean Floud and C. Arnold Anderson (eds) (1961). *Education, Economy, and Society*. New York: The Free Press of Glencoe, p. 214.

5 Brian Jackson and Dennis Marsden (1962). *Education and the Working Class*. London: Routledge & Kegan Paul, p. 224.

6 Max Wolff and Annie Stein (1967). *Six Months Later: A Comparison of Children Who Had Head Start, Summer 1965, with Their Classmates in Kindergarten*. Washington, DC: Office of Economic Opportunity.

7 James S. Coleman *et al.* (1966). *Equality of Educational Opportunity*. Washington, DC: Department of Health, Education and Welfare.

8 Peter W. Airasian *et al.* (1979). *Concepts of School Effectiveness as Derived from Research Strategies: Differences in Their Findings*. Washington, DC: National Institute of Education, pp. 4–5.

9 John Vaizey and C. F. O. Clarke (1976). *Education: The State of the Debate in America, Britain and Canada*. London: Duckworth, p. 1.

10 Christopher Jencks *et al.* (1972). *Inequality: A Reassessment of the Effect of Family and Schooling in America*. New York: Basic Books; Harper & Row edn (1973), pp. 37, 41, 94–5, 158–9, 261–3.

11 Wilma S. Longstreet (1973). *Beyond Jencks: The Myth of Equal Schooling*. Washington, DC: Association for Supervision and Curriculum Development, pp. 3–5; Patricia Cayo Sexton (1973). 'The *Inequality* affair: a critique of Jencks', *Social Policy*, **4** (2), 53–5; Edmund W. Gordon (1975). 'New perspectives on old issues in education for the minority poor', *IRDC Bulletin* (Institute for Urban and Minority Education), **10** (1), 15.

12 Roger C. Barker and Paul V. Gump (1964). *Big School, Small School: High School Size and Student Behavior*. Stanford, Calif.: Stanford University Press.

13 George Weber (1971). *Inner-City Children Can Be Taught to Read: Four Successful Schools*. Washington, DC: Center for Basic Education, p. 4.

14 Ibid., pp. 1–3, 7–8, 25–6.

15 For example Gilbert R. Austin (1979). 'Exemplary schools and the search for effectiveness', *Educational Leadership*, **37** (1); Robert E. Klitgaard and George Hall (1973). *A Statistical Search for Unusually Effective Schools*. Santa Monica, Calif.: Rand Corporation.

16 Austin, 'Exemplary schools', p. 12.

17 Seymour B. Sarason (1971). *The Culture of the School and the Problem of Change*. Boston: Allyn & Bacon.

18 Austin, 'Exemplary schools', p. 12.

19 Thomas L. Good, Bruce J. Biddle and Jere E. Brophy (1975). *Teachers Make a Difference*. New York: Holt, Rinehart & Winston, pp. 5–7, 22, 232.

20 Charles E. Bidwell and John D. Kasarda (1975). 'School district organization and student achievement', *American Sociological Review*, **40**, 55–70.

21 See Austin, 'Exemplary schools', p. 11.

22 Michael Cohen (1982). 'Effective schools: accumulating research findings', *American Education*, **18** (1), 14–15.

23 Anita A. Summers and Barbara L. Wolfe (1977). 'Do schools make a difference?', *American Economic Review*, **64**, 639, 649.

24 Joan Shoemaker (1986). 'Developing effectiveness in the district, school and classroom'. In Institute for Responsive Education, *Equity and Choice*, Boston, Mass.: Institute for Responsive Education, pp. 1–2.

25 Ronald Edmonds (1979). 'Effective schools for the urban poor', *Educational Leadership*, **37** (1), 16–18.

26 For example Wilbur B. Brookover and Lawrence W. Lezotte (1977). *Changes in School Characteristics Coincident with Changes in Student Achievement*. East Lansing: Michigan State University; Wilbur B. Brookover *et al.* (1979). *School Social Systems and Student Achievement: Schools Can Make a Difference*. New York: Praeger; Ronald R. Edmonds and John R. Frederiksen (1979). *Search for Effective Schools: The Identification and Analysis of City Schools That Are Instructionally Effective for Poor Children*. Cambridge, Mass.: Harvard University Center for Urban Studies.

27 Brookover and Lezotte, *Changes in School Characteristics*.

28 Brookover *et al.*, *School Social Systems*, pp. 1–2, 5–7, 135–9, 142.

29 Edmonds and Frederiksen, *Search for Effective Schools*, pp. 1–6, 12, 37, 47–50.

30 Edmonds, 'Effective schools for the urban poor', pp. 15–24.

31 For example, Julienne Ford (1969). *Social Class and the Comprehensive School*. London: Routledge & Kegan Paul.

32 Central Advisory Council for Education (England) (1967). *Children and Their Primary Schools* (Plowden Report). Vol. 1: *Report*, esp chs 3, 16–20.

33 M. J. Power *et al.* (1967). 'Delinquent schools?', *New Society*, October, 542–3.

34 David Reynolds (ed.) (1985). 'Introduction'. In *Studying School Effectiveness*. London: Falmer Press, pp. 1–5.

35 David Reynolds *et al.* (1976). 'Schools do make a difference', *New Society*, July, 223–5.

36 Neville Bennett (1976). *Teaching Styles ad Pupil Progress*. London: Open Books, pp. 251–3 and *passim*.

37 Maurice Galton *et al.* (1980). *Inside the Primary School*. London: Routledge & Kegan Paul, pp. 156–7; Jane Herbert (1981). 'When best is not good enough', *Times Educational Supplement*, 17 July, 15.

38 Barry MacDonald (1978). 'Accountability, standards and the process of schooling'. In Tony Becher and Stuart Maclure (eds), *Accountability in Education*. Windsor: NFER-Nelson, pp. 128–30.

39 Alan Brimer *et al.* (1978). *Sources of Difference in School Achievement*. Slough: NFER.

40 See Michael Rutter *et al.* (1979). *Fifteen Thousand Hours: Secondary Schools and Their Effects on Children*. London: Open Books, pp. 1–21 for a survey of existing literature at that time.

41 Ibid., pp. 177–9.

42 Tony Burgess (1980). 'What makes an effective school?' In Barbara Tizard *et al.*, *'Fifteen Thousand Hours': Secondary Schools and Their Effect on Children*, London: University of London Institute of Education, pp. 11–13.

43 Michael Rutter *et al.* (1980). 'A response to the discussion papers'. In Tizard *et al.*, ibid.; Michael Rutter *et al.* (1980). 'Educational criteria of success: a reply to Acton', *Educational Research*, **22** (3); Michael Rutter (1983). 'School effects on pupil progress: research findings and policy implications', *Child Development*, **54**.

44 Peter Mortimore *et al.* (1988). *School Matters: The Junior Years*. London: Open Books, pp. 1–6, 207–20, 262 and *passim*. See also Peter Mortimore *et al.* (1987). 'For effective classroom practices', *Forum*, **30** (1).

45 Reynolds, *Studying School Effectiveness*, p. 1.

46 Ken Reid *et al.* (1987). *Towards the Effective School: the Problems and Some Solutions*. Oxford: Blackwell.

47 David J. Smith and Sally Tomlinson (1989). *The School Effect: A Study of Multi-racial Comprehensives*. London: Policy Studies Institute; John Tomlinson (1990). *Small, Rural and Effective: A Study of Six Small Secondary Schools in a Remote Area of England*. Coventry: University of Warwick Institute of Education.

48 Smith and Tomlinson, *The School Effect*, pp. 300–1.

49 J. Gray, A. F. McPherson and D. Raffe (1983). *Reconstructions of Secondary Education: Theory, Myth and Practice since the War*. London: Routledge & Kegan Paul, pp. 271–93.

50 J. Douglas Willms and Peter Cuttance (1985). 'School effects in Scottish secondary schools', *British Journal of Sociology of Education*, **6** (3), 302.

51 Peter Cuttance (1986). *Effective Schooling: A Report to the Scottish Education Department*. Edinburgh: University of Edinburgh, Centre for Educational Sociology, pp. vi–vii.

52 Scottish Education Department (1988). *Effective Secondary Schools: A Report by HM Inspectors of Schools*. Edinburgh: HMSO.

53 National Commission on Excellence in Education (1983). *A Nation at Risk: The Imperative for Educational Reform*. Washington, DC: US Department of Education.

54 William E. Bickel (1990). 'The effective schools literature: implications for research and practice'. In Terry B. Gutkin and Cecil R. Reynolds (eds), *The Handbook of School Psychology*, 2nd edn. New York: Wiley p. 862.

55 Cohen, 'Effective schools', pp. 13–16.

56 Edward A. Wynne (1980). *Looking at Schools: Good, Bad, and Indifferent*. Lexington, Mass.: D. C. Heath; Joan Shoemaker and Hugh W. Fraser (1981). 'What principals can do: some implications from studies of effective schooling', *Phi Delta Kappan*, **63** (3), 181.

57 Gregory Stefanich (1983). 'The relationship of effective schools research to school evaluation', *North Central Association Quarterly*, **58** (3); Richard P. DuFour and Robert Eaker (1987). *Fulfilling the Promise of Excellence: A Practitioner's Guide to School Improvement*. Westbury, NY: Wilkerson.

58 Regina M. Kyle (ed.) (1985). *Reading for Excellence: An Effective Schools Sourcebook*. Washington, DC: National Institute of Education.

59 For example John I. Goodlad (ed.) (1987). *The Ecology of School Renewal*. Chicago: National Society for the Study of Education (including Paul Heckman, 'Understanding school culture').

60 Gretchen Rossman *et al.* (1988). *Change and Effectiveness in Schools: A Cultural Perspective*. Albany: State University of New York.

61 David L. Clark *et al.* (1984). 'Effective schools and school improvement: a comparative analysis of two lines of enquiry', *Educational Administration Quarterly*, **20** (3).

62 For example S. Raudenbush and A. Bryk (1986). 'A hierarchical model for studying school effects', *Sociology of Education*, **59**; Charles Teddlie *et al.* (1989). 'Contextual differences in models for effective schools in the USA'. In Bert Creemers *et al.* (eds), *School Effectiveness and School Improvement*. Amsterdam: Swetz & Zeitlinger.

63 Eugene E. Eubanks and Daniel U. Levine (1983). 'A first look at effective schools projects in New York City and Milwaukee', *Phi Delta Kappan*, **64** (10).

64 Edmonds, 'Effective schools for the urban poor', p. 22.

65 Stewart C. Purkey and Marshall S. Smith (1983). 'Effective schools: a review', *The Elementary School Journal*, **83** (1), 429.

66 Ibid., pp. 440, 447 and *passim*.

67 Larry Cuban (1983). 'Effective schools: a friendly but cautionary note', *Phi Delta Kappan*, **64** (10), 695; Larry Cuban (1984). 'Transforming the frog into a prince: effective schools research, policy, and practice at the district level', *Harvard Educational Review*, **54** (2), 131. See also Brian Rowan *et al.* (1983). 'Research on effective schools: a cautionary note', *Educational Researcher*, **12** (4).

68 Ann Lieberman (1986). 'School improvement: common knowledge, common sense, uncommon practice'. In Sandra Packard (ed.), *The Leading Edge: Innovation and Change in Professional Education*. Washington, DC: American Association of Colleges for Teacher Education, p. 98.

69 Lawrence C. Stedman (1985). 'A new look at the effective schools literature', *Urban Education*, **20** (3), *passim*.

70 Lawrence C. Stedman (1987). 'It's time we changed the effective schools formula', *Phi Delta Kappan*, **69** (3); Wilbur B. Brookover (1987). 'Distortion and overgeneralization are no substitute for sound research', *Phi Delta Kappan*, **69** (3); Lawrence C. Stedman (1988). 'The effective schools formula still needs changing: a reply to Brookover', *Phi Delta Kappan*, **69** (6).

71 David Reynolds (1985). 'The effective school', *Times Educational Supplement*, 20 September, 25.

72 Burgess, 'What makes an effective school?', p. 11.

73 Stephen Ball (1988). 'Comprehensive schooling, effectiveness and control: an analysis of educational discourses'. In Roger Slee (ed.), *Discipline and Schools*. London: Macmillan, pp. 132–4.

74 Michael Young (1980). 'A case study of the limitations of policy research'. In Tizard *et al.*, '*Fifteen Thousand Hours*', p. 33.

75 David Hopkins (ed.) (1987). *Improving the Quality of Schooling*. London: Falmer Press, p. 5.

76 David Reynolds *et al.* (eds) (1989). *School Effectiveness and Improvement*. Cardiff: University of Wales College of Cardiff, School of Education; Creemers *et al.*, *School Effectiveness and School Improvement*.

77 Philip Gammage (1985). *What Is a Good School?* [University of Nottingham]: National Association for Primary Education, pp. 1–15.

78 Carl D. Glickman (1987). 'Good and/or effective schools: what do we want?', *Phi Delta Kappan*, **68** (8), 622–4.

79 Barry W. Holtz (1981). 'Can schools make a difference?' (review of Rutter *et al.*, *Fifteen Thousand Hours*), *Teachers College Record*, **83** (2), 300–7.

Chapter 7

Implementation, Policy and Judgement

Inspectors' reports or Royal Commissions in nineteenth-century Britain, and the effective schools research movement in the twentieth-century United States, are examples of processes by which contexts and public criteria for the making of judgements about schools have been established. Parental, community or media judgements of schooling, mainly but not exclusively public schooling, have been more and more conditioned by agendas and attitudes set by policy-makers and interest groups, both to some degree permeable by research or interpretations of research. In the late twentieth century policy-makers and researchers have become more involved in confronting two distinct but interrelated aspects of the research – how any school manages its affairs in such a way as to 'succeed' with its pupils, and how one school's 'success' or 'failure' might be compared with that of another school.[1] British government enthusiasm in the 1980s and early 1990s for publishing inspectors' reports and compiling league tables of schools' examination results seemed to combine both of these, while in fact emphasizing the importance of national, statistically based comparisons. The analysis of any one school must ultimately point to the 'value added' contribution it makes to pupils' achievement, taking account of the characteristics of its particular pupil constituency. It cannot be sufficiently overemphasized, however, that judgements of an educational system, its sectors and individual schools in the late twentieth century have been strongly influenced by criteria defined by government and its policy-related agencies, sometimes taking account of (without necessarily accepting) the relevant research, and often bruisingly misrepresented by the media. In terms of the way these frameworks are established, particularly in the implementation of policies, the United States and Britain provide two quite different case studies in the 1980s and 1990s.

The example of the effective schools research is internationally unusual. Researchers in education, as more widely in the social and political sciences, do not commonly have the privilege of seeing their work readily and directly translated into policy. When it does happen there are high-profile economic or political reasons. There is a considerable literature exploring the conditions in which research may influence or infiltrate policy, or the policy process or environment, and there is a variety of models of how it may do so. Most of the literature is American, not only because of the scale of the American policy operation and of the American policy-related community. The reason lies essentially in the relatively diffuse decision-making nature of many areas of American life, especially education, and the profusion of directions – including the federal one – from which attempts are made to shape or reform procedures and practices. Countries with more centralized systems are not immune from policy-related research, but the pressures and opportunities for it, and for it to be heard, are fewer than in the United States. In European countries, for example, where such areas of public life are more subject to national control, finance, coordination and regulation, policy debate tends to be more constrained, often more confrontational, but less penetrable by research-based effort. The directions of research itself are in the latter case more influenced by the availability of government-controlled or government-provided finance, which forms a higher proportion of the funding available and which can more easily define the objectives to be pursued. This is especially true in a period like that of the 1980s when powerful central government policy-making weakened the impact of research and its ability to compete with or influence ideologically driven educational change.

In countries where research is to any serious extent an institutionalized feature of the academic fabric, educational research has a strong policy-related strand. Research may sometimes indeed be summoned to the service of educational change – perhaps most commonly in the recent past in the form of evaluation of policy implementation. Or research may seek with some degree of independence, and often with rapidly changing emphases, to describe and explain the enormous range of elements and interactions of educational processes. In the past century in many countries, but principally in the United States, a major development has been the establishment of policy analysis as a research activity, in a broad territory between theories of organizational behaviour and what James Q. Wilson believes it is most competent to offer – 'evaluations of policies that have already been implemented', not 'speculations about what may happen in the future'.[2] An important feature of educational structures and debate in the twentieth century, as we have seen, has been the increasing presence of research-based criteria for judging educational processes, initiatives and outcomes at all levels of systems and in all aspects of schools.

The concept of 'research' has itself covered a variety of activities, characterized in such terms as 'conclusion-oriented' and 'decision-oriented', or 'non-mission research' and 'mission research', 'fundamental' and 'applied', or a range of other possible typologies.[3] 'Policy' similarly has been seen as decision-making by government and official institutions, and as almost any kind of planned change in any institution or organization – a process which may also have unplanned and unexpected outcomes. What policy researchers have struggled to ascertain in recent decades has been the extent to which policy processes (whether in a school district, a hospital or a government department) have been directly or indirectly affected by research, and at the same time to understand the nature of relationships between policy-makers and the research community.[4] They have considered research knowledge in competition with other sources of information and evidence, and the means by which research knowledge can in some way become part of policy agendas – and ultimately, in connection with our issues here, become a feature of public debate and awareness, and attitudes towards the 'delivery' of policies in schools or other institutions. Analysts have also, of course, explored the kinds of research and research findings that are unwelcome where policy is formulated, including the historical research that competes with the future orientation that is basic to policy-making.[5]

The research that is absorbed into American federal or state policy-making in education arrives under a variety of sponsorships. James A. Smith maps out the changing roles of the academic specialist, the research bureau, the think tank, the advocacy organization or group. The sponsorship of ideas and directions has included the most academically respectable as well as advocates who use selective research to establish their own legitimacy. With the proliferation of research and evaluation groups in the 1970s particularly, research was to be found amidst 'the cacophony of experts and ideologues'.[6] How research has been commissioned, the authority of its provenance, the ability of the researchers to use channels of influence, and the constraints placed on research findings by those commissioning or funding it may affect the degree to which the research is heard and used.[7] All such considerations, however, apply to the routine processes by which research and politics meet or pass by each other in those places where policy is negotiated, formed and implemented, or where it fails to survive. One of the critical points about public policy in the 1970s and 1980s, however, is that research was not confronting routine processes. It was operating in, or stimulated by, rapidly changing economic and political conditions, resulting in fundamental shifts in the prevailing assumptions on which policy was built. Public services and agencies were under attack from government and other directions, international competition and assertive conservative ideologies were provoking a reordering of national priorities, and education particularly – in the United States, Britain and other countries – faced new pressures and expectations. Education was exposed to blame for failing to provide a competent workforce, demands for greater accountability or 'value for money', the hostile clamour of governments and publics looking for causes of and solutions to poor economic performance and intensified social problems and dislocations. This political context was an important factor in the emergence of the effective schools research movement in the 1970s. To identify those characteristics of schools that make for 'effective' procedures and outcomes could be one way of countering criticism. As we have seen, however, there were other explanations, especially in the United States, with the interest in the school as an institution that followed from evaluations of the education policies of the war on poverty. One important feature of the panorama of educational activities from the 1960s was the emphasis on parents. The poverty programmes placed parent involvement centrally in their concerns. The effective schools research moved to embrace perceptions of schooling by the participants, including parents.

The main focus of the American effective schools research as perceived from outside was the identification of school differences, explained not by a single factor but by a 'critical mass of positive factors which, when put together, make the difference'.[8] By the beginning of the 1980s the research dissemination processes had brought the formulations involved to the attention of state educational officials, and the publications, conferences or other machineries of research permeation were proving very successful. Exactly how successful can be judged by the acceptance of the effective schools research as a basis for planning in some of the states from the early 1980s. In some cases the Edmonds formula was taken more or less intact, but in others it was extended to incorporate elements from other research or from the policy contexts in which particular Departments of Education worked. Edmonds's work to foster effective schools in New York was sending out signals, as were the developments in Michigan. In 1981 the Ohio Department of Education began a series of publications and training strategies predicated explicitly on the research, summarizing it in seven principles drawn from the versions of the research in circulation:

> A growing body of research indicates that for like populations of students, some schools are more instructionally effective than others. While identified factors among the factors vary in number, all seem to contain these basic seven principles. The basic premise for all is that children can learn and that schools do make a difference.

Ohio's own version of these principles contained a sense of mission; strong leadership by principals; high expectations for all students and staff; frequent monitoring of student progress; a positive learning climate; sufficient opportunity to learn; and parent/community involvement. An internal Department document urging the effective schools idea acknowledged the sources and the action taken by the Department's Division of Equal Educational Opportunities to develop programmes from the fall of 1981: 'extensive examinations were made of effective schools research (particularly research conducted by Ron Edmonds, Larry Lezotte and Jerry Brophy) and interviews were conducted with practitioners in the States of New York and Connecticut.'[9] By the end of the decade well over 75 per cent of Ohio's schools were 'implementing some form of the effective schools process'.[10]

Michigan had been working on the collection of 'uniform achievement data' from the mid-1960s, and in 1970 the Michigan Educational Assessment Program conducted the first state assessment of basic skills to provide achievement information to parents, students and their teachers. Through the 1970s it evaluated its compensatory reading programmes and drew on the work of Edmonds and Brookover. From Edmonds, then working in Michigan, it took his analysis of what contributed to high achievement by schools with substantial minority and low socioeconomic populations. From Brookover it took his analysis based on 'improving' and 'declining' schools and school climate. These and a further survey of the literature resulted in the adoption of a school effectiveness policy encapsulated in the State Board of Education's *School Effectiveness: Eight Variables That Make a Difference*. Faced with the question of how change could best be introduced, the Department 'again turned to research findings to answer this question'. The state therefore combined an effective schools programme with a School Improvement Program, the latter of which drew on a participative model of development, together with emphasis on effectiveness variables and a focus on 'organizational climate assessment and commitment'.[11] The emphasis in Michigan throughout was on identification-plus-improvement, the former being only a step to the latter. The research had identified factors outside and inside the school that were important, and the emphasis on within-school factors meant that educators could be influential: 'the principles can be influenced by educators and should be used to improve the schooling process. All children learn, and educators can improve schools to help them learn even more.'[12] The Department structured its improvement programme to avoid what it considered 'the trap of being prescriptive' into which, in 1982, Lezotte was considered to have fallen, a trap which could engender 'reluctance or resistance on the part of school staffs'.[13] Other states, including Ohio, followed a similar path in collecting data, determining principles, and involving the different levels of partnership in workshop, institute and other activities. Two related leaflets issued by Michigan in 1989 read:

> AN EFFECTIVE SCHOOL: A school that sets both quality and equity goals in teaching for learning and demonstrates with observable and measurable student outcomes that it is achieving both.

> SCHOOL IMPROVEMENT PROCESS: A collaborative process through which staff identifies strengths and weaknesses of the school program and uses that information as a basis for making positive changes in observable and measurable student outcomes.

Ohio's 'Building Leadership Model' in 1983 also accepted that the characteristics of school improvement activities had been well documented: 'what has been missing has been the implementation strategy to move from theory to practice', and the 'building' (or 'school') model was intended to answer the question: 'How do I start?'[14]

South Carolina and Connecticut made direct use of Edmonds's formulation of the effective schools criteria, and particularly his central message. South Carolina issued an *Effective Schools Training: School Improvement Model* statement, listing six indicators of an effective school: instruction leadership by the principal as 'the firm foundation', together with emphasis on 'academics', high expectations, positive school climate, frequent monitoring, and positive home–school relations. It based its training programme on a combination of quality and equity, and for its definition of the latter it turned to Edmonds:

> Ron Edmonds's classic definition of an effective school defines equity: one in which the percentage of low socio-economic status students who master basic skills equals or exceeds the percentage of middle-high socio-economic status students who master basic skills.[15]

For South Carolina the effective schools step proved to be the first in a more comprehensive policy direction. In 1984 it passed an Education Improvement Act, raising the state sales tax by one cent, the proceeds to help elementary and secondary education, and involving a wide range of pre-school, curricular, vocational, remedial, care, teacher incentives and other measures.[16] Connecticut's School Effectiveness Project was explicitly based on the 'pioneering research' of Brookover, Edmonds and Lezotte, and 'reinforced by the evolving research on educational change, organizational excellence, leadership, curriculum and teaching'. Its definition of an effective school was the Edmonds one of 'a school which brings low income children to the mastery level which now describes successful performance for middle income children'. The characteristics of effective schools were seen as: safe and orderly environment, clear school mission, instructional leadership, high expectations, opportunity to learn and student time on task, and frequent monitoring of student progress and home–school relations. The State Board's procedure from 1978 was to commission papers, bring in consultants, design a Connecticut School Effectiveness Program, establish a strong School Effectiveness Unit, and develop an implementation and monitoring pattern that closely followed what impact participating schools had, particularly on children from low-income families.[17]

Throughout the 1980s, therefore, a number of states were adopting and implementing effective schools policies with explicit or implicit reference to their targeting minority and low socioeconomic status populations, on the basis of within-school strategies encompassing all children. Compensatory, Chapter 1, policies remained. Chapter 2 of the 1981 Education Consolidation and Improvement Act (which had replaced the 1965 Elementary and Secondary School Act) was concerned with school development, and at the federal level it was through Chapter 2 that the effective schools developments of the 1970s and 1980s entered national policy-making. By the mid-1980s the United States was in the grip of educational 'reform' fever, in which the failures of America's schools and the imminent disasters of 'a nation at risk' were being probed from many directions. The federal and state governments, educational policy agencies, industrial organizations, *ad hoc* pressure groups and others were demanding, advocating and recommending specific changes in education at all levels. States and school boards selected differently from the diverse reform strategies emanating from political and educational directions, relating to curriculum revision, length of school day or year, teacher professional development, testing procedures, and a variety of others. States imposed requirements on schools or on teacher education. New alliances of schools and states were established in pursuit of particular reform efforts, new proposals for school restructuring or for change of direction were developed and implemented by individual schools or consortia of schools. Within the complexities of this situation the effective schools movement, however, held and gained ground. News of the research and of its adoption by some of the states had been heard in Congress, and devotees there succeeded in including in an Act of Congress in 1988 – the Hawkins–Stafford amendments – a provision to define, support and subsequently fund school improvements that were based on an effective schools formula.

Public Law 100–297 made, in fact, a variety of references to 'school effectiveness', which could be increased 'through effective schools programs to improve student achievement, student behavior, teaching, learning, and school management'. The Act was intended to fund the initiation of programmes that could be taken over by the states and local sources when they had been 'demonstrated to be effective'. Assistance would go to 'innovative programs designed to carry out schoolwide improvements, including the effective schools program'. One section of the Act set out in detail that funds would be available to 'plan, implement, support, evaluate, revise, and strengthen effective schools programs', including various training, technical, community involvement and other relevant activities. The crux, however, was a section which defined the purpose of such programmes as being, at all levels of schooling, those of 'promoting school-level planning, instructional improvement, and staff development . . . increasing the academic achievement levels of all children and particularly educationally deprived children', and achieving as 'ongoing conditions' in schools the factors 'identified through effective schools research as distinguishing effective from ineffective schools'. The factors were:

(A) strong and effective administrative and instructional leadership that creates consensus on instructional goals and organizational capacity for instructional problem solving;

(B) emphasis on the acquisition of basic and higher order skills;

(C) a safe and orderly environment that allows teachers and pupils to focus their energies on academic achievement;

(D) a climate of expectation that virtually all children can learn under appropriate conditions; and

(E) continuous assessment of students and programs to evaluate the effects of instruction.[18]

In 1964–5 committees of the House and Senate had taken an extensive interest not only in expert opinion but also in research, at a particularly active period of policy development. In 1988, against a backcloth of less propitious and less optimistic economic and political circumstances, an Act of Congress was able to base policy on factors which had been 'identified through effective schools research', and to enumerate them almost verbatim in Ronald Edmonds's formulation. Congress authorized the funding to support schools designated to adopt these factors as defining their activities. The National Center for Effective Schools issued a leaflet announcing that the funds would be available during the school year 1989–90, 'for school improvement based on Effective Schools Research. . . . The Augustus F. Hawkins–Robert T. Stafford Legislation (PL 100–297) specifically targets Effective Schools Research as a basis for school improvement and mandates the sequential, collegial process which is used in its implementation.'[19] As with all such legislation from the mid-1960s Congress required evaluation of the programmes, and funds were allocated in fiscal year 1990 for a national study of effective schools. This was intended to examine the extent to which the programme, under Chapter 2 of the Act, 'has encouraged and/or supported the initiation, continuation, and/or improvement of effective schools programs, particularly in schools with high proportions of students from poor families'.[20]

The Act and subsequent funding decisions meant that states were henceforward required to spend not less than 20 per cent of their Chapter 2 funding on effective schools programmes as described in the Act, unless they were already spending double that amount on effective schools or similar programmes. Eight states, including the four described above, qualified for waivers. Rhode Island, for example, was already developing an 'Essential Schools' programme, modelled on a somewhat different set of principles in Ted Sizer's Coalition of Essential Schools run from Brown University. The state was able, however, successfully to present its application for a waiver and for the full Chapter 2 funds on the basis of its existing and planned activities.[21] Augustus Hawkins, who chaired the House of Representatives Committee on Education and Labor, had been active in promoting the inclusion of the effective schools principles in the Act, and his committee commissioned a national study of effective schools programmes. Reporting in 1989, the US General Accounting Office underlined that such programmes were 'school-based programs to improve the academic achievement of all children, regardless of socioeconomic status or ethnicity, and particularly educationally deprived children'. In those schools where at least 75 per cent of children were from low-income families, Chapter 1 (compensatory education) funds could also be used for effective schools work. Using free or reduced-price lunch in schools as an indicator, it was clear that the programmes were serving a mix of children from low- and higher-income families.[22] From its starting point, and notably from Edmonds's attempt to combine effective schools with equity principles, the American effective schools research and movement had successfully penetrated state and federal educational policy, and the focus and formulations of effective schools analysis had in part replaced but had largely supplemented the existing Title I and other compensatory approaches to targeted provision for disadvantaged children.

The model of research contribution to policy as a cumulative one, or as one which helps to change the policy environment, to some extent fits this particular case, if the policy process is taken to include the work of influential school board or state officials, the activities of state Departments of Education, and the routes by which state experience is recognized in the offices, committee rooms and House and Senate debates in Washington, DC. Research does not often, however, ripple in accordance with such a model. That it can do so in the American conditions, at times of rapid economic and political change, when legislators are anxiously looking for solutions is evident from both the mid-1960s and the 1980s examples, though the coalescence of political and research aspirations is brought about by more complex factors than the determined use of either political or research antennae. The effective schools research resonated amidst complex national and international uncertainties, at a time when educational policy-making was especially fragmented and weak, and when the research offered glimpses of confidence. It became a feature not of prominent public debate but of cumulative political and bureaucratic action. It did, however, influence the declared direction of school improvement, itself a factor in the way schools are judged. It also influenced the very way in which opinions about schools were formulated, in terms, for example, of factors, principles, indicators, and in this case a combination of characteristics and capacities. In 1989 the Kentucky Supreme Court declared the whole of the state's school system to be unconstitutional because its financing was not uniform. A previous court decision had listed seven 'capacities' that all students should obtain from education in an 'efficient' school. The Supreme Court agreed, and added nine '"essential and minimum characteristics" that could bring about efficient common schools'. An 'adequate education' was one 'that has as its goal the development of the seven capacities'.[23] The basic vocabularies of analysis and judgement had changed, and the effective schools developments had been one of the contributory factors.

Even in the United States, therefore, the relationship between research and policy has pointed further, in the late twentieth century, towards system-wide considerations in making judgements about schools. The educational basis of the war on poverty and the concern with effective schools characteristics intersected most visibly in Ron Edmonds's 1979 essay on 'Effective schools for the urban poor', and although the policy emphasis of the states and Congress included the equity implications, on the whole educational policy in the 1980s was more directly concerned with issues of efficiency and manpower, standards, curriculum and testing. In the late 1980s, however, for reasons different from those prevalent more than two decades earlier, and without the same repercussions at federal level, poverty began to re-emerge as a motivating issue for educational reform. In this 'rediscovery' there were indicators, coming from a variety of directions, of ways in which poverty-related issues might more firmly enter the policy process than they had done in the 1970s and early 1980s. One such indicator was a document on *Investing in Our Children: Business and the Public Schools*, produced by a working group of the Committee for Economic Development in 1985. Clearly having in mind the labour market needs of the next century, and the need to improve the educational attainment levels of those poor and minority children on whom the manpower supply would increasingly depend, the report spoke in language not unlike that of the 1960s. Extra help had to be directed towards children in need of more resources and attention to prepare them for life in a 'free and open democracy'. The report emphasized the importance of preschool education and adopted as an essential focus the need for 'well-designed preschool programs for children from disadvantaged backgrounds'. It picked up in particular the relevance of the Perry Preschool Project and Head Start, and it called on school districts to 'undertake a serious and systematic investment in enriched early childhood education for children from poor families'.[24] For somewhat different reasons, the business community of 1985 was reiterating the objectives and emphases of two decades earlier.

The following year James Comer at Yale was defending Head Start, Follow Through and other 'war on poverty' programmes as ones that can work. From another perspective Henry Levin, in a 1986 publication of the National Education Association, talked of the failure of recent policies to help the disadvantaged – what was needed was more attention to pre-school and its enrichment possibilities, as well as parent education and involvement. Compensatory education programmes, he suggested, 'are not new to schools, but they are neither as extensive nor as imaginative as they might be in addressing the needs of the disadvantaged'. The title of Levin's publication, *Educational Reform for Disadvantaged Students: An Emerging Crisis*, was itself an indication of the strength with which the 1960s interests had survived and were being reinterpreted.[25] In 1987 Kagan and Zigler were emphasizing that in current conditions pre-school provision should be targeted on low-income, bilingual and handicapped children. There were proven lasting benefits from special programmes for disadvantaged children. In the same year William Julius Wilson published *The Truly Disadvantaged*, arguing that 'disadvantaged' was not synonymous with 'black', and offering an interpretation of an 'underclass' that had not yet been reached by past policies, including those of the war on poverty.[26] The 1988 Hawkins–Stafford amendments addressed not only effective schools but also other policies concerning 'children living in areas with high concentrations of low-income families' and the children from low-income families themselves. The Act, in the words of the counsel to the House Committee on Education and Labor, 'put an end to the retrenchment of federal support for education' that had occurred in the 1980s. It included new measures to monitor and improve the use of Chapter 1 funding for 'educationally disadvantaged children'.[27] In a commission report on youth and young families in the same year, the William T. Grant Foundation related its findings to the fact that the poverty rate had declined from 18.5 per cent in 1959 to 8.8 per cent in 1973, but had then risen in stops and starts to 12.3 per cent in 1983.[28]

A revealing contribution to this reawakening interest in education and poverty was a book in 1989 edited by George Miller, Democratic congressman and chairman of the House Select Committee on Children, Youth and Families. In *Giving Children a Chance* Miller championed Head Start as a programme that worked – but only 18 per cent of eligible children were enrolled. What was needed was 'time, money, and imagination by every community, every organization, every business and every level of government'. Contributors to the volume pointed out how, in the late 1980s, state governors, the press and business had argued for increased attention to early childhood programmes and poverty, had underlined the positive outcomes of the Perry and other such programmes, the crucial importance of involving parents, and – this from James Comer – 'early childhood programs must be at the heart of any effort to reduce poverty in this country'. A group of young business leaders stressed child care and education as a means of breaking the 'cycle of poverty'.[29] Poverty was clearly on the national agenda, though hedged around with policy hesitations and difficulties. A researcher at the US Office of Educational Research and Improvement summarized the position at the beginning of 1989, when all the signs were

> pointing toward a willingness to provide new programs for young
> people identified as disadvantaged or 'at risk'. . . . Momentum to
> improve education for disadvantaged children is gathering.

One difficulty lay in the less precise definitions currently in use than had been the case in the 1960s.[30] The momentum was gathering in fits and starts at other levels. In 1990 the Governor of New York State was attacking narrow 1980s versions of accountability and basic competence, and the Governor of New Jersey reversed previous efforts to promote 'basics' and tests, and focused on the effects of poverty. He moved state aid for education away from wealthy to poor districts, on the grounds that the previous state administration had failed to address 'the underlying cause of the most serious educational ills: poverty'. Previous emphasis on standardized tests had left the poorest inner-city districts untouched.[31]

By the end of 1990 Congress was taking new 'steps against poverty', approving major expansions of Head Start for the following years, as well as improvements in the fields of health insurance and child care. The problems addressed in the 1960s had not gone away, and policy concerns were either resurfacing or being reinvented. Practical efforts and specific, often research-based, recommendations were also receiving publicity. Early intervention and pre-school 'for all children' were being designed to ensure that disadvantaged and 'at risk' children (whether for reasons of poverty, race or developmental difficulties) benefited, and new projects drew directly from the most successful experiences of Head Start, and such long-standing initiatives as the Perry Project.[32] One of the outcomes of the Perry and similar projects, reported in the 1970s and 1980s, was the influence on the new business and economic concern with pre-school programmes, as well as new policy directions and intervention programmes. What the results indicated was that by the age of 19 there were 'lasting beneficial effects of preschool education'

> in improving cognitive performance during early childhood; in
> improving scholastic placement and achievement during the school
> years; in decreasing delinquency and crime, the use of welfare
> assistance, and the incidence of teenage pregnancy; and in increasing

high school graduation rates and the frequency of enrollment in postsecondary programmes and employment.

Pre-school attendance had altered performance on four major variables by nearly a factor of two – for example, the rates of employment and attendance at college or vocational training were 'nearly double for those with preschool as compared with those without preschool', and similar figures applied to teenage pregnancy and the number of years spent in special education classes. Those attending pre-school were also at the age of 19 doing better on tests of functional competence, had had lower high school dropout rates and a lower detention and arrest rate.[33] An increasing literature at the end of the 1980s and in the early 1990s was concerned with parent involvement, improving the delivery of Chapter 1 programmes, raising the sights for the teaching of disadvantaged children, criticizing schools for failing to adapt to known needs, and urging an extension of Head Start and other pre-school programmes to cover an increased percentage, if not all, of eligible children.

While there were also voices of caution about the dangers of exaggerating what schools could achieve, the rediscovery of poverty as a basis for aspects of educational policy coincided with these efforts to promote new or stronger commitments, and with the sense generated by school effectiveness and improvement interests that attention should be focused in a major way on the nature and quality of the within-school process. Concerns about child care and about the roles of schools were also coming together in much-publicized developments. James Comer's work in New Haven, Connecticut, from 1968, was a comprehensive project bringing together school administrators and teachers, parents, and guidance counsellors, mental health and other professionals. The core of Comer's relatively structured approach was for the school to take account of all the factors, home and others, influencing the child's behaviour and learning. The results of the programme in higher attendance, fewer behaviour problems and improved academic performance gained a high profile. The Rockefeller Foundation put $15 million into the scheme and the strategy was eagerly taken up by other school systems (165 schools were using the programme at the beginning of the 1990s). Among the publicity being received at the beginning of the 1990s was a major feature in the *New York Times*, under a front-page headline: 'A New Road to Learning: Teaching the Whole Child'.[34]

Also from Yale, 'The School of the 21st Century' was launched in 1987 by Edward F. Zigler, a veteran of the Head Start programme and first director of the US Office of Child Development. The intention was to use existing school buildings as a focus for implementing good-quality, stable, comprehensive child care, which was seen as being just as important as education. The system consisted of all-day child care for 3–5-year-olds on school premises, before- and after-school and vacation care for children aged 6 to 12, and programmes of family guidance for new parents, support and training for family day-care providers, and informal and referral services: 'child care programs should address the entire range of human development, not only cognitive development, but also physical and social development and mental health'. The General Assembly of the state of Connecticut supported the plan and itself coordinated and funded (initially with a grant of $375,000) a group of nine such centres.[35] Schools, commented Thomas Sobol, Education Commissioner for New York State, 'must take on more of what the family and the community can't provide', acting as a broker for other services and expanding the traditional role of the schools.[36]

The important feature of all of these developments for our discussion here is the renewed focus on the need for schools to adapt in order better to serve children from backgrounds which often placed them at risk in pre-school and school settings. While the effective schools movement, various kinds of restructuring and other reform developments of the 1980s aimed at improving schools for all, some of these other approaches adopted similar aims but took more conscious and direct account of the needs of the children most at risk. Not all drew self-consciously on the legacies of the 1960s; some, like Comer's, had origins in that period but elaborated strategies which also drew on other or newer research, and set new targets. This was also true of the Accelerated Schools strategy, aimed explicitly at disadvantaged and at-risk students, developed by Henry Levin at Stanford. Levin defined the programme as one 'for transforming existing schools that have high concentrations of disadvantaged youngsters. . . . The Accelerated School is a transitional elementary school that is designed to bring disadvantaged children up to grade level by the completion of the sixth grade.' The aim, derived in part explicitly from Comer's work, was to be based on three major assumptions: 'unity of purpose among all of the participants', their 'empowerment', and building on their strengths 'rather than decrying their weaknesses'.[37] Extra resources and effort, and a different set of assumptions, aimed to speed up progress for such students, asking what children should know in order to be academically able, and completely restructuring schools in order to achieve what was intended:

> Restructured schools are characterized by high expectations on the part of teachers, parents, and students; deadlines by which students are expected to meet particular educational requirements; stimulating instructional programs; planning by the educational staff; and the use of all available resources in the community, including parents, senior citizens, and social agencies.

By 1991 some 40 of these schools had been established, and in describing the development Levin cited Edmonds's 1979 essay as a foundation document.[38] Here again, reform of the school reached beyond cognitive or academic targets, important though these were, to wider issues of teacher and community involvement – one of the forms of 'empowerment' that became a prominent concept in the literature of the late 1980s and 1990s.

The imperatives that drove changes in educational policy and school-related research and initiatives were, as we have seen, of various kinds. The panorama of activity in the 1980s included both attempts to understand existing provision and attempts to find methods of 'reform' in a country without a central driving mechanism. The reform movement was one of diverse and invariably impatient ideas, experiment at the level of committed educators, and often hasty and optimistic planning and replanning at the level of states and school districts. The problems of schooling were often portrayed, with more or less accuracy, as acute, relating to drugs, violence and delinquency, with guards patrolling the corridors and schools trying to cope with a breakdown in discipline. Market research, reported annually in the *Phi Delta Kappan*, however, suggested that high proportions of parents were in fact relatively satisfied with their children's schools. Differences between schools and school districts were analysed along the dimensions we have discussed, and many others. New strategies of schooling sought to solve one or more of the salient issues which touched both social dilemmas and school behaviours. Particular prominence was achieved by research findings on differences in performance between public and private, notably Catholic, schools, and the much publicized controversy which followed.

At the centre of the debate was a 1981 research report by Coleman, Hoffer and Kilgore, 'Public and private schools', followed by other publications from Coleman and colleagues, critiques from a large number of directions, and further responses. The Coleman research was based on data collected in High School and Beyond (HSB), a statistical study of nearly 60,000 students in over 1,000 high schools. The 1981 study was an initial draft, and a fuller analysis was contained in *High School Achievement*, published the following year.[39] The analyses conducted by Coleman and his colleagues between 1980 and 1985 produced what they considered to be consistent results, showing that 'Catholic high schools are more effective than public high schools'. One of their conclusions was that Catholic high school attendance was particularly advantageous for black, Hispanic and in general minority and lower socioeconomic status students.[40] They concluded that in a variety of ways and for a variety of reasons the Catholic school sector was outperforming the public school sector with all of its students, and in almost all subject areas (science was an exception). The results showed that there was 'greater discipline, greater academic demands, and greater achievement in the private schools'.[41] Since the research appeared at a time when the question of public funding for Catholic schools was being debated, the findings had obvious policy implications.

The research methodology, contested even more strongly than Coleman's 1966 report *Equality of Educational Opportunity*, is not our direct concern here. More important are the grounds on which explanations were sought both by the Coleman team and by the critics, and the questions raised by the controversy for making judgements about sectors of schooling and individual schools. The Coleman researchers explained the success of the Catholic schools by the fact that they were more demanding (including by requiring more homework), and benefited from more supportive family backgrounds. Over the previous 20 or so years there had been a weakening of 'the consensus among parents about maintaining authority and responsibility for their adolescent children's activities', a trend which had affected the public more than the private schools. This had in general 'reduced the effectiveness' of secondary education in the United States. The schools were most effective where they were based on 'value communities', which provided a consensus of values or interests on which schools could operate. In the private sector these included free schools, basic-education schools, conservative Christian schools, Nation of Islam schools, and Jewish schools. In the public sector they included magnet schools, where there were shared interests, parent–school contracts, and agreed values. The Catholic schools similarly had strong shared values, and the greater authority of parents over their children was one of the contributors to the greater achievements of these schools, and the improvement of their status over recent decades.[42] Catholic schools, for reasons such as this, were able to make greater demands on their students, and they were unsuccessful in science precisely because this was the one area in which they did not make greater coursework demands than the public schools.[43]

Many commentators found the basic findings of the Coleman research to be flawed, with particular emphasis placed by most of them on the failure of the methodology adequately to deal with differences in the competence and attainment of students before entering the two sectors of schooling. Coleman had, indeed, looked carefully at racial, ethnic and socioeconomic factors affecting entry to the two sectors, but the critics did not believe that this had gone far enough. Noell, in 1982, argued that if four other variables – sex, handicap status, region of residence, and early college expectations – were taken into account, the 'superior achievement of Catholic school pupils is not confirmed', and broadly speaking Catholic school pupils did no better or worse than those in the public schools.[44] What Noell and others were underlining was the likelihood that the student population of the Catholic schools was self-selected on the basis of pre-high-school attainment. The Coleman research, suggested Alexander and Pallas in 1983, had not dealt satisfactorily with 'the issue of selection biases arising from differences in the mix of students attending schools in the public and private sectors':

> Probably the single greatest burden of school effects research is to distinguish convincingly between outcome differences that reflect simple differences in the kinds of students who attend various schools from differences that are attributable to something about the schools themselves. . . . Put simply, when good students go to good schools, how are we to know which is responsible for the good performance that is likely to be observed?

Coleman, Hoffer and Kilgore had allowed for differences involving social, race and ethnicity background, but neglected differences 'in competency or achievement levels that predate high school'. Their finding that students in the private sector scored 'modestly better on standardized tests than students in the public sector . . . is equivocal'. The socioeconomic controls in the research did not allow for such initial differences. Two years later Alexander and Pallas pointed out that the original research had not had available 'measures of test performance' before students entered high school, and so the researchers did not know whether the Catholic schools were simply enrolling better students in the first place. What was surprising, given the advantages of the Catholic schools, was that they did not outpace the public schools by a greater margin.[45] Willms similarly deduced that the better performance of the Catholic schools was a result of 'differential selection . . . students who have higher initial ability, are better disciplined, and come from families that have higher expectations and provide considerable encouragement and support'.[46] He calculated differences between the schools, not just the sectors, and found that the best and the worst schools were found in the public sector. For the average child there was no 'pervasive private schooling effect'.[47] He found the same lack of any 'pervasive Catholic-school effect on academic achievement' when he re-examined the curriculum-specific data.[48]

What these commentators generally found was that the Coleman findings were unproven, uncertain or misleading, and they warned against using the findings as a basis for policy changes that would channel public funds into the private schools, or indeed as a basis for any policy decisions at all.[49] What is important here is the way in which the controversy over the public and private schools focused attention from another direction on what constituted school effectiveness and how it could be accounted for, including the Coleman team's own search for explanations. These reached out into family values, the changed status of the adolescent, the expectations of the students and the schools, and the nature of the demands placed on the students. The critics argued with the methodology and the findings, focusing particularly on the difficulty of separating effects due to the school from those due to the prior experience and attainment levels of students, as well as on reliance on broad correlations between racial and socioeconomic groups on the one hand and sectors of schooling on the other. Questions to be asked about good outcomes included whether they resulted from 'good students going to good schools', and whether a comparison of schools produced the same messages as a comparison of sectors. The analysis of the HSB data had produced evidence of what one summary described as 'small, systematic differences', and evidence tracing the differences to such matters as patterns of course-taking, 'tracking', discipline and amount of homework. The Coleman findings had been obtained by examining differences between the public and Catholic sectors, but they also 'have application at the level of schools, classrooms, and individual students'.[50] When, as amidst the complexities of the 1980s, research fed so directly into controversy, its ability to influence policy or choice depended increasingly on the power to be heard. Research findings such as those of the Coleman Report *Public and Private Schools* in the United States, or those of Bennett's *Teaching Styles and Pupil Progress* in Britain received wide and selective publicity and left important public signals behind. Critique and controversy, cautions and warnings, in the *Harvard Educational Review* or *Sociology of Education* would not be easily heard outside the academic community.

From the late 1980s notions of school reform on the grand scale moved in two opposite directions: towards weakening the commitment to public education as it had been known, and towards strengthening it. A comprehensive argument for judging public schools as inevitably inadequate in their existing framework came in 1990 in *Politics, Markets and America's Schools*, an important book by Chubb and Moe. Their work, based at the Brookings Institution, had its preliminary airing in 1986 and 1987, when they dismissed research on within-schools factors to enhance effectiveness, as well as state and local policy-making based on such factors. Well intentioned though these were, they would not work:

> We believe that schools are largely products of their environments
> and that the fundamental determinants of school effectiveness are to
> be found in the larger setting or system in which schools operate.
> Weak leadership, principal–teacher conflict, and other problems do
> not plague our public schools through inadvertence or
> misunderstanding or because the people involved are not highly
> trained or motivated. In most cases no one is really at fault – the fault
> lies with the system. Until educational reforms move beyond a narrow
> focus on schools *per se*, they are doomed to the treatment of
> symptoms rather than causes.[51]

This was not an appeal for 1960s-style interventionist policy-making, but in fact the reverse. Good schools were autonomous schools. There was a great deal to be learned from the record of the private schools. Devolved school-based management and other tinkering with the system still did not leave schools and teachers as free as those in private schools to create their own ethos and work as a team free of bureaucratic controls. The problem as Chubb and Moe defined it was, paradoxically, the 'direct democratic control of the schools', which could not succeed in effecting reform, since it was reform from the top, attempting to impose change. Freedom for schools was the freedom of the market-place, a benign and partially directed market. Existing controls were extensive and stultifying:

> mechanisms for approval and veto, rules for budgeting and accounting, and annual performance reports – in which the school provides a compendium of data on its activities, staff, student test scores, parent and staff satisfaction, and future plans – authorities at the district and state level hold school decisionmakers accountable for the school's choices and performance.

School-based management, for example, might improve the position somewhat, but such reforms did not result in institutional change and improved student achievement as fundamental as its advocates intended, since they left 'the traditional institutions of democratic control intact. The schools remain subordinate in a democratic hierarchy.' The answer was to *eliminate* democratic public control of the schools and transfer authority to schools, parents and students. Schools would become free

> to govern themselves as they want, specify their own goals and programs and methods, design their organizations, select their own student bodies, and make their own personnel decisions. Parents and students would be legally empowered to choose among alternative schools, aided by institutions designed to promote active involvement, well-informed decisions, and fair treatment.[52]

Catholic schools, Chubb wrote, were less subject to demands from outside authorities than were the public schools, with the result that by comparison with a public school counterpart the private school principal was better able to create a team with shared values and skills and a willingness to work together. Private schools therefore provided a model of what the school effectiveness and improvement research aimed to achieve. Their team qualities – 'strong leadership, shared goals, cooperative decision making, collegial relationships, mutual trust, widespread efficacy' – were precisely those identified by school improvement research as essential for student achievement.[53] Working with the same HSB data as Coleman and his colleagues, Chubb and Moe moved more determinedly in the direction of decoupling schools from public scrutiny. Their argument was listened to by British Conservative policy-makers looking for ways of reducing the power of local education authorities over the schools (though not, as it turned out, that of central government).

A kind of war to influence the 'system' of American schooling was taking place. Judgements of schools were concerned not only with 'effects' but also with the providers most likely to produce different versions of them. Schools, their aims, their curricula and organization, the roles of teachers, support staff, parents and administrators were all subjects of the galaxy of reports on education that appeared mainly in 1983 and soon after.[54] Reviews of the implementation of school improvement policies by individual states followed, as did case studies of individual schools. One study, by the Education Commission of the States, monitored 'state strategies to support local school improvement', focusing especially on the nature of effective school improvement strategies at the state level, and the conditions under which state-level strategies worked effectively in schools. Case studies of 40 schools in ten states in 1983–5 looked at factors relating to implementation – the state environment, the local environment, the school improvement programme as the state intended it to operate, the programme as it actually operated, and programme outcomes. The study took account of conditions at the state level, both within and outside Departments of Education, and included the kinds of activity we have seen developed in Ohio, Connecticut and other states in support of school effectiveness and improvement programmes. It was concluded that when these varieties of supportive environment existed, 'school improvement efforts had the greatest chance of success. Fortunately, nearly all these conditions are within the control of state and local education leaders.'[55]

Reform efforts included not only the kinds of effective, essential, accelerated or other strategies for networking and developing schools generally or for specific school populations, but also changes targeted on specific aspects of school behaviour and organization. Comer's School Development Program was concerned with 'school-based management teams' which paralleled 'quality circles' developing in Japanese and American manufacturing industry, focusing on 'child development and learning, utilizing management, child development concepts, and support staff to make this focus possible'.[56] The more 'focused' a kind of school the more its advocates believed it likely to be in terms of student motivation and achievement, as we have seen in the case of Catholic and other schools, and as was considered to be the case with magnet schools, which provided specialized vocational or academic programmes.[57] School 'restructuring', which could mean many things, was widely addressed in terms of the empowerment of teachers, devolution of aspects of decision-making to the schools, new approaches to planning and operation at the school level.This would ideally produce what Linda Darling-Hammond, co-director of the National Center for Restructuring Education, called 'a new model of school reform' that would seek to develop 'communities of learning grounded in communities of democratic discourse . . . an education for empowerment and an education for freedom'.[58] New and intense debates and district- or state-wide decisions ranged over all the possible means of raising national standards – assessment, curriculum, length of school day or year, requirements for college entry or teacher certification. These were models of reform, modest or ambitious, which pointed to the regeneration of the public schools as 'communities of democratic discourse', though not on the basis of taking the schools out of public democratic control.

This climate of competing practicalities and panaceas for school reform led in 1989–91 to a climacteric in federal efforts to set targets which would, in President Bush's words, 'make existing schools better and more accountable'.[59] The debate

123

about what is and what ought to be assumed the grand scale in September 1989 when state governors joined the President in Charlottesville, Virginia, for an 'education summit', and agreed to 'establish a process for setting national education goals' and for promoting the means of attaining them.[60] The following year the President and governors adopted six 'National Education Goals':

By the year 2000:

1 All children in America will start school ready to learn.

2 The high school graduation rate will increase to at least 90 percent.

3 American students will leave grades four, eight, and twelve having demonstrated competency in challenging subject matter including English, mathematics, science, history and geography; and every school in America will ensure that all students learn to use their minds well, so they may be prepared for responsible citizenship, further learning, and productive employment in our modern economy.

4 U.S. students will be first in the world in science and mathematics achievement.

5 Every adult American will be literate and will possess the knowledge and skills necessary to compete in a global economy and exercise the rights and responsibilities of citizenship.

6 Every school in America will be free of drugs and violence and will offer a disciplined environment conducive to learning.[61]

In 1991 President Bush announced the publication of *America 2000: An Education Strategy*, aimed at moving towards the six goals, including the establishment of at least 535 'New Generation of American Schools' to set the pattern for achieving 'world class standards'. The 1989 statement had acknowledged common features of some of the successful 'restructuring efforts' already taking place – including an emphasis on school accountability for results not compliance with regulations, decentralization of authority and decision-making to the schools, a rigorous programme of instruction, a professional environment for teachers and active parent and business involvement.[62] *America 2000* also acknowledged the initiatives taken by Sizer's Coalition of Essential Schools, Comer's School Development Program, Levin's Accelerated Schools and others. Traditional assumptions were to be set aside, the mould was to be broken, and the New American Schools were expected 'to produce extraordinary gains in student learning'.[63] Intentions, of course, were not the same as outcomes. Start-up funds for the 535-plus New American Schools were rejected by Congress, the level of private funding necessary to develop the whole programme failed to materialize, and a New American Schools Development Corporation set up to promote the scheme funded 11 initial projects in 1992, instead of the planned 20–30.[64] The much publicized 'reinvention' of America's schools received some applause and as much hostility. Harold Howe II, for example, condemned *America 2000*'s failure to recognize diversity and poverty, as well as the maldistribution of revenues across the states:

How could a serious group of policy makers looking broadly at the problem of inadequate schooling have ignored this issue? Weren't they aware that both Kentucky and Texas have had their systems of school finance declared unconstitutional by their state supreme courts or that some 23 other states have similar cases pending?[65]

The importance of the targets and plans elaborated in *America 2000* and related activities lies in the basic judgements being made about the system, and the elements of what at this level of policy-making were considered to be the features of 'better schools'. In the United States, as in Britain and other industrialized countries, amid the continuing economic and social difficulties of the late 1980s and early 1990s criticism of the schools' performance went together with hasty redefinitions of the purposes of schooling and a search for 'national' solutions. Diverse views of the future reflected views of what schools were for and what they ought to be. Judgements of schools were caught up in the warfare, some of it on the grand scale, over the nature of standards and their relationship to political and economic aims and anxieties.

Within the warfare the research-based reform efforts were delivering mixed messages. The positive references to restructuring in *America 2000* bypassed the controversy and often agony that accompanied the reforms encompassed by the concept,[66] and did not go as far as the more radical proposals offered by Chubb and Moe. Researchers were reporting the progress or 'success' of schools based on effective schools principles, for example in Louisiana.[67] A study between 1986 and 1990 of eight schools in the Coalition of Essential Schools found weaknesses, difficulties, a lack of consensus and in some cases deepening divisions between teachers. Change was political, and even where

> the rhetoric of an organization suggests that everyone can benefit from school reform, we observed that efforts to create change in specific settings simultaneously created a sense that some people benefit while others were disadvantaged . . . even when there seems to be consensus that change is needed and even when dedicated and well-intentioned people are trying to bring it about, issues and problems – often unanticipated – arise that threaten and impede the change process almost from its inception.[68]

Projects foundered on a lack of sustained will or resources, changes in administrative or teaching personnel, or contradictory messages about 'what works' or what might receive state or federal funding. New attempts to create private and profit-making schools or to bring the public schools more firmly into the market-place were taking shape. Competition for a hearing, for funds and for credibility had moved with the policy clamour into the 1990s. The election of a Democratic President in 1992 brought new policy personnel and ideas to Washington, and an intention to bring the multiple existing strands of educational policy into a new shape. Priorities were being re-examined, and though the realities of the classroom and the school had not changed, the frameworks of judgement and planning were set to change. Other continuing realities should not be forgotten – for example the criteria of churches and communities, the expectations of students and parents. One reminder comes from a seven-year study conducted by SchoolMatch, a private firm in Columbus, Ohio, that helps parents choose schools and school systems for their children:

> Few parents want their child in the most academically rigorous school or the one with the highest test scores. Parents want their children in an environment that allows the children to excel and develop confidence in their abilities. . . . It is more important to parents that their children are successful than that the school earns the highest marks. It is a myth that we can simply look to the schools with the highest test scores as the best for families.

The best environment was one where schools and classes were small enough for the talents of individual children to be recognized.[69] The old criteria of what was meant by children excelling or being successful might be modified, but did not disappear in the new frameworks.

This outline of the competition of ideas and reforms in the United States in the 1980s and 1990s traces some of the threads of policy, implementation and ideal. American educational research and debate, more than those of any other country, are a kaleidoscope of alternative interpretations and futures. Embedded in American views of the next reform or the next decade or century are clear messages about the present. As much as does the direct critique of current problems and failures, they explain the prevailing or changing frameworks of judgement. The kaleidoscope contains fragments of parents' support and fears; contending claims of the public and the private; employers' dilemmas, present and anticipated; controversies of researchers and their critics; and increasingly the voices of policy and public opinion demanding 'better' and more, and in some cases less, accountable schools – accountable for their 'standards' and for service to the nation's acute economic and social needs. It is a case study of schools, and judgements of schools, not just as part of twentieth-century pluralisms, but also as part of changes in the power to influence judgement and direction. The same was true, in response to similar dilemmas, in a very different environment and with even more discernible shifts of power and direction, in the Britain of the 1980s and 1990s.

NOTES

1 See discussion of 'atomistic' and 'relational' approaches to research in Andrew McPherson and J. Douglas Willms (1986). 'Certification, class conflict, religion, and community: a socio-historical explanation of the effectiveness of contemporary schools', *Research in Sociology of Education and Socialization*, **6**.

2 James Q. Wilson (1981). ' "Policy intellectuals" and public policy', *The Public Interest*, **64**, 41.

3 Lee J. Cronbach and Patrick Suppes (eds) (1969). *Research for Tomorrow's Schools: Disciplined Enquiry for Education*. New York: Macmillan, pp. 19–21; David Donnison (1972). 'Research for policy', *Minerva*, **10** (4), 520; Maurice Kogan *et al.* (1980). *Government's Commissioning of Research: A Case Study*. Uxbridge: Brunel University Department of Government, p. 10.

4 Including in Canada; see Peter Coleman (1977). 'Policy research and educational policy formation: a case study'. Calgary, Alberta, mimeo; Edward A. Holdaway (1982). 'The relationship between research in education and policy formation', University of Melbourne, Centre for the Study of Higher Education, mimeo; E. A. Holdaway (1983). 'Educational policy and education research', *Education Canada*, Winter.

5 David K. Cohen and Michael S. Garet (1975). 'Reforming educational policy with applied social research', *Harvard Educational Review*, **45** (1); Jerome Bruner (1975). 'The role of the researcher as an adviser to the educational policy maker', *Oxford Review of Education*, **1** (3), 187–8; Nathan Caplan *et al.* (1975). *The Use of Social Science Knowledge in Policy Decisions at the National Level*, Ann Arbor: University of Michigan, Institution for Social Research.

6 James Allen Smith (1991). *The Idea Brokers: Think Tanks and the Rise of the New Policy Elite*. New York: Free Press (the quotation is from p. 223).

7 Cf. Janet Finch (1986). *Research and Policy: The Use of Qualitative Methods in Social and Educational Research*. London: Falmer, for a discussion of the British 'research tradition'.

8 Gilbert A. Austin (1979). 'Exemplary schools and the search for effectiveness', *Educational Leadership*, **37** (1), 12.

9 Ohio Department of Education (1981). *Effective Schools Process* (trifold). Columbus, Ohio; Hazel P. Flowers and James P. Jilek (n.d.). '*An Academic Model for Instructionally Effective Schools*'. Columbus: Ohio Department of Education, mimeo.

10 Private communication, Chief of Executive Schools Section, Division of Equal Opportunities, Ohio Department of Education, June 1990.

11 Michigan Department of Education (1980). *All Children Can Learn: Schools Do Make a Difference* (trifold). Lansing; Michigan State Board of Education (n.d.). *School Effectiveness: Eight Variables That Make a Difference*. Lansing: Michigan Department of Education (n.d.). 'Effective schools research: Michigan's approach', internal memo.

12 Michigan Department of Education, *All Children Can Learn*, p. 1.

13 Michigan Department of Education (1982). 'The Michigan School Improvement Program: a description of a structured approach for school improvement', mimeo, p. 4.

14 Ohio Department of Education, Division of Equal Educational Opportunities (1983). *Ohio Building Leadership Model* (trifold). Columbus.

15 South Carolina Department of Education (n.d.). *Effective Schools Training* (trifold). Columbia.

16 South Carolina Department of Education, Division of Public Accountability (1990). *South Carolina Education Act 1984, as Amended*. Columbia; South Carolina State Department of Education (1989). *What Is the Penny Buying for South Carolina?* Columbia.

17 Connecticut State Board of Education, School Effectiveness Unit (1989). 'A guide to the Connecticut School Effectiveness Project'. Hartford, mimeo; Connecticut Department of Education (1984). 'An evaluation of school effectiveness programs in Connecticut: technical report', mimeo; Connecticut Department of Education, School Effectiveness Unit (1989). 'The School Effectiveness Report: history, current status, future directions', mimeo.

18 Public Law 100–297 (1988), Ch. 2, Secs 1501, 1531, 1541, 1542.

19 National Center for Effective Schools (1988). *Special Notice: Funding for School Improvement Based on Effective Schools Research*. Madison.

20 US Department of Education, Office of Planning, Budget and Evaluation (1988), internal memo stating Ch. 2 grants for 1990; Department of Education, Applications Control Center (1990). 'Effective schools programs under Chapter II', Attachment A, mimeo, 31 May.

21 Rhode Island Department of Elementary and Secondary Education (1989). 'Application: Chapter 2, federal, state and local partnership for educational improvement'. Providence, mimeo; interview, Chris O'Neil, Executive Assistant to the Commissioner, responsible for the Essential Schools Program.

22 US General Accounting Office (1989). *Effective Schools Programs: Their Extent and Characteristics.* Washington, DC, pp. 10, 15–16, 27.

23 Quoted in Chris Pipho (1989). 'Entire Kentucky education system unconstitutional', *Phi Delta Kappan*, **71** (1), 6–7.

24 Committee for Economic Development (1985). *Investing In Our Children: Business and the Public Schools.* New York, pp. 9, 22–3, 43–6.

25 James Comer (1986). 'Education for community'. In Alvin L. Schorr (ed.), *Common Decency: Domestic Politics after Reagan.* New Haven, Conn.: Yale University Press, p. 200; Henry M. Levin (1986). *Educational Reform for Disadvantaged Students: An Emerging Crisis.* West Haven, Conn.: National Education Association, pp. 21–5.

26 Sharon Kagan and Edward F. Zigler (1987). *Early Schooling: The National Debate.* New Haven, Conn.: Yale University Press, pp. 31–3, 100; William Julius Wilson (1987). *The Truly Disadvantaged: The Inner City, the Underclass, and Public Policy.* Chicago: Chicago University Press.

27 Public Law 100–297, Section 1512 (b) (2) (A); John F. Jennings (1988). 'Working in mysterious ways: the federal government and education', *Phi Delta Kappan*, **70** (1), 63.

28 William T. Grant Foundation Commission on Work, Family and Citizenship (1988). *The Forgotten Half: Pathways to Success for America's Youth and Young Families.* Washington, DC, p. 20.

29 George Miller (ed.) (1989). *Giving Children a Chance: The Case for More Effective National Policies.* Washington, DC: Center for National Policy Press (Miller, Introduction, pp. x–xiv; Bernice Weissbourd and Carol Emig, 'Early childhood programs for children in poverty: a good place to start', pp. 1–10; James Garbarino, 'Early intervention in cognitive development as a strategy for reducing poverty', p. 35; Appendix, 'Investing in prevention: tomorrow's leaders and the problem of poverty', p. 204).

30 John Ralph (1989). 'Improving education for the disadvantaged: do we know whom to help?', *Phi Delta Kappan*, **70** (5).

31 Diane Hofkins (1989). 'Shared concern on inner-city failure', *Times Educational Supplement*, 9 March, 9 (reporting Governor Sobol of New York State); Peter Kerr (1990). 'Florio shifts policy from school testing to more aid to poor', *New York Times*, 14 May, A1, B3.

32 For example, Nancy A. Madden (1991). 'Success for *all*', *Phi Delta Kappan*, **72** (8); Harry Carthum and Paula Akerlund (1991). 'Meeting the future: the Aberdeen Preschool Project', *Phi Delta Kappan*, **72** (9).

33 John R. Berrueta-Clement (1984). *Changed Lives: The Effects of the Perry Preschool Program on Youths through Age 19.* Ypsilanti: High/Scope Press, p. 1.

34 *New York Times* (1990). 'A new road to learning: teaching the whole child', 13 June, A1, B7; Caroline St John-Brooks (1992). 'How to work a miracle', *Times Educational Supplement*, 23 October, 14.

35 Yale Bush Center in Child Development and Social Policy (n.d.). *The School of the 21st Century* (trifold). New Haven; *Hartford Courant* (1991). 'For families, a fun place to learn', 16 October, 2; Edward F. Zigler and Matia Finn-Stevenson (1989). 'Child care in America: from problem to solution', *Educational Policy*, **3** (4).

36 Reported in Hofkins, 'Shared concern on inner-city failure', p. 9.

37 Henry M. Levin (1988). *Accelerating Elementary Education for Disadvantaged Students.* Stanford, Calif.: Center for Educational Research, pp. 11–12.

38 Henry M. Levin (1991). 'Educational acceleration for at-risk students'. In Aletha C. Huston (ed.), *Children in Poverty: Child Development and Public Policy.* Cambridge: Cambridge University Press, pp. 225–6.

39 James S. Coleman, Thomas Hoffer and Sally Kilgore (1982). *High School Achievement.* New York: Basic Books.

40 Thomas Hoffer, Andrew M. Greely and James S. Coleman (1985). 'Achievement growth in public and Catholic schools', *Sociology of Education,* **58** (2), 74.

41 James Coleman, Thomas Hoffer and Sally Kilgore (1981). 'Questions and answers: our response', *Harvard Educational Review,* **51** (4), 545. (This was a special issue on 'Report analysis: public and private schools'.)

42 Ibid., pp. 544–5.

43 Hoffer *et al.* (1985), pp. 96–7.

44 Jay Noell (1982). 'Public and Catholic schools: a reanalysis of *Public and Private Schools*', *Sociology of Education,* **55** (2/3), 131–2.

45 Karl L. Alexander and Aaron M. Pallas (1983). 'Private schools and public policy: new evidence on cognitive achievement in public and private schools', *Sociology of Education,* **56** (4), 170–1; Karl L. Alexander and Aaron M. Pallas (1985). 'School sector and cognitive performance: when is a little a little?', *Sociology of Education,* **58** (2), 115.

46 Doug Willms (1982). 'Is there a private school advantage? Measuring differences in student achievement', Stanford, Calif.: Institute for Research on Educational Finance and Governance *Policy Perspectives,* 1–2.

47 J. Douglas Willms (1984). 'School effectiveness within the public and private sectors: an evaluation', *Evaluation Review,* **8** (1), 132–3.

48 J. Douglas Willms (1985). 'Catholic school effects on academic achievement: new evidence from the High School and Beyond follow-up study', *Sociology of Education,* **58** (2), 112.

49 For example Alexander and Pallas (1983), p. 178; Willms (1985), p. 113.

50 Edward H. Haertel (1985). *Academic Achievement in Public and Catholic Schools: What Do the Analyses Mean?* Stanford, Calif.: Institute for Research on Educational Finance and Governance *Policy Perspectives,* 8.

51 John E. Chubb and Terry M. Moe (1987). 'No school is an island: politics, markets and education'. In W. L. Boyd and C. T. Kerchner (eds), *The Politics of Excellence and Choice in Education* (special issue of *Journal of Education Policy,* **2** [5]), 131.

52 John E. Chubb and Terry M. Moe (1990). *Politics, Markets and America's Schools.* Washington, DC: Brookings Institution, pp. 199–200, 221, 226.

53 John E. Chubb (1988). 'Effective schools and the problems of the poor'. In Denis P. Doyle and Bruce S. Cooper (eds), *Federal Aid to the Disadvantaged: What Future for Chapter 1?* London: Falmer Press, pp. 252–7.

54 For a review of these reports see Barbara Z. Presseisen (1985). *Unlearned Lessons: Current and Past Reforms for School Improvement.* London, Falmer Press, Part II.

55 Beverly Anderson and Allan Oddin (1986). 'State initiatives can foster school improvements', *Phi Delta Kappan,* **67** (8), 578–81. For examples of case studies cf. Eleanor Farrar and Patricia Flakus-Mosqueda (1986). 'State-sponsored schoolwide improvement programs: what's going on in the schools?', *Phi Delta Kappan,* **67** (8), 586–9.

56 Comer, 'Education for community', pp. 203–6.

57 Anthony Green (1988). 'The power of magnets', *Times Educational Supplement*, 6 May, 23; Hilary Wince (1990). 'Top marks for mission schools', *Independent*, 6 December, 21.

58 Linda Darling-Hammond (1993). 'Reframing the school reform agenda', *Phi Delta Kappan*, **74** (10), 761.

59 George Bush (1991). 'Remarks by the President announcing America 2000'. In US Department of Education, *America 2000: An Education Strategy*. Washington, DC, p. 49.

60 US Department of Education (1991). *America 2000: An Education Strategy. Sourcebook*. Washington, DC, p. 73.

61 US Department of Education, *America 2000*, p. 3.

62 US Department of Education, *America 2000. . . Sourcebook*, pp. 78–9.

63 US Department of Education, *America 2000*, pp. 19–21.

64 James A. Mecklenburger (1992). 'The braking of the "break-the-mold" express', *Phi Delta Kappan*, **74** (4), 2–4.

65 Harold Howe II (1991). 'America 2000: a bumpy ride on four trains', *Phi Delta Kappan*, **73** (3), 200; Harold Howe 11 (1991). 'Seven large questions for *America 2000*'s authors'. In William T. Grant Foundation and the Institute for Educational Leadership, *Voices from the Field*. Washington, DC, p. 26. ('The Bush administration strategy to "reinvent" America's schools' is part of the subtitle of this publication.)

66 For the long reform attempts to restructure the public schools of Chicago, for example, see G. Alfred Hess, Jr (1991). *School Restructuring, Chicago Style*. Newbury Park, Calif.: Corwin Press.

67 For example, Sam Stringfield and Charles Teddlie (1990). 'School improvement efforts: qualitative and quantitative data from four naturally occurring experiments in phases III and IV of the Louisiana School Effectiveness Study', *School Effectiveness and Improvement*, **1** (2).

68 Donna E. Muncey and Patrick J. McQuillan (1993). 'Preliminary findings from a five-year study of the Coalition of Essential Schools', *Phi Delta Kappan*, **74** (6), 486–9.

69 Quoted in Evans Clinchy (1993). 'Needed: a Clinton crusade for quality and equality', *Phi Delta Kappan*, **74** (8), 608.

Chapter 8

Government, Market and Frameworks of Judgement

It is as difficult to generalize about policy-making internationally and over time as it is to generalize about the 'standards' of schooling. The effective schools research in the United States reached into diverse and influential centres of policy-making which left research and policy to compete within states and localities. The effective schools research therefore competed for influence on the pattern and quality of schooling at the same time as the directions of politics and national priorities themselves changed. In Britain the effective schools research did not reach into the sources of policy energy, unable to compete at a time when such energy was increasingly being controlled by central government.

Conservative educational policy in the 1980s and 1990s was aimed at developing national structures and procedures which would change the control and content of schooling and simplify judgements about schools. Although the vocabulary of the dominant policies included that of 'better schools', what was at stake was in fact the reconstruction of the system to produce schools that would be judged by their responses to a more market-oriented context. The intentions were not unlike those of American policy-making at the end of the 1980s, but the structures and strategies were different. If certain prescribed information about individual schools was made public, Conservative ministers believed, judgements in comparison with other schools could more easily be made, and schools could then become more amenable to parental choice. The vocabulary of 'good' or 'effective' became almost irrelevant, except in relation to simple, comparative data. The purposes of a school under such policies were to be defined in market-oriented and market-responsive terms, and schools were to be 'successful' by publicly defined criteria and publicly established data.

The market-place, however, was never pure. The 1980s policies did move state education into Local Management of Schools, with devolved budgets, setting the stage for competition amongst schools. The information available about individual schools was widened to include the publication of examination results (in the case of secondary schools) and of inspection reports. Parental choice was embodied in legislation. The more open the market was to be, however, the stronger were the symbols of its establishment by central government – the 1988 Education Reform Act, strongly worded White Papers, a new breed of government-sponsored schools known as City Technology Colleges, ministerial decisions, Department of Education and Science (later Department for Education) regulations. One view of Edwin Chadwick's pioneering efforts for sanitary reform in the first half of the nineteenth century was that his efforts seemed to spring from 'a desire to wash the people of England all over, every day, by administrative order'.[1] The paradox of Conservative policy in the 1980s and 1990s was that it sprang partly from a desire to free the schools from existing (especially local authority) controls, and partly from a desire to 'wash the children of England all over' with market-driven forms of education, established 'by administrative order'.

The path chosen for Conservative education policy from the early 1980s meant that in practice, whatever the market intentions, alternative approaches to the analysis and improvement of schools could not penetrate to the centre. The British parallel to the nationwide American debates about competing programmes for educational reform and restructuring was an intensification of central decision-making. In some respects the position in Britain was more like that in those American states which opted for strong requirements of their publicly provided schools. Individual states had objectives relating to school improvement, parental choice, school-based budgeting, economic renewal, racial equality and opportunity. The British national policies stemmed from similar economic anxieties and financial constraints, but were more encased in tighter ideological, if sometimes contradictory, frameworks. The new Conservatism wanted a free market, yet it imposed a National Curriculum based on a government-selected pattern, with associated plans for national testing. It wanted schools freed from local authority control, but strengthened the roles of central government itself in creating and sustaining City Technology Colleges, technical and vocational education, relations between schools and industry, and perspectives of enterprise. Judgements about schools became more and more dependent on centrally determined criteria, and on types of data promoted and sanctioned by government.

The essential change in the policy-making that affected judgements about the aims and performance of schools in the public sector was the move away from concentration on the social contexts of schooling towards a focus on their economic accountability. The former had taken two forms in the period after the Second World War and up to the late 1970s. The first was the movement for the comprehensive reorganization of secondary schools, which saw the comprehensive school as a contribution towards greater social fairness and equality. The second was the emphasis placed by the Plowden Committee on primary schools in 1967, and by the 'educational priority area' policy which followed, on the importance of placing schools within area-focused strategies for urban improvement and the fight against disadvantage and poverty. At the heart of the social or sociological approach to judgements about schooling in the 1960s was an attempt to find ways that might, to use the American vocabulary, 'compensate' for a variety of disadvantages. For the Newsom report in 1963, *Half Our Future*, the constituency under scrutiny was 'pupils aged 13 to 16 of average and less than average ability', five out of six of whom 'are likely to be children of manual workers skilled, or unskilled', and reaching this age group from poverty-stricken social and educational environments. It was easy enough to establish general educational objectives, suggested the committee, but it was less easy to provide a school experience that took account of the particular talents, experience and expectations of these pupils. 'Human justice' and national 'economic self-interest' coincided to require more help for the pupils and the schools concerned.[2]

The Plowden Report, four years later, considered how to balance the need to develop what it considered to be 'good' or 'quality' primary schools with the needs of children in deprived neighbourhoods. The committee placed the more than

20,000 primary schools in England in nine categories, ranging from Category 1, 'in most respects a school of outstanding quality' (109 schools) and Category 2, 'a good school with some outstanding features' (1,538 schools), through to Category 9, 'a bad school where children suffer from laziness, indifference, gross incompetence or unkindness on the part of the staff' (28 schools). Category 6, 'a decent school', contained the largest group, 6,058 schools. The judgements were made partly on the basis of the committee's own visits, but mainly on a survey conducted by HM Inspectors, and related to such factors as atmosphere and relationships, curriculum, children's progress, and 'awareness of current thinking on children's educational needs'. While it was possible to categorize schools roughly in this way on the basis of their educational characteristics, the report focused massively on the differences between schools that resulted from their social situation:

> In a neighbourhood where the jobs people do and the status they hold
> owe little to their education it is natural for children as they grow
> older to regard school as a brief prelude to work rather than an
> avenue to future opportunities. Some of these neighbourhoods have
> for generations been starved of new schools, new houses and new
> investment of every kind.

What such deprived areas needed were 'perfectly normal, good primary schools alive with experience from which children of all kinds can benefit'. Schools in these areas placed 'special and additional demands' on teachers. The children were often backward, and current educational policies were unlikely to lessen the inequalities in the system:

> If the fruits of growth are left to accumulate within the framework of
> present policies and provisions, there is no assurance that the living
> conditions which handicap educationally deprived children will
> automatically improve – still less that the gap between these
> conditions and those of more fortunate children will be narrowed.

The situation called for 'a new distribution of educational resources'. The committee called for 'positive discrimination' in favour of schools needing such special help. This was in many respects the kernel of the report, and of many of the educational and urban policies that emerged simultaneously and subsequently: 'The proposition that good schools should make up for a poor environment is far from new. It derives from the notion that there should be equality of opportunity for all, but recognises that children in some districts will only get the same opportunity as those who live elsewhere if they have unequally generous treatment.'[3] A 'good school' in these terms was one that benefited from a policy which took account of the socially derived needs of the classroom. This was as true of judgements of primary schools that stemmed from considerations of disadvantage and poverty as it was of judgements of secondary schools that stemmed from injustices in provision and the selection of children based on or biased by social class.

These were not, of course, the only policies and developments of the 1960s impinging on notions of the aims and qualities of schooling – others were concerned, for example, with new types of examination and the increasingly prominent issues relating to immigration and race. The emphasis on social and educational priority as defined in area, and particularly urban, terms was, however, the dominant one under a Labour government in the mid-1960s; it declined as economic circumstances changed in the 1970s and received its death knell under a Labour government in 1977. *Education in Schools* was a consultative Green Paper issued that year, and, as much as the Conservative administration's policies from 1979, signalled a new framework for making judgements about schools. A policy shift was already apparent in a speech given at Ruskin College, Oxford, in 1976 by Prime Minister James Callaghan, which was followed by what was termed a 'great debate'. The Green Paper spelled out the shift. It acknowledged criticisms of schools – including the underlying feeling that 'the educational system was out of touch with the fundamental need for Britain to survive economically in a highly competitive world through the efficiency of its industry and commerce'. Debate and planning had hitherto been dominated by the reorganization of the school system and increased numbers, and the document set out a number of aims against which schools could 'judge the effectiveness of their work'. The suggested aims ranged widely, including – to help children develop lively, enquiring minds; to instil respect for moral values and tolerance of other races, religions and ways of life; to help children understand the world in which we live; to help them to use language effectively; and to provide a basis of mathematical, scientific and technical knowledge. One stated aim which was indicative of the accelerating change in economic and social priorities read: 'to help children to appreciate how the nation earns and maintains its standard of living and properly to esteem the essential role of industry and commerce in this process'. *Education in Schools* did express the government's continuing commitment to 'discriminating in favour of children who are underprivileged for whatever reason', and one of the aims of schools was to help 'the development of children whose social or environmental disadvantages cripple their capacity to learn, if necessary by making additional resources available to them'. How far the balance of policy-making had begun to change, and was soon to change more radically, can be seen from the section of the Green Paper entitled 'School and working life', which set out a series of strategies for improving contacts between schools and the world of employment, and for improving general understanding of 'the nation's industrial and commercial well-being'. The important central paragraph stressed that young people needed to reach maturity

> with a basic understanding of the economy and the activities, especially manufacturing industry, which are necessary for the creation of Britain's national wealth. It is an important task of secondary schools to develop this understanding, and opportunities for its development should be offered to pupils of all abilities. These opportunities are needed not only by young people who have careers in industry later but perhaps even more by those who may work elsewhere, so that the role of industry becomes soundly appreciated by society in general.[4]

It is of especial importance in understanding the changed context in which judgements of schools were being made in the 1980s and 1990s to have in view the massive importance attached to vocational issues from this point in the 1970s. Changes in approaches to the curriculum, school financing and control, assessment, teacher education and other related features of education were not governed solely by the economy, but the impetus for moving the focus of school policy from disadvantage and injustice to economic performance came directly from the declining economy that Britain confronted most critically in the 1970s. Not that vocationalism was new to education or to Britain. There were, as we have seen, strong traditions of vocational relevance in medieval, church-related and other strands in the history of education. Preparation for employment, whether manual or professional, was a constant element in the provision of types of school, curriculum and qualification. The struggle to include modern subjects, science, crafts and other elements in the curriculum was a response, often extremely belated, to changes in the employment market, in technology, in the social status of occupations old and new.

The purposes of vocationalism and its surrounding policies have at different times meant different routes through curricula, schools and post-school institutions. Vocationalism has often been an instrument in a search for rapid solutions to problems of modernization and economic difficulty. It has been presented as an imaginative approach to a practically based, activity-oriented curriculum, or as a crude additive or alternative to an 'academic' curriculum. It has been seen as an instrument of democratization, and as a weapon of social control. It has been offered as a component of a liberal education, or as a framework for liberal education itself. An outstanding aspect of the development of modern versions of the vocational has been their place in the adaptation of the British independent school in recent decades. These schools have often been in the forefront of innovations in science and technology, and their teachers have played a role in these connections beyond the independent schools. The recent history of these schools involves a serious diminution of emphasis on the traditional classical curriculum which had served as a model of upper- and middle-class culture, in favour of a curriculum which included subjects and examinations which enabled their students to compete adequately in a modern economy.[5]

Vocationalism, given that it is related to preparation for employment or takes account of the applications of knowledge, skills and understanding, has as an important context the different stages of education. Historically there have been debates about the relevance of employment considerations at these different stages, depending on school-leaving ages, opportunities for transfer to secondary or some form of post-secondary education, and the availability of employment opportunities after secondary or higher education. All of these have been governed by differential access to educational and employment opportunities by different social groups. In the nineteenth century the concept of the vocational changed markedly.[6] Education at all levels had for centuries had defined and employment-related outcomes, whether for religious functions in the case of cathedral song schools, or domestic service in the case of charity schools. Underlying the concept of the grammar school or the mass elementary schools of the late eighteenth and early nineteenth centuries were concepts of social roles to be filled, as there was in the case of private schools for girls, or the employment of private tutors. With the growth of industrialism established types of school encountered, and resisted, pressures to relate to a changing world of work. The battles over whether science, modern subjects such as history and modern languages, and even commercially oriented subjects such as book-keeping, should be incorporated into the grammar school curriculum straddled the century, leading to the creation of rival, 'modern'-subject-oriented schools. At the end of the century higher elementary schools with vocationally oriented programmes emerged. Neither then, nor for most of the twentieth century, did specifically technical or trade-oriented schools survive comfortably in the British setting.

At some points in the twentieth century in Britain, as in the United States, attempts to override such dichotomies as liberal versus vocational, academic versus practical and technical were indeed made. 'Vocational education' and 'vocational training' were strengthened in both countries early in the century. The arguments of John Dewey, A. N. Whitehead and British, European and American 'progressive' educators were directed against what they saw as false dichotomies. Their arguments fed into new approaches to school and to work, and asserted the possibility of a vocationalism that would be integral to a rounded education, not a discrete and low-level training.[7] Attempts of this kind from the 1920s met, however, with little success. In Britain, by the Second World War, and then in the implementation of the 1944 Education Act, different 'types' of children were being channelled into different types of school, heading for different outcomes. The grammar school track was targeted on access to university, with a curriculum largely structured on that assumption – even though the majority of its students were not university-bound. The secondary modern school curriculum adopted a structure that was to some extent similar, but which also encompassed elements of a vocationally oriented curriculum suited to the needs of a clientele with different social destinies from those of the majority of the grammar school population. The comprehensive schools were to grapple with the complexities of combining two somewhat different traditions.

By the 1940s the vocational had become identified with those skills and areas of study pertaining to such precise occupational outcomes as typing and shorthand, technician training and the various 'practical arts'. Post-war governments made limited attempts to rescue a wider understanding of the vocational and to promote an improved status for it, but divisions between the academic and the vocational, symbols of 'success' and 'failure', remained. Hierarchies of jobs meant hierarchies of institutions, programmes and subjects. By the second half of the century institutional structures reflected the academic/vocational divide with remarkable clarity. Experiments with 'junior technical schools' between the wars, and secondary technical schools after the Second World War, were never widely adopted.[8] When the British economy shuddered under the impact of the oil crisis and international competition in the 1970s, the country's 'institutionalized anti-vocationalism' began to be subjected to the first major policy scrutiny of the century. The 'great debate' on education inaugurated in 1976 produced government documents which advocated bringing the world of work more directly into the classroom. There were already demands in circulation for greater curriculum 'relevance', and the Labour government's consultative document *Education in Schools* reflected the sense that the curriculum in many schools 'is not sufficiently matched to life in a modern industrial society'. It advocated not the preparation of pupils for specific jobs but 'studies and activities that are practical and obviously relevant to working life'.[9] From this point there was to be some confusion regarding work-relatedness, relevance and the vocational. The Department of Education and Science and the Inspectorate took a more active part in promoting ideas of curriculum change, including the possibility – also pursued in the mid-1970s – of a common or core curriculum in which science, mathematics and other essential subjects would form a secure part. 'It helps neither the children, nor the nation,' said the DES in 1984, 'if the schools do not prepare [pupils] for the realities of the adult world.' Parents, employers and the public rightly expected the curriculum to pay regard to 'what the pupils will later want and be called upon to do'.[10] As in the 1880s or the 1920s, the economy was compelling attention to be directed to the purpose, content and outcomes of the system.

The Conservative government of Margaret Thatcher in 1979 inherited the educational traditions within which vocationalism had a pariah status. It directed efforts increasingly to reducing public financial support and setting education in a market economy framework, though one with strong central government controls in the field of education. Through the Manpower Services Commission it introduced an alternative curriculum for 14–18-year-olds: the Technical and Vocational Education Initiative. TVEI aimed to attract more of this age group 'to seek the qualifications/skills which will be of direct value to them at work', be better equipped 'to enter the world of employment', and to use their skills and knowledge 'to solve the real-world problems they will meet at work'.[11] It entailed work experience for the students, and collaboration between local education authorities, industry and public services. It developed – differently in different authorities and schools – options in such areas as information technology, craft and design technology and business studies. TVEI was received at first with suspicion or hostility by many for its utilitarian undermining of the curriculum, but it was also seen to have merit in correcting the traditional curriculum imbalance and in re-evaluating the 'vocational' potential of other areas of the curriculum.

The TVEI policy and implementation were an important element in the reframing of popular perceptions of the purposes and quality of schooling. It strengthened the focus on the curriculum, and confirmed the trend towards government intervention in establishing how judgements of schooling were to be made. In this as in other cases, however, initial policy intentions and the forms of implementation were not necessarily the same. Nor were policy aims necessarily well thought out, and there was always scope for unexpected or unintended outcomes. An early comment by a comprehensive school principal suggested that it was important for such schools to translate the aims of TVEI into forms that would give 'access to all pupils, of all abilities, without closing down their options, or depriving them of a balanced education which included expressive and creative elements as well as basic skills and competencies'.[12] An evaluation of TVEI in 1987 emphasized its ambiguities and the basis on which it had achieved wider support:

> Its greatest success so far seemed not to have been in its content of
> technical, vocational or pre-vocational training, nor – as yet – in its
> broader aim of increasing the status of these subjects among young
> people or their future employers or teachers. . . . Rather, it lies in the
> personal and social development and motivation of young people
> whose interests were not adequately stimulated by the traditional

academic curriculum and the didactic teaching methods normally used to convey it.[13]

TVEI had proved to be open to wider interpretation than had originally appeared possible, or had been intended. It did not have to mean a divisive curriculum for the disadvantaged and less able.

Under the Education Reform Act of 1988 technology became one of the mandatory 'foundation subjects' in all state-funded schools. As a result of government and other pressures stronger links were being established between industry and the schools. Educational objectives were being framed at least partly in relation to the 'enterprise culture' the government was committed to promoting. The 'new vocationalism' was strongly criticized from some directions as being instrumental and philistine, and for aiming to produce an uncritical labour force. While sometimes accepting the expansion of vocational education, critics objected to the penetration of narrow views of enterprise and work into even the primary classroom. The attack on the 'new vocationalism' weakened as schools and post-secondary education made their adjustments. If the cruder versions of an economy-driven vocationalism could be averted many saw in the new programmes much that might be welcomed. TVEI courses proved to be popular with students from a wide range of ability,[14] but its adaptability and integration into school curricula did not disguise the fact that the basis of attitudes to school provision and performance was being significantly altered.

The vocational issue was not, of course, the only determinant of changes in perceptions of schools. In the 1970s and 1980s policy-makers moved in other directions to influence what schools did and how they and others judged their work. Questions of accountability became increasingly prominent. Curriculum content and structure, the quality of teachers and teacher education, the pattern of public examinations, the roles of teachers, local authorities and Her Majesty's Inspectorate in monitoring school standards, and the roles of parents and employers in judging the appropriateness of school outcomes, all assumed new importance. Education itself became interpreted more and more as the provider of the kinds of skill necessary for economic revival. After 1979, the more the future was interpreted in terms of market competition, the more government saw education as the only contributory force which it could and should manipulate directly. At the heart of the changes influenced and directed from the mid-1970s were both this attempt at economic rescue and doubts constantly expressed by industry and the media about the performance of schools in relation to entry into and performance in employment. The question, at various levels of policy-making, was what kinds of strategy might be used to induce improvements; unlike the position in many of the American states, research on school effectiveness was to play little or no part in the requirements that were introduced. At the level of government and local authorities, for example, criticism of the quality of education lay behind Education Acts in 1980 and 1981 which 'required schools to provide parents with more information about the curriculum and school organization and to publish their results in public examinations'. HMI reports on schools were to be published, and schools were being made responsible in the late 1970s and early 1980s for 'systematically reviewing their own performance'. In 1982, 80 per cent of the local authorities in

England and Wales had been involved in the process of 'school self evaluation' known at the time as 'school based review'.[15] An important feature of debates about schools in the 1970s was, however, the variety of searches for criteria of quality, some of which reverberated through the research-based findings of Rutter's *Fifteen Thousand Hours* at the end of the decade, and the work of Reynolds and others which we have discussed, but which also resulted from processes of inquiry of a different kind by HM Inspectorate and others.

In 1975, for example, the Inspectorate published a paper entitled *Ten Good Schools*, resulting from visits to discover what constituted a 'successful' school. Their conclusions about the schools visited were that, though these varied,

> each can demonstrate its quality in its aims, in oversight of pupils, in curriculum design, in standards of teaching and academic achievement and in its links with the local community. What they all have in common is effective leadership and a 'climate' that is conducive to growth. The schools see themselves as places designed for learning: they take trouble to make their philosophies explicit for themselves and to explain them to parents and pupils; the foundation of their work and corporate life is an acceptance of shared values.[16]

Another study by HM Inspectors four years later, *Aspects of Secondary Education in England,* found teachers and pupils working hard in most schools, with 'solid achievements'. The great majority were 'orderly communities' and all were anxious 'to secure basic skills and to enable their pupils to obtain examination qualifications which may be important to their future. They are sensitive to public expectations and aware of the need to prepare their pupils for the responsibilities of adult life.'[17] At this stage of public scrutiny of the schools there was still an available emphasis on 'shared values', the range of aims on the basis of which the achievements of schools and pupils could be judged. The long-term goals of education, for the Warnock Committee which published its report *Special Education Needs*, were twofold: to 'enlarge a child's knowledge, experience and imaginative understanding, and thus his awareness of moral values and capacity for enjoyment'; and to enable the child 'to enter the world after formal education is over as an active participant in society and a responsible contributor to it, capable of achieving as much independence as possible'. The goals were the same for all children, even if the obstacles to be overcome and the help to be given were different.[18] A grammar school becoming comprehensive was, as Elizabeth Richardson discovered in a study of a school in a situation of change, vulnerable to parents' and official anxieties about its standards – standards of work as demonstrated by examination results and the number of university places obtained, and standards of personal behaviour as demonstrated 'by dress and hair style or by "good" or "bad" manners inside and outside the school premises'.[19] Such aims and the criteria of judgement had not changed.

The point from the mid-1970s was the extent to which such criteria of judgement were eclipsed by others. The HMI study of secondary education at the end of the 1970s indicated how far the question of standards, at least at the official level, had become identified with that of the shape and communication of the curriculum. In 1980 the Department of Education and Science and the Inspectorate published discussion documents on the curriculum, and the following year the DES published, in *The School Curriculum*, a response to the discussion, offering local authorities guidance on how the school curriculum might be improved. Schools prepared children for adult life and responsibilities as active members of society, with 'proper regard to what the pupils will later want and be called upon to do'.[20] Although a number of processes clearly contributed to the notion of standards achieved, the emergent diagram had become one in which the curriculum had moved to the centre, and debates about standards had to a substantial extent become debates about the purpose, structure and content of the curriculum. A new academic concern with curriculum studies emerged particularly strongly in the 1970s, and a new urgency surrounded the issue of where control of the curriculum lay. A 1977 report of a Committee of Enquiry on the management and government of primary and secondary schools in England and Wales included an extensive discussion of the relationships between governors and school staffs, including in relation to the curriculum. The committee conceived of the curriculum as 'the sum of the experiences to which a child is exposed at school', and moved from there to define the role of the school governors as a partnership (which included teachers) with responsibility for 'the whole curriculum'. The framework was decided by national and local education authority policies, and within it the committee recommended that the governing body should have responsibility 'for setting the aims of the school, for considering the means by which they are pursued, for keeping under review the school's progress towards them, and for deciding upon action to facilitate such progress'. In doing so the governors were not to 'assume the mantle of teachers, still less that of inspectors'.[21] The report proved controversial, especially for the teachers' unions, with regard not only to the future composition of governing bodies, but also to the extent of the intervention by lay members, including parents, that these proposals represented in the professionals' decision-making authority over the curriculum. Other issues were to surface, but the curriculum was to be of paramount concern in making policy and judgements about schools in the 1980s and 1990s.

The debates about secondary schooling suggested a range of difficult questions regarding the quality of schooling. These focused, for example, on school sub-structures (such as year groups and counselling provision), the roles of head-teachers, classroom teachers and teachers with a variety of responsibilities, and the choice of assessment techniques and examinations. Questions of streaming, mixed-ability grouping, setting for specific subjects and other aspects of the management of learning and experience had indeed been intensified by the comprehensive school, and the question of 'shared values' was basic to critiques of the comprehensive school and its standards. The demand that the grammar school tradition should live on 'into the new scheme of things'[22] had not disappeared, and was itself a way of suggesting that the comprehensive school could only work by reflecting the former tripartite divisions. The grammar school tradition was not easily translated into the values of the comprehensive school. The most cogent opposition to the notion that the comprehensive school *could* represent shared values, or a 'common culture', came from a series of writings by G. H. Bantock portraying 'the educational dilemmas of our democratic way of life', and attacking the sociological approach to schooling as a contribution to social equality. Children were growing up, in Bantock's descriptions, in different social and intellectual cultures, influenced to different extents by the mass media, the 'yobbo' behaviour of the Beatles, the 'boy-next-door' image of Tommy Steele, and successful assaults by popular culture. In educational terms the comprehensive school meant for Bantock (and from 1969 for the sequence of *Black Papers*, to which he contributed) an experiment which could only undermine the high culture, without doing anything for the victims of the mass culture:

> Educationally, we have to face the inescapable inequality of the children sitting before us, unequal in attainments and in motivation, facts which a mere glance at the exercise books forces on our attention, however much, ideologically, we may seek to deny the patent evidence. It is not simply a matter of one child's demonstrably *knowing* more than another. It is also that part of the inevitable result of the educative process is to produce inequalities of sensitivity, or understanding, of 'taste' and responsiveness.[23]

What was needed, Bantock argued, was 'ample opportunity to achieve the highest level of realization which very diverse natures can encompass'. This meant accepting education's 'primary datum', and not hiding the truth 'in a mistaken philanthropy of an excessive "equality of opportunity"'.[24] The implication was a diversity of 'natures' best provided for in a diversity of schools, or at least with a diversity of curricula, and this was one of the threads which became apparent in the attempts by Conservative ministers and cabinets to define ways forward for the system of education in the 1980s. The Conservative approach to appropriate schooling had to confront such ideas of separatism and a return to grammar school provision, alongside other notions of how the whole system of public education was best financed and controlled if it was to meet the skills and personnel needs of the end of the twentieth century and beyond. The result was a sustained effort to reshape the system in such a way that the quality of individual schools could be determined by the combination of government-promoted frameworks and definitions, and the operation of the market.

It cannot be overstressed that the major development in considerations of school quality in the 1980s and 1990s was the intensity of government commitment to altering not only the system of education but also the identity of schools and ways of perceiving their activities. Criteria which had entered into official judgements from the late 1960s, and which had affected the operation of large numbers of schools, were eroded and abandoned. The concepts of educational or social priority schools and schools of exceptional difficulty, underpinned by notions of positive discrimination, disappeared from the policy agenda. The main criteria of judgement which came to dominate government thinking about public education, and which were embodied in a series of parliamentary Acts and ministerial decisions, were: implementation of a detailed National Curriculum and its attendant assessment provisions; maximum opportunity for schools to be free of local authority control; parental choice, and maximum information by which parents and others could judge the 'performance' of schools. Contingent on or parallel with these were measures to provide for the appraisal of teachers, to move teacher education into closer collaboration with schools or to remove it completely from universities and colleges, and to transfer the inspection of schools from the HMI tradition into a more *ad hoc*, competition-driven form of inspection. Within this pattern of change a new sector, City Technology Colleges, was created, to promote technological and design studies in a number of semi-independent secondary schools. When the intended commercial sponsorship of the CTCs failed to materialize on the scale planned, the numbers were supplemented by government finance – but the sector remained small. The intention across all of these developments was to replace local authority control with school-based financial control, and governing bodies under the dominant influence of employers and parents.

The new policies and structures were designed to convey, indeed to be, the message regarding quality. All were enacted in the name of increasing standards. A good school would be defined by the financial autonomy of its principal and governing body, the public availability of its examination and inspection results in simple comparative tables (bypassing consideration of school intake and social composition or other 'contextual' factors), and therefore its success in competition for status and students (and the funds that accompanied them). Within these frameworks a perpetual policy war was waged against 'progressive' ideas and practices – often characterized as '1960s' legacies in teaching and organization. The schools were called on to reinforce 'traditional values', to provide a basis of knowledge, skills and understanding, and to turn education away from the social purposes once becoming prominent towards those of a new individualism. As Kenneth Baker, when Secretary of State for Education and Science, put it in 1986:

> While socialists see education as a means of social engineering, we [the Conservative Party] see education as a springboard for individualism, opportunity and liberty. By creating opportunities for the child it confers freedom of choice and action for the young adult. For us, education must fulfil the individual's potential, not stifle it in the name of egalitarianism. Education can no longer be led by the producers – by the academic theorists, the administrators or even the teachers' unions. Education must be shaped by the users – by what is good for the individual child and what hopes are held by their parents.[25]

The focus here, as in the New Right thinking generally from the 1980s, was neither directly on the child's social background and opportunities, nor on the effectiveness of the school and the classroom, but on the opportunities which lay in increasingly unfettered competition. Part of the strategy to provide 'what is good for the individual child' was to diminish or destroy the powers of the administrators (that is, the local authorities), of the teachers' unions (but also of the teachers, as the attacks on them continued throughout the 1980s), and of the 'academic theorists' (and their research, as distinct from the political theorists advancing the new messages). It is for these reasons that the Education Reform Act of 1988 and other legislation can be seen not merely as a blueprint for change, but also as a means of establishing a pattern of provision free of the influence of the three groups. The government wished to remove from judgements about schools a great deal of what had previously informed the judgements of 'users'.

The embodiment of a National Curriculum in the 1988 Act is crucial to this process because it indicates the way in which an emergent debate was interpreted, and the way in which a generation of parents and others were being trained not just to accept 'a curriculum', but also to respond to a battery of related principles and policies aimed at reinterpreting the notion of standards. There had been in the 1970s and into the mid-1980s a considerable debate about a 'common' or 'core' curriculum, engaging those in favour, those opposed, and those willing hesitantly to accept with reservations. The more the government in the late 1980s defined its version of the National Curriculum, the more difficult it became for those in the third category to accept, given the increasing strength of their reservations. Participants in the debate in the 1970s had assumed that moves in this direction were concerned with a core curriculum. In 1975 Rhodes Boyson, former comprehensive school headteacher and Conservative MP (later to be a Conservative government minister) related such a concept to a breakdown of an 'understood' national curriculum that existed until the beginning of the 1960s, with almost all schools covering the same 'basic curriculum'. The position now was that compulsory education was 'a farce and morally indefensible unless all schools cover the same basic syllabus as preparation for society'. He interpreted a common curriculum as one which would contain agreed elements up to the minimum school-leaving age:

> A basic curriculum in certain subjects would be laid down and
> examined in all schools, the rest would be at the discretion of the
> individual schools. . . . Such basic specific curricula which would be
> examined could occupy 30 to 40 per cent of the time of academic
> pupils, 50 to 60 per cent of the time of average pupils and 80 per cent
> or more of the time of the less able.[26]

Beginning with working papers entitled *Curriculum 11–16* in 1977 and culminating in a document of the same name with the subtitle 'Towards a statement of entitlement' in 1983, a group of HM inspectors doggedly sought, in collaboration with some local authorities and secondary schools, to define 'a coherent common curriculum in secondary education'. Its basic premise was that curricula should be based 'on a common framework which provides coherence, and, while taking account of individual needs and abilities, still ensures the provision of a broadly based common experience'. The crucial point about the final document was that it offered an 'outline specification' whose aims were presented in terms of skills, attitudes, concepts and knowledge. The balance was in terms of allocation of time for 'areas of experience' (the aesthetic and creative, the ethical, the linguistic, the mathematical, the physical, the scientific, the social and political, and the spiritual), and the structured provision was to occupy some 70–80 per cent of the time available, the remainder to be used by pupils according to their individual interests.[27] James Callaghan's Ruskin speech and the consultative document *Education in Schools* provoked considerable discussion around the curriculum issue.

This Green Paper talked of a need to investigate what role might be played by a ' "protected" or "core" element of the curriculum common to all schools. . . . The creation of a suitable core curriculum will not be easy', and there was to be consultation on the possibility of reaching agreement on the translation of common aims into such a 'core' or 'protected part' of the curriculum.[28] Alan Beith, Liberal spokesman on education, agreed that it was necessary to 'get agreement on a core curriculum covering basic skills', but criticized the Secretary of State, Shirley Williams, for not indicating how far the Department would go in assuming 'direct powers' over the curriculum. One teachers' union spokesman thought the references to a core curriculum were 'profoundly unhelpful'. After eight regional conferences during the 'great debate' and 'months of earnest study by the department I would have expected something a little more analytical'.[29] This kind of debate was projected into the 1980s in a number of forms. The Inspectorate and the DES continued to pursue ideas about what gradually became termed a National Curriculum, searching for forms of breadth, balance and, controversially but increasingly, relevance.[30] There were, however, three major steps to the form finally taken by the National Curriculum. The first was the government's 1985 White Paper *Better Schools*, which confessed that 'successive generations may differ in how they define standards at school and how they measure changes in standards'. It argued that school standards were generally not 'as good as they can be, nor as good as they need to be', to equip young people for the next century, and to ensure the nation's economic prosperity. The White Paper identified two characteristics of the best schools that were present in most schools – 'the commitment of the teachers to the education of their pupils and the orderly and civilised relationship between teachers and pupils', but there were too many wide variations amongst schools to be acceptable. It welcomed what it saw as wide agreement to plan a curriculum that would be common to all pupils – containing English, mathematics and physical education or games, elements from the humanities and arts, practical and technological work, together with religious education (which was statutory) and a foreign language for most pupils. If planned on these lines, 'it is likely that 80–85 per cent of each pupil's time needs to be devoted to subjects which are compulsory or liable to constrained choices'. It underlined the importance of examinations in raising standards.[31]

The second step was a 'consultation document' entitled *The National Curriculum 5–16* in 1987, echoing *Better Schools*. Eighty-five per cent of the curriculum was to be devoted to the 'foundation subjects', and the objectives of the National Curriculum were to be met by a programme of Attainment Targets and 'clear assessment arrangements'. The aim was to 'raise standards consistently, and at least as quickly as they are rising in competitor countries'.[32] Standards were deeply enmeshed with subjects, stages, attainments, assessment, in order to provide pupils with standard opportunities and enable schools to provide what was needed to meet international competition. It was this version of the National Curriculum that carried over into the third step, the Education Reform Act 1988, which laid down in detail what were to be the three 'core' subjects, mathematics, English and science (a fourth, Welsh was laid down for Welsh-speaking schools), together with six 'foundation subjects' (plus a modern language at certain stages, and Welsh for non-Welsh-speaking schools). The Act also laid down Key Stages, and gave the Secretary of State authority to specify Attainment Targets, Programmes of Study and assessment arrangements 'as he considers appropriate' for each subject. Religious education was to be given and a daily act of collective worship, controversially defined as 'of a broadly Christian character', was to take place. Many of those who had supported the idea of *a* national curriculum found it difficult to support significant features of *this* National Curriculum. In the 1987 consultation phase, the Labour Party's education spokesman, Jack Straw, for example, strongly supported the idea of a national curriculum (as many in the Labour Party had previously done), but on condition that it left professional discretion in the hands of the teachers, and was not tied to the proposed testing at the ages of 7, 11 and 14.[33] Also during the consultation phase, Denis Lawton, director of the University of London Institute of Education and a leading contributor to curriculum issues, summarized the position of supporters-with-reservations with regard to the document, reservations that were to be made about the Act itself:

> I long ago came to the conclusion that some kind of national
> curriculum was desirable. Some of the arguments in favour are set out
> in the consultation document but mostly it ignores the debate on
> curriculum which has taken place over the last 20 years. I have two
> specific complaints. First, the draft is entirely subject-based in its
> thinking. Second, important areas of human experience such as
> politics and economics are almost completely neglected.

No justification had been presented for the foundation subjects, and the emphasis was outdated.[34]

A central aim of the National Curriculum was to provide precise objectives for the schools, precise targets for the pupils, and clear information for parents. In the period since James Callaghan's Ruskin speech, in which he referred to the 'core curriculum of basic knowledge', and the Green Paper which extended the discussion in the following year, an entirely new basis for planning and judging schools and their curricula had been laid. The opting-out and budgeting arrangements were intended to bring new constituencies into positions of influence and control, and these were directly indicative of the new role of government in shaping attitudes towards schools' operations. These, with the National Curriculum, pointed more towards strategies for achieving school effectiveness, without using the term, than towards a picture of what it was. The subject-based curriculum structure and the intricate pattern of Attainment Targets and assessment were based on a wholly different approach to judging and improving schools from that contained in the effective schools and school improvement research. The proposals and the decisions on the curriculum were controversial (and were as divisive within the government as elsewhere). Initial resistance by teachers and others to the National Curriculum was based on its perceived rigidity, its lack of attention to previous debate, experience and change. The National Union of Teachers described it as

> more of a step back to the 1950s than forward to the 21st century. The
> core and foundation subjects identified in the text of the Reform Act
> would not have been out of place in the grammar school timetable 30
> years ago . . . a subject focus has been chosen in preference to
> education based on the process of learning and on areas of
> experience. There is no clear analysis of what the entire educational

experience of a pupil should include other than in terms of narrow subject specialism.[35]

In practice, during the next five or so years, the implementation process had to respond, albeit slowly, to these and other criticisms, including the overloading of the prescribed curriculum and the complexity of the testing. The National Curriculum Council that was established by government almost immediately began to focus on the need for what it described as 'the whole curriculum context', including 'cross curricular provision':

> The whole curriculum of a school, of course, goes far beyond the formal timetable. . . . Above all, schools need to give the curriculum structure and coherence, thus demonstrating the elements and strands which bind it together. . . . To achieve these whole curriculum aims, schools need to ensure that the planned contribution of different subjects is not made in isolation.

The NCC focused on cross-curricular dimensions ('the intentional promotion of personal and social development through the curriculum as a whole'), cross-curricular skills and cross-curricular themes, and by recognizing these teachers could have a clear view 'of how their teaching contributes to the whole curriculum experience of their pupils' and could achieve a 'cohesive structure'.[36] The parallel School Examinations and Assessment Council set the monitoring of pupil progress within what it called a 'whole-school approach to formative assessment'.[37] The structure of the National Curriculum as defined by subjects did not, the Department of Education and Science emphasized in 1989, 'mean that teaching has to be organised and delivered within prescribed subject boundaries'. The Act did not require teaching to be provided 'under the foundation subject headings'.[38] There were, however, continuing government pressures for non-'progressive' forms of teaching, especially in the primary school.

Parents and the public continued, of course, to make judgements of schools based on established criteria, or what came to be called 'performance indicators'. In a crude form, said one commentator, 'raw exam results, pupil behaviour, sports results or the annual school concert have always been regarded by the public, rightly or wrongly, as indicators of a school's performance'. Attempts were being made, through the legislation and in other ways, to suggest to schools and others more comprehensive ways of measuring schools' performance. One leaked DES document suggested that schools could gather information about pupils' social behaviour (truancy, lateness, behaviour on leaving school), staff demeanour, police records, and so on.[39] The government's favoured device for indicating comparative performance came to be the 'league table', by which the results of tests and examinations could be compared from school to school, and Secretaries of State who developed the idea, notably John Patten, were anxious that the simple data should be made available, not complicated by information relating to other school or social factors. Experts in the field, however, attacked the attempt to publish such raw data or averages as unjust, since schools might well be labelled as ineffective or failing simply because of the quality of their intake. The National Foundation for

Educational Research derided the attempt to make such 'simplistic' judgements through league tables:

> An example of a school league table would be the total number of GCSE passes, perhaps expressed as a mean number per head. It is scarcely necessary to explain that, as a measure of school effectiveness, this is seriously flawed, and unfair. It takes no account of the quality of the intake, either in terms of ability or special circumstances.[40]

As was widely pointed out, the real measure of achievement was some form of 'value added', since a school might well be doing a great deal better in producing a modest set of results with initially low-achieving pupils, than in producing excellent examination results with students starting from a much higher baseline. An American psychologist, discussing the possibility of separating genetic from environmental effects, commented when looking at the British scene in 1993, that 'instead of a Patten-type plan of the week for ranking schools according to tests of scholastic achievement, it ought to be possible to separate out the school's achievement from the ability which the pupils have when they arrive.'[41] British policy-making had, as we have seen, become increasingly impervious in the 1980s and early 1990s to research and arguments from what Kenneth Baker had labelled the 'academic theorists'. The criticism of an overloaded curriculum, excessive testing and the intention to publish league tables of test results came under increasingly bitter resistance, however, from the schools. Teachers boycotted the tests, the organizations of teachers, headteachers, parents and others mounted an offensive which, by the middle of 1993, led government to retreat from some of the more stringent of its positions on the curriculum, testing and the publication of raw data in league tables.

The small number of British researchers who had retained a commitment to understanding the structures and processes which constituted an 'effective school', or the bases on which 'school improvement' might take place, had continued to pursue the targets that were identified by research mainly at the end of the 1970s and in the early 1980s. The question was – was anyone listening? From the 1980s the schools were overwhelmed with curricular and other organizational changes, and work on school improvement unrelated to the immediate National Curriculum targets seemed peripheral. The schools and the local authorities were battling against constant budgetary pressures, and the difficulties of resources and physical conditions constantly underlined in reports by the Inspectorate. The late 1980s and 1990s have been a period of the most intensive and complex changes schools have ever been called on to face, including changes which modified previous changes. These pressures on the schools and local authorities, combined with the strength of government policy-making, have made the context of research vastly different from that in which the effective schools researchers worked in the same period in the United States. There were still in Britain, as we have seen, a small number of focal points of continued research on effective schools and school development issues, including the Centre for Educational Sociology at the University of Edinburgh, and the journal and other publications associated, for example, with David Reynolds and David Hopkins.[42] The context of the government's policy preoccupations also made it more difficult in the United Kingdom for issues relating to poverty and disadvantage to re-emerge in relation to education as they were doing in the United States. Poverty in the 1980s increased sharply, as it did in many other countries, and new constituencies were brought below the poverty line – 'a broad and growing fringe of people of all ages who are excluded from the mainstream of their societies: unemployed or intermittently employed workers, lone parents, physically and mentally handicapped people, ethnic minorities and pensioners whose pensions are low because they were on the margins of the economy during their working lives'.[43] The gap between the affluent and the poor was widening, but national policies – educational and other – were directed not towards poverty issues but towards specific economic and ideological targets. In research and other terms the educational implications surfaced, but not with the same urgency as in the United States.

Research sponsored both by the European Commission and others revealed, for example, that Britain had an 'educational under-class' for whom nursery education was provided on a much smaller scale than in other European countries, with fewer places, great disparity of provision across the country, and a high proportion of part-time provision.[44] A report from a Conservative-led House of Commons Select Committee in 1989 called for greater effort to attain the targets that had been set out in Margaret Thatcher's 1972 White Paper *A Framework for Expansion*. Education for the under-fives, it emphasized, could contribute to a number of 'social, educational and compensatory objectives', and provision needed to be expanded until it was available for the children of all parents who wished it; in the meantime resources should continue to be targeted on 'children with priority need'.[45] The American message that pre-school education could reduce school failure and crime was heard to some extent in Britain, and the Home Office responded by supporting some pre-school inner-city projects,[46] but the scale of such targeted projects was small. An Edinburgh project stressed the impact of family, school and neighbourhood forms of deprivation on attainment. Opportunity in Britain, it found, was 'polarising, socially and geographically'. How neighbourhood deprivation affected attainment was not clear, but 'families, schools and neighbourhoods are all implicated', and remedial policies therefore needed to be directed at all three.[47] The implications of poverty and racial and gender disadvantage for social and economic futures were not surfacing as clearly for British policy-makers (in politics or in industry) as they were in some areas of American life. Remedial policies featured either little or not at all in late 1980s and 1990s Conservative government policy directions. Developing the strategies laid down in the 1988 Act, government policy in the 1990s continued to be directed towards restructuring the system, encouraging schools to opt out of local authority control, and remoulding the financing process. It did so, for example, in the White Paper *Choice and Diversity* in 1992, including, as part of its process of raising the standards of all schools, creating a framework for taking over the management of 'at risk' or 'failing' schools, as identified particularly by inspection reports.[48] A leader in *The Times* when the White Paper was published began: 'The government is dismayed at Britain's poor education record and has responded as governments always respond. It has blamed everybody but itself, and decided to nationalise the schools.'[49]

The acceleration of these forms of policy-making for education in Britain in the 1980s and 1990s changes the focus in the recent history of judging the quality or effectiveness of schools. The nineteenth- and earlier twentieth-century components and constituencies remain visible – the views of parents, teachers and publics, governments, inspectors and employers, and a concern with examinations and inspection, process and attainment. The surface similarities, however, mask profound changes. The important questions in this period relate not so much to what judgements were being made, but to how judgements *should* be made, and who has the power to make and shape them. There are basic differences between, on the one hand, the dominant criteria being developed for judgement (and the controversies surrounding them), and the provenance of the criteria in the 1980s and 1990s, and on the other hand, those of earlier decades. The roles of teachers in curriculum design and pupil assessment have been diminished. The judgements of parents about schools (even as policies aimed to give parents greater power to choose and be represented in school governance) have been made increasingly in relation to the powerful policies, values and information provided or moulded by government. The 150 years of HMI involvement in judging schools was brought to an end, as their ability to evaluate the quality of schools was marginalized, the number of inspectors was drastically reduced, and their roles redefined as supervision through an Office for Standards in Education (OFSTED) of teams of inspectors with no necessary professional experience. The role of local authorities was severely restricted as new forms of school budgeting were introduced, new powers were given to school boards of governors with non-political majorities, and the provision of services by local authorities was limited or endangered as schools were invited by government to opt out of local authority control. The community role of schools that was being enhanced in earlier decades was underplayed as government policy increased emphasis on formal academic processes, examinations and assessment. The importance of community relationships was heavily redefined in terms of partnerships with industry and the world of work in general. At a time when unemployment was increasingly common for school-leavers, popular expectations and judgements of schooling were naturally heavily influenced not just by pupils' acquisition of the knowledge, skills and understanding necessary for competition to obtain and keep jobs, but also by the kinds of measure of attainment emphasized in the publicized national policies. The cautions expressed by researchers and 'academic theorists' about the measures of effectiveness being adopted, and about the comparative judgements being made, were either unheard or heard too late in the clamour of determined, centrally driven change.

The paradoxes of centralized attempts at decentralization and the increase in standardization in the name of diversity were devices adopted within the particular traditions of schooling, and took different paths from the changes debated and made in the United States in the same period. Different versions of vocationalism took shape, embodied in different opportunities for central policy machineries to influence – and ultimately control – the directions of curriculum change. The United Kingdom and the United States experienced in the 1980s different versions of conservatism-in-practice, different ways of exercising leverage on education-for-the-economy. There were some parallels, including American attempts to formulate national curricula and more standardized forms of assessment, the British attempt to use City Technology Colleges in ways and for purposes similar to those advocated by Chubb and Moe and others, and the move to forms of school-based management and budgeting in both countries. Ways of thinking about schools and their effectiveness were conditioned differently in the two countries, however, by the different roles of central government and the ways policy-makers interpreted their opportunities to change the provision, content and evaluation of schooling. Ways of developing and debating interpretations of the aims, practices and outcomes of schooling were widely different in the two sets of structures and traditions. The American concern with school renewal in the 1980s and 1990s has been based on the relatively weak capacity of central government to effect change amidst the competing models and alternatives. Its role has therefore been the difficult one of attempting to influence and provide the leverage of change. The British equivalent has been based on a determination to make powerful use of central opportunities to restructure the system. In both cases the criteria for making judgements about schools were enmeshed in developments on the grand scale.

NOTES

1 G. M. Young (1936). *Victorian England: Portrait of an Age*. London: Oxford University Press, p. 11.

2 Central Advisory Council for Education (England) (1963). *Half Our Future* (Newsom Report). London: HMSO, p. 10, chs 4 and 5.

3 Central Advisory Council for Education (England) (1967). *Children and Their Primary Schools*, Vol. 1: *Report* (Plowden Report). London: HMSO, pp. 101–2, 50–7.

4 Secretary of State for Education and Science and Secretary of State for Wales (1977). *Education in Schools: A Consultative Document*. London: HMSO, pp. 2–4, 6–7, 34–5.

5 Cf. Geoffrey Walford (1986). *Life in Public Schools*. London: Methuen, pp. 186, 205–12.

6 Jürgen Herbst (1980). 'The liberal arts: overcoming the legacy of the nineteenth century', *Liberal Education*, **66**.

7 Harold Silver (1983). *Education as History: Interpreting Nineteenth- and Twentieth-Century Education*. London: Methuen (cf. ch. 7, 'The liberal and the vocational').

8 For a full account see Gary McCulloch (1989). *The Secondary Technical School: A Usable Past?* London: Falmer Press.

9 *Education in Schools*, p. 11.

10 Department of Education and Science and Welsh Office (1981). *The School Curriculum*. London: HMSO, p. 1.

11 Manpower Services Commission (1987). *The TVEI Operating Manual*, quoted in Oliver Fulton, 'The Technical and Vocational Education Initiative: an assessment', *Education and Training UK 1987*. London: MSC, p. 103.

12 Anne Jones (1983). 'Door need not close when Young comes in', *Times Educational Supplement*, 7 January, 4.

13 Fulton, 'The Technical and Vocational Education Initiative', p. 108.

14 Mike Leach (1986). ' "TVEI will fail" ', *Times Educational Supplement*, 31 October, 22.

15 Philip Clift (1987). 'LEA initiated school-based review in England and Wales'. In David Hopkins (ed.), *Improving the Quality of Schooling*. London: Falmer Press, pp. 45–6.

16 Quoted from *Ten Good Schools* (1975). In W. S. Fowler (ed.) (1988). *Towards the National Curriculum*. London: Kogan Page, p. 36.

17 Department of Education and Science (1979). *Aspects of Secondary Education in England: A Survey by HM Inspectors of Schools*. London: HMSO, p. 260.

18 Committee of Enquiry into the Education of Handicapped Children and Young People (1978). *Special Educational Needs* (Warnock Report). London: HMSO, p. 5.

19 Elizabeth Richardson (1975). *Authority and Organization in the Secondary School*. London: Macmillan Education, p. 63.

20 Department of Education and Science, *The School Curriculum*, p. 1.

21 Department of Education and Science and Welsh Office (1977). *A New Partnership for Our Schools* (Taylor Report). London: HMSO, pp. 52–3.

22 J. N. Hewitson (1969). *The Grammar School Tradition in a Comprehensive World*. London: Routledge & Kegan Paul, p. 4.

23 G. H. Bantock (1968). *Culture, Industrialisation and Education*. London: Routledge & Kegan Paul, pp. 60–3.

24 G. H. Bantock (1963). *Education in an Industrial Society*. London: Faber & Faber, pp. 224–5. In 1977 Bantock wrote: 'For nearly twenty years now I have been arguing that the crisis in our secondary education is cultural and cannot be met by the organisational device of the comprehensive school': in 'An alternative curriculum'. In C. B. Cox and Rhodes Boyson (eds), *Black Paper 1977*. London: Temple Smith, p. 78.

25 Kenneth Baker (1986). Speech to Conservative Party conference, in *Times Educational Supplement*, 10 October, 10.

26 Rhodes Boyson (1975). 'Maps, chaps and your hundred best books', *Times Educational Supplement*, 17 October, 21.

27 Department of Education and Science (1983). *Curriculum 11–16: Towards a Statement of Entitlement. Curriculum Appraisal in Action*. London: DES, pp. 15–17.

28 *Education in Schools*, pp. 11–12.

29 *Times Educational Supplement* (1977). 'Short on ideas, say Liberals and Tories'; 'Unions blow hot, cold, but mostly lukewarm', 29 July, 5.

30 For example, Department of Education and Science (1981). *The School Curriculum*. London: HMSO, pp. 12–13 for common, balanced curriculum; Department of Education and Science (1984). 'The organisation and content of the 5–16 curriculum'. London, mimeo pp. 6–10, for broad and balanced curriculum; Department of Education and Science (1985). *The Curriculum from 5 to 16* (Curriculum Matters 2, An HMI Series). London: DES, p. 54, for 'coherent, broad and balanced' curriculum; Department of Education and Science (1988). *The Curriculum from 5 to 16: an HMI Report* (responses to previous document), p. 3, for 'breadth, balance, relevance, differentiation, progression and coherence'.

31 Secretary of State for Education and Science and Secretary of State for Wales (1985). *Better Schools*. London: HMSO, pp. 1–5, 22, 29.

32 Department of Education and Science (1987). *The National Curriculum 5–16: A Consultative Document*. London: DES, pp. 2–3 and *passim*.

33 Reported in the *Guardian*, 5 September 1987, 4.

34 Denis Lawton (1987). 'Fundamentally flawed', *Times Educational Supplement*, 18 September, 31.

35 National Union of Teachers (1990). *A Strategy for the Curriculum*. London: NUT, pp. 11–12.

36 National Curriculum Council (1989). *Circular No. 6: The National Curriculum and Whole Curriculum Planning: Preliminary Guidance*. York: NCC.

37 School Examinations and Assessment Council (n.d.). *A Guide to Teacher Assessment: Part B, Teacher Assessment in the School*. London: SEAC, p. 2.

38 Department of Education and Science (1989). *National Curriculum: From Policy to Practice*. London: DES, paras 3.7, 3.8, 4.3.

39 Paul Harrison (1988). 'Winning points', *Times Educational Supplement*, 27 May, A23.

40 National Foundation for Educational Research (1991). 'Assessing the effectiveness of schools', *NFER News*, **55**, 11. For discussion of value added cf. Andrew McPherson (1992). 'Measuring added value in schools.' In *NCE Briefing No. 1*. London: National Commission on Education.

41 Robert Plomin, Pennsylvania State University, speaking at a conference on giftedness, reported in *Times Higher Educational Supplement*, 5 February 1993, 5.

42 Cf. David Reynolds and Peter Cuttance (eds) (1992). *School Effectiveness: Research, Policy and Practice*. London: Cassell (an international symposium containing ten contributions, six by British authors).

43 David Donnison (1991). 'Squeezed and broken on the brink', *Times Higher Education Supplement*, 19 April, 13.

44 Judith Judd (1988). 'Britain's educational under-class', *Observer*, 10 April, 7 (reporting a study by the European Commission on child care and equality of opportunity).

45 House of Commons Select Committee on Education, Science and the Arts (1989). 'Under 5s', reported in *Times Educational Supplement*, 13 January, 6–7.

46 Nicholas Pyke (1992). 'Under-5 education can cut crime', *Times Educational Supplement*, 23 October, 3; *Times Educational Supplement* (1993). 'An American way of infancy', 23 April, 10.

47 Catherine Garner (1989). *Does Deprivation Damage?* Edinburgh: Centre for Educational Sociology, University of Edinburgh, pp. 3–5.

48 Secretaries of State for Education and Wales (1992). *Choice and Diversity: A New Framework for Schools*. London: HMSO, pp. 48–50 and *passim*.

49 *The Times* (1992). 'State knows best', 29 July.

Chapter 9

'We Already Know'?

The quality of schooling, and the vocabularies involved in judging it, became increasingly subordinated in the 1970s–90s to the contexts established by political conservatism internationally. In the making of judgements about schooling the political dimension has always been important, but in the contest to shape attitudes and judgements the rules became more stridently laid down by the governments, ministers and policy power-houses of the political right. The protagonists in such contests have changed markedly across the time scales and frontiers we have considered, and the rules of engagement have changed as the aims, evidence and its sources, and strategies, have been redefined. The history of judgements is above all the history of those powerful enough to challenge or to defend prevalent aims, evidence and strategies. We have seen at different times and for different constituencies how the inputs to influence judgements have been made, and the ways in which the understandings of parents, publics and others have become dependent less and less on reconciling diverse messages, and more and more on powerful simple politically and economically based signals.

Before we leave this central theme it is important to emphasize that the ability of research to influence policy and judgements depends on the nature of the research, the communication context within which it operates, and the directions and balance of popular and political opinion. The effect of the sociology of education in Britain from the late 1950s and the 'war on poverty' in the United States in the 1960s was to refocus attention on the school in its social setting. The most important role of the effective schools research from the 1970s was to refocus attention on the inner workings of the school. Whether or not the particular research effort had serious impact on attitudes and judgements depended on its acceptability in dominant policy-making environments, or on its ability and opportunity to compete for influence amid the dominant policy concerns. Research-based school effectiveness and improvement ideas might find little or no place where strong policy frameworks based on other considerations were designed to obstruct their entry, or they might have only short-lived impacts. A major difficulty in gaining attention for newly developed research-based understandings arises when the policy heights are captured for absolutes. The commanding heights were less open to alternatives in the Britain of the late 1970s and 1980s than in the United States.

The political battlegrounds on which opinion was moulded in both countries had not been empty in previous decades. In both cases prior battles had been fought under banners of 'progressive' and 'traditional' (or 'conservative') education. Admiral Rickover and others in the United States had fought what they considered a 'progressive orthodoxy' in the schools and teacher education. The battle on similar terrain in Britain was won partly by the 'Black Paper' attacks and then by a Conservative government, but also by the lethargy of progressive educators and their failure to recognize fundamental changes in the world around them. 'Progressive' in this context is inevitably a shorthand for a range of positions, subsuming what has been known since the end of the nineteenth century as, for instance, 'child-centred' or 'radical' education. The progressive movement of the twentieth century has never been homogeneous, and has often been profoundly divided – as in the United States between the wars, when the choice lay between emphasis on the child or on democracy and the social order. In the 1960s and 1970s progressive educators were involved in curriculum reform, the development of new pedagogies, the exposure of educational and social inequalities, the explanation of disadvantage and under-achievement, campaigns for new school and university structures and the redistribution of administrative power. They were interested in the defence of children's rights, interpreting the multi-racial classroom, or the development of the personalities and capabilities of all or specific groups of children in schools and other educational settings. The agenda of the progressive educator has been long and complex, and it has often had to resist or adapt to changing and often hostile conditions. From the 1960s, however, the progressive movement gradually lost its sources of energy, failing to see through its inertia the strength of emergent conservative values and policies.

In Britain as in many other countries progressive educators failed to see not only the seriousness of the challenge of traditionalist views, but also the changing economic circumstances that would make them more assertive and acceptable. In the United States Rickover and the Council for Basic Education may have provoked irritation amongst many American educators, but what they represented was not seriously analysed and understood at the time. From 1959 Rickover was making a sustained attack on the spirit of Dewey, which 'permeates our teachers' colleges and state boards of education ... it makes its pernicious influence felt in the steady deterioration of secondary-school curricula'.[1] He went on in 1962 to use European models to attack the 'change-over in this country from traditional to progressive concepts of public education',[2] and the following year he described as a dogma the progressive educators' view centred on children's ' "democratic" right to study only what interests and pleases them'.[3] The campaign of Rickover, A. E. Bestor[4] and others against the backcloth of Sputnik, international competition, technological rivalry, cold war and social upheaval sought to establish that in the United States there was an established, progressive orthodoxy that was responsible for the nation's economic and social ills.

In Britain the parallel did not emerge until the end of the 1960s, with the appearance of the first of the 'Black Papers'. The time lag may be explained as a result of the strength of the sociology of education which the Black Paper authors attacked, and the more general acceptability in Britain of 'open' primary education. In both countries, as we have seen, the 'progressive orthodoxy' and the prevalence of progressive practices was more often myth than reality. The first Black Paper in 1969 included amongst its targets the 'comprehensive disaster' and the 'assumptions on which "progressive" ideas, now in the ascendant, are based'.[5] The second continued and widened the attack, and – with a mirror image of Rickover's discovery of Europe – found in the United States a classroom reaction 'against "progressive" teaching methods'.[6] The response in Britain was partly derision, partly silence and expectation that the new threat would go away, partly political anger at the attempt to undermine the widespread consensus in support of the reforms being attempted. This faith in a broad, continuing educational consensus was not shaken until the general election of 1979, and the arrival of Margaret Thatcher's government, not only sympathetic to Black Paper views, but containing a minister who had co-edited *Black Paper 1977*. The Black Papers had been dismissed as irrelevant to the 1960s efforts to erode such established structures and processes as selection for secondary education, streaming, or examinations at 16-plus. Progressive education had become sanguine to the point at which it no longer felt the need seriously to defend existing or prepare for new positions. Political radicalism was reflected in educational radicalism only in relation to long-debated issues, including the future of the independent schools. The field was left clear for other, more combatively prepared positions.

A new contest of values had surfaced. Judgements made about schools in the 1980s and 1990s have been against a backcloth of the powerful changes of direction that we have seen. Our attempt to set these changes in a longer perspective suggests that there are important continuities and discontinuities, though the former are often difficult to discern amidst the changes in policies, systems and institutions, and amid the changing strengths and tones of dominant voices. The nature of the continuities is well illustrated by an official report which included an account of current criticisms of the schools:

> Public education of the present time is subject to searching criticism with respect to purpose, organization, administration, curriculum, teaching methods, and results . . . much of the criticism of the public schools to-day is due to a marked change in the purpose of public education. Thus the charge of a curriculum 'behind the times', and the demand for vocational subjects, represent no mere call for different school subjects as such, but a complete transformation in the idea of what . . . schools should do.

Most criticism was being directed against the curriculum, 'because here is where the changing purpose of the school shows itself most clearly'. The 'bookish curriculum' of the schools was under attack, and some responses were aimed at preparing children directly 'for the kind of life, economic and social, which they will lead when they leave schools'. Other critics went in the opposite direction, and schools attempted to put their theories and practices 'to every conceivable test and change their methods whenever necessary'. This account of the perceived weaknesses of the schools, the criteria by which they were judged and the nature of the debate around them was in fact written by the American Commissioner of Education in 1912. In many respects it could have been written towards the end of the twentieth century, in the United States, in Britain or in many other countries.

The commissioner believed that the validity of much of the criticism would be 'admitted or not according to the belief or nonbelief in a changed purpose for the schools',[7] and this could be a permanent slogan for school systems everywhere, as their controllers seek to balance the need to respond to the new and defend traditional goals and procedures. The criticisms of 1912 are reflected in the policies

155

adopted in the 1980s to sharpen definitions of curricula and outcomes and to address the means of attaining them. The British National Curriculum and *America 2000* addressed issues seen as acute in 1912. What parents have wanted from schools in recent decades includes many of the elements – moral, cultural, economic – that were wanted by their own parents. In the twentieth century as in the nineteenth, countries try to use educational systems to win wars and trade wars, to serve purposes that seem pre-eminent to those able to influence change or the maintenance of the status quo. However the realities of judging standards may change, the language and sub-texts of standards have many elements of continuity.

As the power of churches or royalty fades, and as the power of governments and bureaucracies increases, discontinuities are not hard to find. The interpretation and value of a liberal or a vocational education change, as do the pattern of schooling and access to its component parts by the privileged and the unprivileged. Control of systems and schools and their purposes changes. Types of school are created and disappear, new teaching methods are introduced, different kinds of expert are heard, and parents are aware that the schools, while in many ways pursuing similar goals, are in important ways also not the same as they used to be. In relation to the second half of the twentieth century particularly our discussion has traced not only some social and political pluralisms, but also the competition of aims and strategies generated. It has not been possible to track systematically some of the important contributors to this competition – for example, the press and 'public opinion', national commissions, or those developing tests or evaluation procedures. For the late twentieth century it has been essential to focus on the frameworks of judgement established by the research which has tackled the issues most directly, and the frameworks developed with increasing power by the state and its agencies.

The issue of who makes judgements, and on what basis, is profoundly affected by the strength of government or other public intervention, since there is a natural tension for parents, school governors and others between their perspective on the day-to-day running and achievements of the school, and the powerful policy imperatives under which they are called to operate. Some forms of restructuring in the United States and Britain have sought to lessen the bureaucratic external pressures of this kind, but they do not remove the policy pressures. In the British case particularly the nationally determined requirements for the curriculum, assessment and reporting continue to mean that teachers, parents and governors have to make their judgements and decisions in response to politically determined and often rapidly changing requirements and concerns. In the United States school restructuring from the late 1980s was similar. The move towards greater school autonomy meant, in Arthur Wirth's positive interpretation,

> incorporating more democratic, participative ways of attempting to
> solve problems. Educational work structures were created that
> respected the capacity of teachers, parents, students, and
> administrators to take creative action for change at the local level. . . .
> Some of the most effective restructuring attempts are being made in
> schools that confront our most intractable problems – the inner-city
> schools in impoverished, blighted neighborhoods.

This response was to what Wirth calls the factors that were making 'the centralized, bureaucratic model of control as dysfunctional in American schooling as it was in American industry'.[8] For the American public schools, however, weakening the state bureaucratic controls still left the schools facing not only intractable problems such as those of poverty, but also the same public pressures for new economic directions, the same difficulties over resources, the same market demands, as in Britain. The pressures might be exerted differently, but the ability of school people to analyse, judge and act was contained within frameworks similarly imposed upon them. Making judgements in both countries was governed by the requirements of new or intensified indicators, what Wirth calls the 'epidemic of testing',[9] an emphasis on competencies and outcomes, an ethos of measurement, a climate of efficiency and cost benefit.

The new climate, with its measurement- and outcomes-oriented policies for schools, meant the marginalizing of concerns relating to the schools' social environments, pointing away from the problems of impoverished families and neighbourhoods and at-risk children. Judgements of the dominant directions of policy-making for schools, including opting out, comparative tables of examination or testing results, and the particular shape of a nationally imposed curriculum, must take account of what the exercise of power in these ways excludes from public consideration. It did so particularly in bypassing the relationship between education and social conditions that had been made prominent in Britain and the United States in the 1960s. One outcome of that emphasis had been the community school, which attempted to break down barriers between the classroom and the questions of welfare, health, leisure provision, adult learning and other aspects of the communities in which schools were situated. The paths along which we have traced attitudes to schools have generally contained a concern with relating them to the wider society, and the contests of judgement surrounding schools have frequently been over the extent to which they have done or should do so. Whether the outcomes of schooling have been seen as service to the church or citizenship or some other abstraction or principle, social and political values have never been far from the provision of education. The community relationship, however, is a specific version of such a relationship, setting the school within a complex local environment. Community schools were central to the work of the Educational Priority Area projects of the late 1960s and continued as a movement beyond, as also in the United States at roughly the same time. Close relationships between schools and parents were a significant feature of the 'war on poverty' programmes, and took forms which were quite different from policies which aimed simply to give parents representation on the bodies that govern schools. Such features and aims of schooling played no part in policies which provided for 'opting out', City Technology Colleges or a National Curriculum.

Fundamental to the discussion of judgements is the notion of encounters or contests of judgements coming from different directions, and the exercise of power in defining the criteria on which judgements are made. Schools are themselves multiple constituencies, often in uneasy relationships, within which consensus may be easy or conflict prevalent. Schools operate in relation to multiple outside constituencies, on a different basis according to the private or public nature of the controls, and with differences stemming from many features both of the schools and of the agencies concerned. And beyond those are the multiple interests involved with the schools and their attainments – parents, employers, colleges and universities, politicians, and the organs of public opinion. The realities within which the schools operate and their qualities are defined fall roughly into three categories – their community location, their public policy contexts, and their internal workings.

This takes us back, first, to the notion of community. The concept is as elusive as that of 'society', which gave rise to some fundamental controversy, including within the Conservative Party, under the new Conservative politics. The fragmentary, market-controlled (within strong politically controlled state oversight) version of social processes associated with Margaret Thatcher was partly responsible for the sustained attack on local government made by Conservative governments, and did much to undermine some traditional local Conservative support. The chairman of the Conservative Education Association, for example, protested in 1993 about centralization having gone too far, and also said that

> The growth of the largely unaccountable grant-maintained schools . . . will throw up serious problems unless further thought is given to how these schools will relate to the community. If you believe, as Margaret Thatcher and some ministers do, that there is no such thing as society then a purely market approach is acceptable. If you do not share this negative view then something is missing. There is a democratic deficit that needs to be addressed. Local government should continue to have an important role in education, especially in its planning.[10]

This Conservative view of community and society may differ in important respects from other versions of the concepts, but it suggests a continuing presence of a view of schools as enmeshed in something beyond their mere market competition. Community location is in fact more than a geographical statement about a school. It is also a statement about how it responds to the social composition and needs of its neighbourhood or the constituencies from which it draws its students. How it responds has often been controversial, since a school's use of its community as a basis for planning its curriculum or teaching approaches may be seen either as a realistic and creative use of the children's experience or as a narrowing of educational horizons. What the community does is define some of the important characteristics, needs and expectations of the children, and strengths and weaknesses which they bring to the process of learning. 'Impoverished, blighted neighborhoods', rural schools and leafy suburbs do so differently. Questions of community raise issues about the school's relationship to, for instance, health, psychological, counselling and physical resources available in the community, under the control either of the same educational authorities, or under other auspices. The Educational Priority Area (EPA) policies and projects in Britain in the late 1960s and early 1970s particularly underlined the potential in these relationships. The reports of the EPA projects pointed to the need to develop 'educationally informed families' and 'socially informed schools'. There were implications for the curriculum and the teacher, the college of education, the social services, the retail market . . . the Town Hall and the industrial enterprise. . . . The viability of the community school rests in part on policies for housing and civic redevelopment. . . . And, where circumstances permit, the architects and planners can create the bricks and mortar of a community school by intelligent grouping of health clinics, shopping centres and recreational facilities with school buildings.[11]

National policies against poverty, racism or unequal opportunities have meaning for schools in local, community terms. Given continued or increasing poverty and equal opportunities issues in both Britain and the United States the questions posed most forcefully in the 1960s are posed similarly, however different the circumstances, in the 1990s.

Whatever the difficulties of defining the concept of community, the school relates to its community and is itself a community primarily with regard to the world outside the school that is brought into the school in the experience of its members. The US Commissioner of Education's report in 1912 quoted the director of the Bureau of Municipal Research of New York City as an observer, 'standing between the schools and the public'. A community needed to understand the fact that 'schools are weakened, not helped, by being separated from the main currents of community life and being protected against problems which play upon and educate the child before going to school and after its few short years of school'.[12] There has been no uninterrupted public recognition in this century, in either the United States or the United Kingdom, of the importance of such a view, but we have seen the ways in which such recognition did surface in the work of British sociologists before and after the Second World War, and in the research and policy-making of the United States in the mid-1960s. It is worth repeating the American view of Rutter's *Fifteen Thousand Hours* in which Barry W. Holtz comments that 'we once hoped that schools would create new models of community, encourage new commitments towards meaningful vocations, end racial discrimination, and open up new avenues out of poverty and unhappiness. Right now, it seems, we rejoice if children can be taught to read.'[13]

The second set of realities for the schools is that of the policy contexts we have explored mainly for the public schools – those which emanate from governments, whether at national or state level. Private schools may fall in part within such contexts but they are framed mostly by their own proprietary or regulatory agencies. Public policy reaches the schools, directly or through intermediaries, in the form of legislative requirements or other official prescriptions. Supervision of policy rests with local authorities or other bodies forming part of the political and administrative structure, or with inspectors acting on behalf of the publicly determined criteria. As we have seen in the case of some recent restructuring approaches, such supervision may be relaxed – and in the case of proposals such as those of Chubb and Moe may be recommended for complete transfer to the school. British policies in the 1980s and 1990s have gone towards the transfer of management decisions to the schools and at the same time towards more visible public accountability. What schools have to do in the policy context is make best sense of what is required of them, respond in necessary ways and leave themselves as much room as possible to interpret policies with insight. How much room they have to interpret and adapt policies in the process of implementation depends on a mix of external and internal factors which varies considerably with circumstances. Since national or other public policies are themselves determined by the zigzags of political and economic change, the complexity of the school's relationship to the policy environment, particularly in the twentieth century, has made it increasingly difficult for them to define clear purposes. This is not the case for schools based on what was called 'value communities', and private Christian, Jewish, Islamic or other schools, and some vocationally specific schools, have been able to maintain and even strengthen their sense of purpose. For public education in general, however, the direction of the schools has been increasingly determined by national decisions or pressures towards structural, curricular or other changes. In the best of cases 'implementation with insight' may describe the extent of the school's ability to find room to interpret and respond.

The third set of realities, the internal workings of the school, are not just the techniques and technologies. They rest on basic assumptions about the purposes and potential effectiveness of the school for its students individually and collectively. Schools have been criticized as mechanisms for sorting children on behalf of the class structure, as training grounds for corporate capitalism, as a mechanism for ensuring that working-class children fail. Different kinds of school have, of course, historically served different populations, and have incorporated the means of 'promoting' particular students or categories of students. They have 'streamed' or 'tracked' students on apparently educational but ultimately social criteria. Schools and their teachers have knowingly or unwittingly adopted methods involving prejudice or injustice. In one way or another, however, it is the destinies of individual children that they work to influence. How much children's learning and achievements are affected by school as compared with family and community is still an open question, but it is clear that the impact of the school is enough to make its choices and procedures important to the outcomes. How a school perceives and acts upon its responsibilities is shaped within the web of its responses to policy and community issues, but it also makes constant decisions on the basis of its own assumptions and ways of operating, the deployment of its resources, its culture – which may be responsive to the best information and advice available, or a form of collective inertia. How a school responds to the presence of children with learning difficulties, or those with physical disabilities, may depend on its interpretation of policy directives or available reports of research or experience. It may equally depend on resources and understandings of how to use them, or its own sense of purpose, or an accumulation of confusions.

Research findings may operate, of course, at the levels of public policy and community relationships, but the kinds of research we have discussed here become important at the point at which they reach into the school, or provoke reflection on the reasons for their failure to do so. The research on school effectiveness and development of the 1970s and after has, as I have suggested, been particularly focused on those specific aspects of school structures and behaviours, and their interrelationships, that may help to explain the levels of students' achievement. That does not make this research, or any other research, the permanent 'truth' about schools. It has been a form of research which has simply responded to what it saw as illogicalities in previous judgements about schools, and has deliberately sought to move on from *ad hoc* and unsystematic notions of what is good or bad, productive or unproductive, about schools. It has extensively explored the implications of its own findings. An American effective schools advocate has expressed the view that it is particularly the movement's emphasis on the aphorism 'all students can learn' that has made it distinctive:

> Schools historically have been organized to produce results consistent with the normal curve, to sort youth into the various strata needed to fuel the economy. There is a deeply ingrained belief that the function of schooling is to sort students into two groups: those who will work with their heads and those who will toil with their hands. . . . The effective schools movement represents a significant departure from this way of thinking. . . . The fundamental belief is that, given appropriate conditions, all students can learn.[14]

If schools wish to use the research and intelligence most likely to inform their decision-making, the research that looks at within-school operations and their implications is the most likely to do so. A large variety of other forms of classroom and school-based research also compete to influence the schools, and schools have difficulty in absorbing the range of research directed towards them.

The effective schools research has figured here because of its international resonance, in terms of research strategies and specifics, and in raising major questions of the relationship between detailed research and judgements of the way schools work to achieve their aims and assess their achievement. Its impact has been blunted in part by exaggerated – particularly American – claims for what has been discovered, and weaknesses in 'school improvement strategies' stemming from the research. David Reynolds comments that these were often 'based upon acquisition of elite knowledge, were "top down" and externally generated in orientation, were individually targeted and were predominantly based out of schools', while there were available at the same time other models of research, relying on 'practitioner knowledge, group improvement activity, internally generated "bottom up" solutions and completely school-based improvement attempts'. Reynolds points to a greater need, in the new educational conditions of the 1990s, to focus on the 'culture' rather than the 'structure' of the schools.[15] What the effective schools research contributed most to the intelligence available to schools and schools systems was not only the strong emphasis that 'all students can learn', but also the sense that all aspects of the school can and need to be studied. The essential difficulty perceived by the effective schools researchers throughout its development has been that of going beyond the clustering of diverse characteristics to their relationships, to explanations of the school 'culture' that can help people in schools to act on their insights and to take advantage of the news that comes from research. A school can best make judgements about itself if it is aware of its purposes, its history, the configuration of experiences that make up its culture.

These are the three frameworks within which schools mainly operate. How they do so gives rise to judgements by others, inside and outside those frameworks. Schools may hold an insecure place in the pattern of judgements, precisely because the component parts of their culture change. An important question is whether, as a

e experience of recent decades, it has become more difficult to make
s because of these complex frameworks and the behaviour of schools
m, or whether there is now so much evidence that it has become easier to
search evidence, interpreted differently in different forms of transmission,
ne fragment of evidence available to those who make judgements. The
noise to most listeners will be a jumble of messages, about parents being
empowered or manipulated, teachers being deprofessionalized, the market being
freed, schools being freed, indicators being strengthened, traditional values being
reasserted or economies being rescued. The noises may be no less complex than
before, but, as we have seen, the relative strength of the signals has changed. In spite
of the difficulties, it has been possible to oversimplify some of this, as of any other,
research. Circumventing the politics, two Australian authors in 1993, with only a
passing reference to the effective schools research, nevertheless use all of its
echoes in expressing the view that 'we already know what makes a good school. The
topic has been extensively researched over the past two decades, and what has
been discovered looks reliable because it is not spectacularly new.' They use the
language of 'good schools' although clearly much of what is described in a passage
by Hedley Beare, one of the authors, replaces the vocabulary of 'effective schools'.
In his relatively long summary he considers that:

> Good schools have clear educational aims. . . . Good schools target
> learning outcomes. They believe that every student can learn and is
> willing to learn. An attitude of success permeates the whole school
> . . . A good school has a good Principal who is an educator rather than
> merely a manager. . . . Good schools . . . understand that their core
> task is educating. . . their teachers direct their energy to academic
> learning. . . . There is a school-wide, systematic, regular assessment
> program. . . . Good schools 'maintain an orderly and safe environment'
> for learning. In good schools, it is safe for a student to be curious, to
> play with ideas, to experiment and to make mistakes. Good schools
> do not burden either their students or their staff so heavily that time
> for enrichment, time to reflect, time to participate in recreation or
> artistic or professional or other educational pursuits are crowded out
> of the program. . . . 'Good schools are good places to live and work
> [in], for everybody'.

So, add Beare and his colleague Richard Slaughter, 'we can recognise what good
schooling is like, its characteristics isolated by more than twenty years of
systematic research and inquiry'.[16]

The Australian commentary is useful both where it is correct and where it is
misleading. It is correct in suggesting the extent to which research findings about
schools have amassed across two decades, and it is correct in suggesting that there
are ways of bringing them together into portraits of schools. It makes, however,
three mistakes. First, it aggregates. It fails to see that piecing these items together
into an understanding of what makes a good school is exactly what the researchers
have achieved to only a very limited extent. Secondly, it fails to look outside the
school gates to consider what constitutes a good school, and how people other than
those in the school itself may perceive its quality. Thirdly, it does not represent the

school reality of 1993. It does not ask whether a good school remains the same at a time when principals may be placed more and more in the position of having to be 'merely managers'. It does not ask about the external forces shaping curricula and turning systematic testing into Arthur Wirth's 'epidemic of testing'. It does not ask how time and space for reflection are to be found in a good school when such time and space are at a premium as a result of external policies, decisions or pressures. Can one say that good schools are good places to work in for everybody without asking about the school's response to its constituency of children who experience poverty, blighted environments, the disadvantages of race, the pressures of unemployment, the competition of purposes? How long does a good school remain a good school by some pleasant set of criteria, and for everybody? There is here what we might call 'a political deficit that needs to be addressed'.

As we have seen throughout this pursuit of the good and the effective, both are conditioned by the source of their definitions, and the power to make and influence them. We have emphasized judgements of schools as a competition or a contest, resulting in consensus only where there is a consensus based on community and shared values. Where there is no such consensus, and such a consensus cannot be artificially achieved simply by marginalizing the pluralisms, parents and publics will find it difficult to know how to allocate priorities in making their judgements. As they move within their three interrelated frameworks in times of rapidly changing operational criteria the schools themselves find it difficult to see their own cultural identity and evaluate their own performance, their own concern for stability in new conditions. An effective school is only one version of a good school, or one contributor to its understanding. The research is one of the signals that may be jammed by the strength of the prevalent politics. The research may even be misrepresented by the researchers themselves, given the powerful policy alternatives against which they have to contend. Schools have their own difficult politics to construct, and a diversity of outside judgements to resist or to influence. Manoeuvring creatively within its three frameworks a school might just succeed in satisfying itself that it is a good school, and might be judged by others to be a good school, not by everyone all of the time, but enough to suggest that it is fulfilling appropriate purposes as best it can, with the people and the resources available to it, and at least for the time being.

NOTES

1 H. G. Rickover (1959). *Education and Freedom*. New York: Dutton, pp. 137–8.

2 H. G. Rickover (1962). *Swiss Schools and Ours: Why Theirs Are Better*. Boston: Little, Brown, p. 146.

3 H. G. Rickover (1963). *American Education – A National Failure: the Problem of Our Schools and What We Can Learn from England*. New York: Dutton, p. 72.

4 Arthur Bestor (1953). *Educational Wastelands: The Retreat from Learning in Our Public Schools*. Urbana: University of Illinois Press; A. E. Bestor (1955). *The Restoration of Learning: a Program for Redeeming the Unfulfilled Promise of American Education*. New York: Knopf.

5 C. B. Cox and A. E. Dyson (n.d.). 'Letter to Members of Parliament'. In Cox and Dyson (eds), *Fight for Education: A Black Paper*. London: Critical Quarterly Society, p. 6.

6 C. B. Cox and A. E. Dyson (n.d.). 'Letter to Members of Parliament'. In Cox and Dyson (eds), *Black Paper Two: The Crisis in Education*. London: Critical Quarterly Society, p. 3.

7 P. P. Claxton (1912). Introduction to the *Report of the Commissioner of Education for the Year ended June 30, 1912*. Washington, DC: Government Printing House, pp. 2–8, 16.

8 Arthur G. Wirth (1993). 'Education and work: the choices we face', *Phi Delta Kappan*, **74** (5), 361, 363.

9 Ibid., p. 364.

10 Demitri Coryton (1993). 'Good policies, bad politics', *Times Higher Education Supplement*, 20 August, p. 10.

11 A. H. Halsey (ed.) (1972). *Educational Priority*, Vol. I: *EPA Problems and Policies*. London: HMSO, pp. 117, 153.

12 William H. Allen, quoted in Claxton, *Report of the Commissioner*, p. 17.

13 Cf. Chapter 6 above, note 79.

14 Joseph Murphy (1992). 'Effective schools: legacy and future directions'. In David Reynolds and Peter Cuttance (eds), *School Effectiveness: Research, Policy and Practice*. London: Cassell, p. 166.

15 David Reynolds and Anthony Packer, 'School effectiveness and school improvement in the 1990s', ibid., pp. 182–3.

16 Hedley Beare (1989). *The Curriculum for the 1990s: A New Package or a New Spirit?*, quoted in Hedley Beare and Richard Slaughter (1993), *Education for the Twenty-First Century*. London: Routledge, pp. 73–4. The final quotation from Clark *et al.* is from 'Effective schools and school improvement: a comparative analysis of two lines of enquiry', in J. L. Burdin (ed), *School Leadership*. Newbury Park: Sage (1989), p. 183.

Index

Index